Blood into Ink

BLOOD
into
INK

*South Asian and
Middle Eastern Women
Write War*

edited by

Miriam Cooke &
Roshni Rustomji-Kerns

Westview Press
Boulder • San Francisco • Oxford

Copyright © 1994 by Westview Press, Inc., except for the Foreword, which is © 1994 by Meena Alexander

Published in 1994 in the United States of America by Westview Press, Inc., 5500 Central Avenue, Boulder, Colorado 80301-2877, and in the United Kingdom by Westview Press, 36 Lonsdale Road, Summertown, Oxford OX2 7EW

Library of Congress Cataloging-in-Publication Data
Blood into ink : South Asian and Middle Eastern women write war /
[compiled by] Miriam Cooke and Roshni Rustomji-Kerns.
    p. cm.
  ISBN 0-8133-8661-6. — ISBN 0-8133-8662-4 (pbk.)
  1. War—Literary collections.   2. Peace—Literary collections.
3. Indic literature—Women authors—Translation into English.
4. Indic literature (English)—Women authors.   5. Middle Eastern
literature—Women authors—Translations into English.   I. Cooke,
Miriam. II. Rustomji-Kerns, Roshni.
PN6071.W35B58   1994
808.8'0358—dc20   94-1770
                                          CIP

Printed and bound in the United States of America

The paper used in this publication meets the requirements of the American National Standard for Permanence of Paper for Printed Library Materials Z39.48-1984.

10   9   8   7   6   5   4   3   2   1

For Goolnar Behram Rustomji (1915–1987)
and Edit Cooke (1921–1989),
two women who witnessed this century's horrors
and did not succumb because they persisted in hope
and trusted in the human spirit

Contents

PART 2   Waging Peace

Foreword: Translating Violence: Reflections After Ayodhya

I am that Tree planted by the River,
Which will not be moved.
I, the Rock, I, the River, I, the Tree
I am yours—your passages have been paid.

—Maya Angelou, 'On the Pulse of Morning'

JANUARY 21, 1993—a day of brilliant blue skies and the somewhat milder weather that can sometimes attend us in mid-winter. I pick up the newspaper and read of children in the Iraqi desert playing with spent shells, abandoned weapons, burnt out tanks: the aftermath of warfare turned into the play of children. I read of a child in Basra who had the idea of turning used uranium shells into handpuppets, using bits and pieces, a tin can, a spent bottle, empty matchboxes, bits of foil—the supernal play of childhood unfolding in the killing fields of the Gulf War.

The writer of this piece, Eric Hoskins, the medical coordinator of the Harvard study team's survey of health in post-war Iraq, alludes to such play in his discussion of the diseases that have struck children under the age of five in that ravaged country. In the first eight months of 1991 alone, he writes, 50,000 children died. The deaths came from the extremely difficult conditions there, the hardships aggravated by the UN sanctions. But the ranks of post-war children dying are increasing, he writes, because of a great increase in cancer and a mysterious epidemic of swollen stomachs that could well be caused by the radioactivity in the shells fired from allied weapons.

Those who live in a war zone cannot prevent their children from playing, nor can they encase their own bodies in lead. Human lives must go on, but the often secret, long-term implications of abrupt violence are painful, difficult to spell out. And we are not just talking about large-scale wars with bombs manufactured halfway across the world falling out of the brilliant blue, but of smaller wars, neighbour battling neighbour in the ethnic violence that is upon us at the tail end of this century.

As a four-year-old child I travelled northward with my mother by train all the way from Kottayam, in Kerala, to the great city of Bombay. We came to catch a steamer that would take us across the Indian Ocean and Arabian Sea, up the Red Sea to Port Sudan. My anxious anticipation of the ocean liner dissolved in the excitement of seeing Bombay. I had never entered a city as seemingly endless. I was struck by the enormous crowded roads, big red buildings with spires and domes, the stone Gateway of India built by the British with cool waters lapping against the sea walls. Over the years, returning to Bombay for brief visits, I was struck continually by the frail yet resilient fabric of that city with its thousands of people thronging the train system, the streets, the buses but still bound each to the other in a civility that sometimes seems harder to come by here in New York, our city of skyscrapers, subways, and burnt-out blocks.

Recently there were communal riots in Bombay, and what was a bubbling, vital, multiethnic, multireligious city was condemned to the brute force of mobs fueled by ethnic hatred. The riots were sparked by the destruction on December 6, 1992, of Babri Masjid. The sixteenth-century mosque in Ayodhya, built by Babur on what is held to be the birthplace of Ram—Ramjanmabhumi—was torn down by right-wing Hindu nationalists, who swore to turn India, the world's most populous democracy, into a strict theocracy, a *ram rajya*. Riots and deaths followed in several Indian cities. In Bombay, which was among the worst hit, Hindu mobs sought out Muslims, and Muslims retaliated. In violence reminiscent of Partition and the bloodshed of 1948, people were killed in slums and in wealthy neighbourhoods, on bridges, on highways, in railway stations. 'We had all heard of Beirut', a long-time resident of Bombay said, trembling with emotion. 'I have never been there. But who thought it would be like that here?'

I listened to those words and was silent. Growing up partly in India, partly in the Sudan, I remembered vividly my childhood visits to Beirut. In the years before the Six Day War it was a dazzling city and, like Bombay, spread out by the sea with the mountains cradling it, higher, more austere than the Western ghats one can reach from Bombay. It was outside Beirut that I first had my glimpse of snow on the outstretched arms of a great cedar of Lebanon. It was the grace, the cosmopolitan fervour of the city that struck me. The bitter dregs of violence that would visit it seemed inconceivable then, as inconceivable as what happened in Bombay.

One cold, damp day, I rode out with a group of other Indians to a small town across the Hudson River. After the chokehold of traffic in downtown Manhattan and the dim half-light of the Holland Tunnel came the New Jersey Turnpike and acres of industrial marshland, smokestacks and bits of old machinery, and the greyness of earth and sky, until suddenly, we turned off and stopped in front of a small, low-lying motel that housed the Akbar Restaurant. The irony of the Bharatiya Janata Party (BJP) meeting in a restaurant named after the great Mughal emperor Akbar, who espoused the ideal of religious tolerance, was not lost on us.

Inside the restaurant the BJP was hosting a Friends of India fundraiser. In the biting cold outside, protesters lined the muddy bank between road and parking lot with raised placards reading 'Hindu-Muslim Bhai-Bhai', 'Rebuild Babri Masjid', and 'Stop Funding Massacres in India'. In the closed conference room of the restaurant, Sikander Bakht, the BJP speaker who had come all the way from India especially for the occasion, spoke warmly of the virtues of *hindutva,* the cultural priority of Hindus, the indissoluble bond between Hindu identity and Indian nationalism. Cries of *'ram rajya',* raised by men some of whom wore the red armbands of the RSS, echoed in the closed room. The speaker's plea to the listeners not to forget their Indian identity had not gone unheeded. In Edison, New Jersey, India was undeniably theirs, its rich, many-faceted religions, its traditions of cultural tolerance, and its modern, secular, multiethnic character expunged forever.

One of the members of the Mosque Committee told me how he was thrown out of the lobby outside the meeting room and threatened by the local police with handcuffs and lockup if he resisted. While two carloads of police watched warily, some of the BJP group came out of the motel, and the two sets of Indians confronted each other on American soil. The riots in Bombay and in Surat were fresh in our minds. The bloodletting of Partition was just behind us. Was India to revert to such violence again? Would mosques, temples, churches, houses, and schools have to be destroyed at whim just because there was a prior claim on the soil? The irony of the BJP speaker inside the Akbar Restaurant invoking Mahatma Gandhi's name was not lost on us. How long did one have to live somewhere to make it one's home? Was there no protection for minorities anywhere? It seemed quite appropriate to protest, to carry on this line of questioning on the democratic soil of New Jersey. The claims to identity that were made within the closed room of the Akbar Restaurant were heard by men and women who in their daily lives were hardly members of a Hindu majority but lived rather as Asian immigrants, a clearly visible minority in America. Why could they not feel the predicament of minorities in their own homeland? Why this terrible need to claim one cultural identity, singular and immovable, for India?

One of the members of the protest group, shivering in the sudden wind, spoke of the 451 Palestinians expelled by Israel, living in makeshift tents in southern Lebanon. 'It's cold there too', she said, smiling bitterly as the cries of 'Down, down BJP' grew louder, and the cars, filled with party supporters, eased out of the parking lot. 'What rights do we have anywhere?' she asked me. 'How will you write this?' she continued. I smiled back at her wryly and stamped my feet, trying as best I could to free myself of the dampness. My toes were frozen and thoughts of writing were far from me.

Like many others, I had grown up at the borders of violent conflict. My mother's parents were Gandhians, believers in *satyagraha*, the way of nonviolent resistance. But even as stories of peaceful resistance in the face of *lathi* charges and mass arrests filled my ears as a child, there were also mutterings about the Indian National Army (INA), of women who armed themselves, of others, too, like Preetilata Wadekar, who threw bombs at the British. The struggle to decolonise took on a different hue in my years of growing up in Khartoum. There was a civil war raging in the south of the Sudan, and students at the university who came from there would tell tales of torture and mutilation. As I left the Sudan to go to study in Britain, I was well aware of the struggles for justice that raged on. In India at the time, there were students my age who joined the Naxalite movement; many others were sympathetic to the cause of an armed struggle for justice. National independence was clearly only a very small first step, and violence, in its multiple forms, would have to be confronted.

The struggle for women's rights, in any case, flowed side by side with the post-colonial struggles for freedom. Even as the girlfriends I grew up with in Khartoum marched with men in the streets, demanding a solution to the 'Southern Question', so those voices, strengthened, were raised against the horrors of clitoridectomy, and varying, personal decisions were made on the tob, whether to cover oneself in it or not. In India, where I returned in the early seventies, a powerful feminism that sought to rewrite the nation in terms of a viable existence for women was taking shape. Friends in Delhi organised against bride burning; friends in Hyderabad collected the stories of women who were active in the armed uprising of the Telengana movement. Within me, too, was the awareness that Gandhi, the apostle of nonviolence, had, in the course of his experiments in community living on Tolstoy Farm in South Africa and in Sabermati Ashram in Ahmedabad, cut off the hair of young women he suspected of sexual misconduct. What place did women have, I wondered, in the new world?

The complexities that underlie women's writing need to be understood in relation to the constraints of power, both patriarchal and colonial. It is through such constraints that the woman's voice works, translating violence.

In his essay 'Representative Government' (1861), John Stuart Mill made the case for despotism. The natives of India were on his mind when he wrote: 'A vigorous despotism is in itself the best mode of government ... to render them capable of a higher civilization.' The strictures of colonialism and patriarchy fused in this belief in the necessary exercise of despotic power, an argument that I sometimes heard voiced in the post-colonial world I grew up in, fused though with a sense of the need to keep women in their place, teach them what to do.

Though the details of the patriarchal argument were not voiced in the precise modalities of Victorian rationality—after all, in India, the elaboration of female sexuality is complex, woven into the fabric of a hierarchical society—still, a colonial sense of maintaining power, of keeping order was critically present. And somewhere in there, too, as an undertone, was the grim feel of progress, a forward march into the new world. But the regurgitation of Victorian rationality hardly suited this new world. The boundary lines of behaviour, for both men and women, were rapidly blurring. There was a curious lack of fit between the corsetlike constraints of dead British rule (one thinks of a garment shredded, shrunk, stays torn and visible but still held up to the living, growing body) and the nationalism that paradoxically permitted such values to be voiced. Perhaps it was no accident that, as Romila Thapar has pointed out, the version of Indian history British colonialism established, indeed required for its legitimation, was one that the *hindutva* forces have used to build on: Golden Age of Hindu Rule, Barbaric Muslim Rule, Progressive British Rule. In each case, the Woman Question must be marshalled into line.

After the destruction of Babri Masjid and the riots that followed, one thinks: What the more extreme factions want is nothing less than the restoration of a mythic Golden Age, whatever the bloodshed involved, with women standing in as mothers of the nation-state or, like the fierce female orators, Sadhvis Uma Bharati and Ritambara Devi, whose voices have been copied out onto countless tapes and distributed in households in India, crying out to raise the saffron flag on the Red Fort in Delhi, wiping clean the slate of history, a cry for a cleansing so pure that all the complexities of a multitudinous, multireligious past are wiped out and history remade in the apocalypse of the mind.

But these writings before us, by women from West and South Asia, embody precisely those complexities that stand opposed to the bloody requirements of an ethnic cleansing, complexities that cannot be lost sight of if we are to survive. If to be female is already to be Other to the dominant languages of the world, to the canonical rigours of the great classical literature of Arabic or Sanskrit or Tamil, then to be female and face conditions of violent upheaval—whether in an actual war zone or in communal riots—is to force the fragmentation both of the dominant, patriarchal mould and of the marginality of female existence. The explosive possibilities, then, of female expressivity become multifarious. As for the old tattered corset of Victorian rationality, it is as if one picked it up and tried to fit it over a female body—vital, magnificent, with as many arms as the goddess Saraswati, and with one of the arms, maimed from a piece of shrapnel, still bleeding.

But how will our goddess speak? In many tongues, in babble, too, we think, a babble mimicking the broken words that surround her.

The bitter translation of self required by violent conflict is clear in all these writings by women from South and West Asia. It is as if the continuous pressure of violence, always already localised, has forged itself into a second language—an Otherness more radical than any the woman writer has been forced previously to feel—and through this anguishing, potentially fatal medium, she is to voice her passions, reconfigure her world. Such expressive acts require fierce labour of the feminine imagination—the walls of domesticity broken down, the retaining walls of desire breached.

In Mridula Garg's powerful short story 'The Morning After' a middle-aged mother of two sons faces a mob in Delhi. The narrative is set during the 1984 riots after Mrs. Gandhi's assassination, when thousands of innocent Sikhs were attacked and killed. Satto Auntie has hidden a young Sikh lad in her cupboard. Helping him escape, she pays with her own life. In Ghada Samman's *Beirut Nightmares*, realism is exchanged for surreal seances of a world in convulsion. As a 'Palestinian saboteur' is crucified outside, none of those who drink and dance inside the luxury hotel realise that the man being crucified is really the Messiah whose birth they think they are celebrating. Given the strenuous nature of such an aesthetic, it is hardly surprising that at times the rituals of terror overcome the everyday world and the Otherness of violence seems to fill the substance of speech.

The very marginality of the female condition becomes highly charged in a world filled with conflict. Women can manoeuvre differently than men, and even fiercely partisan women can use their mnemonic powers, not to paint a nostalgic foyer from which the female self has been brutally evicted, but rather to fuse together fragments of a difficult world. Ancestral memory must be recast so that innocence, however frail, might survive. In Samira Azzam's story 'On the Road to Solomon's Pools', the deep sense of belonging that the Arab family feels even as it is forced to flee ancestral lands is exploded by Israeli gunfire; and while the death of the young child has no possible consolation, nationalism, the naming of this land as ours, provides the narrator with a momentary hope: 'Look, this is the mountain. The day will come when we will turn it into an Arab mountain.' The issues of territory and nationhood become intertwined.

Territoriality then, in these post-colonial writings by women, becomes not just an issue of what Benedict Anderson has called the 'ghostly imaginings' of nationalism but a flesh and blood issue—literally, flesh and blood. For it is through the border crossings undertaken by the female body, the living 'I', that the creative potentiality of the world is inscribed afresh. In 'Parbati' by Farkhanda Lodhi, the metamorphic nature of the female self is made visible. Crawling through the barbed wire into no-man's land, Parbati changes her name, her whole identity refashioned under the heat of passion. Her border crossing and return precipitate a questioning of woman's place in the already-constructed world. Indeed here as in several of the other works, the radical disruption of life in the war zone permits an escape from the strict feminine mould of ordinary life and opens up explosive possibilities of freedom. In Nuha Samara's 'Two Faces, One Woman', the protagonist, left alone by her husband in war-torn Beirut, sits in front of a mirror and cuts off her long hair. As she bleaches it, she sees her face harden and feels herself beginning to look like a Nazi officer. She takes her old father to a hospital; she learns how to shoot; she takes a lover. The release of sexuality that both Lodhi's and Samara's protagonists feel signals a dissolution of the old patriarchal bondage, the radical possibility of female independence in a splintering world.

What becomes of so-called 'normalcy'? How shall we continue to cross the street, wash vegetables, bring our children home from school, approach our lovers, bury our dead? Life needs to go on, particularly the kinds of ordinary care that stitch the world together. The contortions of the everyday caused by multiple forms of violence—bombardment, mass shootings, curfews, riots, rapes, the forced exodus of civilians—when crystallised into art, reveal not merely the extreme, enforced condition but also the hidden structures of a world previously taken for granted, a world in which women have not often been at ease.

What does it mean to speak out in a time of violence? What becomes of the lyric voice fronting war? These are not questions to which quick answers can be found. But they are questions we are forced to ask ourselves at the tail end of the century, our earth torn up by multiple wars. Sometimes women's writing works through radical negativity, and we witness the nightmarish logic of war, a surreal theatre of cruelty that fractures identities, the sudden eruption of sexual desire, the explosion of pleasure, or then again, the body turned to a brutal instrument. At other times the fragility of helpless children, the instinct for natural beauty, the tenderness toward all of existence that makes us truly human are illumined. At such times the second language of violence only serves to force into visibility the longing for love.

In her poem from Beirut, Huda Naamani evokes the excess of cold:

'We write our bodies with snow, the soul
remains a horizon'.

But the voice continues in the longing for peace, for perfection:

'each stone we will heal
its wound, each grape vine we will prune it
with our lashes'.

Amrita Pritam, a generation earlier in Punjab, during Partition, noted peepul trees smashed, swings broken, the Chenab flooded with blood and cried out to her dead predecessor in the terrible hope that time might be remade:

> 'Today I asked Waris Shah
> Speak from your grave
> Open a new chapter
> In the Book of Love'.

If there were a Book of Love, such voices that tell of violence, would surely be recorded on its covers.

In the poem she read at the 1993 presidential inauguration in Washington, Maya Angelou spoke with lyric intensity of the mixed multitudes of America—the living, whose voices and bodies cry out for change. 'Arriving on the nightmare' the poet dares to hope that they are bought out of mental and physical slavery: Their 'passages have been paid'. On the inside back page of the newspaper that carried the text of Angelou's poem, I read of Iraqi children dying from spent shells spat out by American missiles. The spirit of Angelou's fierce compassion forces me back to the desolation of the actual—radioactive shells mimicking nature, contortions that the innocence of childhood could never decipher. Children dying now of the games they played in a war-ravaged land: Who will pay their passages?

Meena Alexander
New York City

Preface

The ink of the pen of scholars is more precious than the blood of martyrs.

—A saying attributed to
Muhammad, the Prophet of Islam

You do not know how hard it is transfiguring blood into ink ...

—Laila al-Saih,
"Intimations of Anxiety"

THIS ANTHOLOGY ARISES out of our own experiences with war and our conviction that conflict should not lead to killing. We are each concerned with women's ways of living and coping with violence and conflict, probably because we have both experienced war in South Asia and the Middle East.

Roshni will always carry with her childhood memories of the Indian struggle for independence from Britain—unending debates at the dining table, exciting glimpses of Gandhi and Nehru, hushed funerals for young men killed in *lathi* charges, her mother's insistence that she say, "Shakespeare was only *one* of the world's great writers, not the greatest," and her memories of being moved by Sarojini Naidu's speeches. She will also always be haunted by the experience of communal violence and the partition of a newly independent nation: more debates, exhortations to eschew religious partisanship, floods of refugees, the formidable presence of Fatima Jinnah and her brother Muhammad Ali Jinnah. Almost half a century later, she is re-membering, in the sense of putting together, disparate aspects of that struggle in the East from the vantage point of living in the West. At the same time, she is realizing that the theme of women and war has always been a part of South Asian writings, whether by men or by women.

Miriam experienced the Middle East as an outsider and war as an adult. She started to study Arabic and Islam at the University of Edinburgh in the immediate aftermath of the Arab-Israeli War of 1967. Two years later, she went to Lebanon to study at the American University in Beirut. When she left, she knew she would return to Beirut. In the intervening eleven years before her return, the simmering turmoil had exploded into civil war. In 1980, she spent three months there. The city was alive with intellectual ferment. New artists and writers, particularly women, were emerging almost on a weekly basis. Miriam met many women writers at literary salons, dinner parties, sidewalk cafes, and sometimes even in swimming pools. She wrote an article for *Middle East* magazine on women's fiction during the war. The article led later to a chapter, that chapter to another. In 1982, supported by a Fulbright scholarship, she returned to complete research for a book. She spent the three months preceding the Israeli invasion interviewing women, including Emily Nasrallah, Ghada Samman, Daisy al-Amir, Laila al-Saih, and Huda Naamani, recovering some of the writings that were already being forgotten and trying to understand the dynamic of women's survival and steadfastness in the chaos that Lebanon had become. The Israeli invasion that June forced her out of West Beirut and eventually out of the country.

We both have witnessed how in war women become the mainstay of their societies as they construct a livable, survivable normality at the heart of the nightmare even while they actively participate in the public domain of the struggle. These personal experiences made us realize that war for women may involve enduring bombardment and torture, protecting children, one's own or those of an "enemy," or it may involve a simple, or often not so simple, matter of daily survival. We have exchanged our stories and learned from each other, but above all we have learned from those women who penned their experiences out of the wars they have lived.

It was in 1988 that we each became aware of the need for women to speak out to each other and across cultural borders. One late evening in November, after the panels and sessions of the Conference on South Asia at the University of Wisconsin, Madison, had concluded for the day, Roshni found herself in a group of Indian, Pakistani, and Bangladeshi women. They were involved in a spirited discussion on cultural traditions and Western as opposed to indigenous feminist approaches to South Asian women. Many of them said that their own voices were barely being heard. It is often dangerous and sometimes ineffectual, they argued, for those who are not participants in its lives and cultures to offer solutions and theories for South Asia. South Asian women should themselves continue to examine and comparatively assess past and contemporary feminist movements and beliefs in South Asia and the West. It is they who should find solutions for revisions and change. This experience was repeated, with greater anger and frustration on the part of the South Asian women, during the 1992 session of the Conference on South Asia in Wisconsin.

Miriam had a similar experience in the autumn of 1988. She attended the second annual gathering of the Association of Middle Eastern Women's Studies, during which debates about who has the right to write about whom dominated the sessions. Some Arab and Iranian women scholars claimed privileged access to the lives of Middle Eastern women. European and American anthropologists, historians, and literary critics who had long been engaged in research on Middle Eastern women felt that their work should have a place and that their perspective was valuable. The debate over identity politics continues, but we have chosen to risk dialogue.

We recognize the differences in our perspectives, but we insist also on the importance of sharing our experiences. We are committed to finding common ground that will help women from different backgrounds to understand and listen to each other. Our personal contribution to providing a cultural bridge is this anthology. But we are not naively optimistic. We know that in the search for freedom, justice, and peace people are often caught in violence and war. Yet, it is precisely this paradox of war and peace that has generated mythologies and literatures. These peace-war paradoxes, mythologies, and literatures are inextricably intertwined. We conclude with a quotation from Meena Alexander's memoir, *Fault Lines:* "True poetry must be attentive to violence. It must listen and hear. Our lines must be supple enough to figure out violence, vent it, and pass beyond." The hope behind our anthology is that by transfiguring blood into ink and death into discourse, we may survive beyond war into peace.

Miriam Cooke
Roshni Rustomji-Kerns

Acknowledgments

WE HAVE RECEIVED invaluable assistance in the course of compiling this anthology. We acknowledge the constant encouragement and support of Dr. Milton Gordon, former vice president of Sonoma State University. A Sonoma State University Faculty Incentive Grant between 1987 and 1989 facilitated the early stages of the compilation. Our special thanks go to Vidyut Aklujkar, Meena Alexander, Jean Arasanayagam, Carlo Coppola, Chitra Divakaruni, Nancy Dupree, Naseem Hines, Roger Kaplan, Anjum Khilji, Muhammad Umar Memon, Farzaneh Milani, Panna Naik, and Tahira Naqvi for their help in the selection process and often also for their translations of individual pieces. We wish to acknowledge Diana Lopez, Shelly Bullen, Patricia Bryant, and Gail Woods for their unfailing help and their countless hours of typing. We appreciate the help and support offered to us by Barbara Ellington, Libby Barstow, and Jennifer Watson. Above all, we want to thank Charles Kerns and Bruce Lawrence, who were always there for us, reading and rereading versions of the manuscript, making useful suggestions, and cheering from the sidelines.

M.C.
R.R.-K.

Credits

The selection on p. 11 is © 1988. Reprinted by permission of the translator, Daniela Gioseffi, from her edited book, *Women on War: Int'l Voices.* ... New York: Touchstone—a division of Simon & Schuster.

The selection on p. 16 is from Salma Khendra Jayyusi, *Anthology of Modern Palestinian Literature,* copyright 1992, © Columbia University Press, New York. Reprinted with permission of the publisher.

The selection on p. 28 is reprinted by permission of Chitra Divakaruni.

The selection on p. 30 is reprinted by permission of Siham Daud.

The selection on p. 32 is from Salma Khendra Jayyusi, *Anthology of Modern Palestinian Literature,* copyright 1992, © Columbia University Press, New York. Reprinted with permission of the publisher.

The selection on p. 35 is reprinted by permission of Ghada Samman.

Meena Alexander's poem, "No Man's Land" [the selection on p. 45], appeared in *NEW LETTERS* (57:1, Fall 1970). It is reprinted here with the permission of *NEW LETTERS* and the Curators of the University of Missouri–Kansas City and with the permission of the author.

The selection on p. 48 is reprinted by permission of Farkhanda Lodhi.

The selection on p. 65 is reprinted by permission of Anne Ranasinghe.

The selection on p. 67 is reprinted by permission of Gynergy Books.

The selection on p. 73 is reprinted by permission of Jean Arasanayagam.

The selection on p. 77 is reprinted by permission of Carlo Coppola.

The selection on p. 86 is reprinted by permission of Aliya Shuaib.

The selection on p. 91 is reprinted by permission of Sri Ramakrishna Math.

The selection on p. 92 is reprinted by permission of Penguin Books. The translation is that of E. Powys Mathers.

The selection on p. 93 is reprinted by permission of Chitra Divakaruni.

The selection on p. 101 is reprinted by permission of Sahar Khalifa.

The selection on p. 105 is reprinted by permission of Nessia Shafran.

The selection on p. 136 is from *Critical Inquiry* by Gayatri Chakravorty Spivak, published by the University of Chicago Press, as republished by Routledge 1988 in *In Other Worlds.* Reprinted by permission of the University of Chicago Press.

The Center for Middle Eastern Studies, University of Texas at Austin, is the publisher of the selection on p. 147. The University of Texas Press markets and dis-

Blood into Ink

Introduction

THE WAR MYTHS OF MANY cultures tell of women who are victims and of men who are heroes, of women who are passive and of men who are active. But these are, after all, only myths. The fact is that women have always been in war. The women soldiers George Bush sent to fight in the 1991 Gulf War did not constitute an unprecedented break in the ways wars have been fought. They merely exemplified the fact that women are increasingly represented as participating in war: U.S. women marines carrying a "full pack" on their way to Saudi Arabia, Israeli military women, Palestinian mothers with their daughters and sons at barricades, Argentinian mothers protesting their sons' and grandsons' disappearance, Pakistani women at target practice, Sri Lankan women caught up in communal violence.

These images and voices come at a time when the culture of war is increasingly under investigation. Throughout the 1980s, feminist scholars revisited wars in history to study their causes and outcomes as well as the ways in which they were fought. Their findings revealed that although war has always been neatly classified as genderless, it is in fact one of the most highly gendered human activities. This new scholarship shows how the deliberate omission of women—except as nurses, long-suffering wives, mothers, sisters, and campfollowers—from the story of war has allowed the fiction of an ungendered domain to persist.

Although stories of World War II did include women, they were represented as mere substitutes for men. They rallied to the national cause, and they filled in for the heroes. Authorities saluted these women as though what they were doing was extraordinary and new, as though they were doing a job of which only men were capable. Many men and women longed for the war to end so that the women might return to their natural domain, the home, where they could resume their invisible role as the family support. Their return to the home symbolized the return of peace and the restoration of men to their visible roles as social managers.

Since the 1940s, this cycle of women's inclusion and exclusion has repeated itself in South Asia and the Middle East,[1] but with a difference. In few cases did the men leave for a front; the war was usually waged at home. During the anticolonial independence wars as well as throughout

1

civil and communal disturbances, women as well as men continued their work at home, in the office, or in the fields while joining demonstrations and carrying bombs, rifles, messages, and medical supplies. Both women and men have integrated their roles in the conflicts into their everyday, traditional activities.

Women's experience of twentieth-century war in South Asia and the Middle East challenges the separation of front and homefront and of family and society common to most modern Western wars. Recent scholarship highlighting the new meanings women assign to their traditional roles reveals that the continuum that connects individual and societal relationships also accommodates individual and societal conflict. War and gender are coming to be recognized as fluid and negotiable structures within which meanings are continuously questioned and contested. The explosion of some dichotomous structures tends to destabilize others; it enables a revisioning of history. Women are seen to have always been in war, and nowhere more so than in conflict that has not been designated a separate space where men splinter lances.

Although women have always been in war, the ways in which they have participated over the past two centuries have changed. There has been a radical shift in the literary and visual representation of women's war participation during this century. Women no longer enter into what was once considered male-only territory in men's roles and often in men's clothes. They are entering as women, and their self-conscious, self-confident presence has changed the nature of that territory. It has become a space that is restricted neither to men nor to women but that openly acknowledges the presence of both.

The situation in South Asia has differed somewhat from that of the Middle East. In the nineteenth century, women as well as men in South Asia became actively involved in opposing the British colonizers. Their joint struggle against an external enemy made them aware of a parallel, yet barely acknowledged, conflict at home. The women who were so essential to the national struggle realized that they were disempowered within their own society. Women and some male reformers began to insist on the importance for women of combining social and political roles. Women in the states of the Middle East, however, did not join the men's anticolonial movements in full force until the twentieth century. And it is only in the postcolonial period that they have begun to articulate the need to conduct simultaneous political and social revolutions. They are insisting that their struggle as women must become part of the nation's and that this integration must be theorized so that both the nationalist and the feminist revolutions are understood to be mutually necessary.

Women have begun to realize that they must record their participation in war. If they do not, no one will. Many women also recognize that if their actions are to change their societies, they must create a new mythology of the war-peace paradox that can effectively challenge the more traditional, male-dominated mythology of wars fought in search of justice, freedom, and peace. These new war stories must be grounded in the reality of women's lives. In the process of creating this new mythology, women have recognized that their involvement with the rituals of violence does not end or even begin with traditional war, that all their battles, whether they be "personal" or "political," are linked. Women's daily struggles for survival—physical, economic, intellectual, and emotional—stretch seamlessly into the more public arena of political war. Their literature on war presents their awareness of involvement in this larger, ongoing context of war.

During the struggle for independence, writers with socialist sympathies began in the 1930s to form Progressive Writers' Associations (PWAs) all over India. Women writers such as Rasheed Jehan, Ismat Chugtai, Sarojini Naidu, Kamaladevi Chattopadhyay, and Mahasweta Devi were active members of these groups. Indian, Pakistani, Bangladeshi, and Sri Lankan women have recorded their experiences and observations of independence, communal, and civil wars in nearly every literary genre and every language of South Asia. In the Middle East, however, women did not publish in significant numbers until the postcolonial period. The poetry of Palestinian women, particularly since 1967, has been universally hailed. During the Lebanese Civil War, a school of women writers known as the Beirut Decentrists emerged. Although some, like Ghada Samman, Emily Nasrallah, Huda Naamani, and Hanan al-Shaykh, were previously known in the Arab world, the war and their joint literary production have given them as well as lesser known writers like Nuha Samara greater visibility at home and abroad. When women write together, they challenge those who would like to appropriate and silence their voices.

But has this attention to women's military and discursive activism in the crisis of war and peace earned them recognition of their value and importance? We believe that it has. As feminist networks spread nationally and globally, many women are learning that they are not alone and that their forms of fighting and resisting can be successful.

The importance of bringing together literary works that express women's experiences in war cannot be overestimated. The works in this anthology demonstrate the multiple ways in which women become active participants in daily and military battles and how they write about war not only as an extraordinary but more importantly as an ordinary experience of coping with conflict and violence on a daily basis. Writing is the recording of experience; it is also the assignation of meaning to an event that once interpreted becomes part of a process that may be transformative.

It is important to note that women's literature on war presents both men and women as active participants. To present women's war writings that feature heroines only would do a disservice to this literature. Whereas men's war literature has usually relegated women characters to the roles of nurse, patient wife or mother, and abused or raped partisan or enemy, women's literature explores the range and variety of roles that war compels everyone to play. The inclusion of a few works with male protagonists highlights the fact that war creates expectations that both men and women may find difficult, if not impossible, to fulfill. We see a Palestinian father who can play neither his ascribed role as guardian of his society nor his adopted role as nurturer and protector of his son. At the same historical moment in India, during Partition, a Muslim soldier tries in vain to save a terrified Hindu girl. An Indian soldier returning home from war accepts his wife's illegitimate son as two more hands to help overcome abject poverty. An Iraqi soldier throws himself heedlessly into battle, desperate for heroism. As he dies from a wound inflicted "below the waist," his wife inadvertently kills their baby in childbirth.

⌁   ⌁   ⌁

Publications on women, war, and conflict, both single-authored monographs and anthologies, began to appear in the 1980s. Most were theoretical, political, and above all, Western, despite frequent claims to universality.[2] *Blood into Ink* is the first anthology to present twentieth-century women's writings about conflict and war outside the West, specifically focusing on South Asia and the Middle East. There can be no question that of all the voices in contemporary fiction, those of women from economically developing countries are the least heard and the least familiar to the Western reader. Most of the writers whose works are included in this anthology are well known at home and in many cases abroad. In some exceptional cases, we chose works by lesser-known authors because we considered the piece to be eloquent and relevant. Although many of the works appear here for the first time in English, the anthology includes important translated works that have been published elsewhere. It should be noted that we were unable to include as many Israeli stories as we would have liked because permission to publish was denied by the Hebrew Translation Institute.

The poems, short stories, and excerpts from memoirs and novels in this volume are not "exotic" products of the "Third World." They are essential for an understanding of the lives of ordinary people caught in the midst of seemingly endless political wars and social conflicts. Although they are often influenced by Western literature, these works are deeply rooted in South Asian and Middle Eastern literary and oral histories, mythologies, and traditions. They derive their strength and importance from art forms and aesthetics specific to their cultures as well as from individual experiences.

Some may wonder why we have selected writings from the Middle East and South Asia. Why juxtapose Arabic, Hebrew, Persian, and Pushto works from Syria, Lebanon, Israel and the Israeli Occupied Territories, Iraq, Iran, and Afghanistan with Hindi, Urdu, Gujarati, Marathi, Bengali, Punjabi, Tamil, Sinhalese, Malayalam, and English selections from Bangladesh, Pakistan, India, and Sri Lanka? What can these distinct literatures have in common? These are fair questions because in the postcolonial era, these geographically contiguous areas have rarely been paired or seen as a block, especially in the West. However, they are integrally connected. They share a long and continuous history of cultural, economic, and political exchanges. Trade, travel, conquests, and alliances have linked these areas from the earliest times. The medieval Islamic Empire that stretched from South Asia in the East through the Middle East to North Africa in the West fostered the interchange of intellectual, religious, and artistic influences. Most of the countries that constituted that Islamic world still retain an Islamicate culture. Some, like Saudi Arabia and Pakistan, were constructed in the twentieth century to be Muslim states with specifically Islamic constitutions. The British and French colonial exploitation of these areas in the seventeenth, eighteenth, and nineteenth centuries served to intensify these links as countries of South Asia and the Middle East confronted the rise of the West as a technological power. The twentieth-century anticolonial struggles for political and economic independence became part of and subject to an increasingly polarized competition for global hegemony.

Blood into Ink takes 1947 as its point of departure. In that year, the British arranged or proposed partition for both a South Asian and a Middle Eastern country in which they had imperialist interest: India and Palestine. In India, partition led to the establishment of the Muslim state of West and East Pakistan (later Bangladesh); in Palestine, partition was not implemented. Partition plans in each case caused immense demographic upheaval. The following year, the British left both places.

Most of the countries of South Asia and the Middle East have witnessed independence struggles against colonial powers, revolutions, civil wars, and postcolonial interstate wars. Many of the independence wars involved a rupture from the land for the indigenous inhabitants as well as for the colonizers. India's 1947 independence from the British was overshadowed by the pain of partition. The establishment of the state of Israel only a year later displaced and exiled the majority of the indigenous Palestinian inhabitants. Although the primary goal of independence wars was the expulsion of oppressive foreigners, an increasingly important concomitant objective was the restructuring of society out of the debris of the colonized past. The newly independent, particularly those who had almost as little at stake in the new system as they had had in the old, came to see that without a revolution in social and gender relationships, nothing would change. Indeed, in most cases nothing did change. Many resistance leaders simply slipped into the shoes vacated by the ex-colonizers. No longer could responsibility for the people's ills be disavowed by blaming the outsider only. Taking their destinies into their own hands, women and men targeted and challenged their new but familiar oppressors, and civil war often ensued. Domestic upheavals in the postcolonial state, like revolution and civil war, have attracted neighbors' and Western powers' attention and appealed to their hope of benefit without risk. Iraq seized the opportunity for quick gain by exploiting the confusion generated by the Islamic Revolution in Iran; all of Lebanon's close and distant neighbors sent military aid to fund useful militias. The Chinese advance in the 1960s toward the northeastern borders of an India still struggling with postindependence socioeconomic problems, the ongoing American policy of promising or withholding financial and military aid to India and Pakistan, the recent Soviet adventure in Afghanistan, and India's intervention in Sri Lankan politics—all continue to exacerbate tensions within South Asia.

We are aware of this sequence. However, we are also aware of the fact that the easy identification of types of wars with historical periods may be misleading. These apparently linear developments can reverse themselves, mutate, and then reappear under new guises that may be variously named. For example, 1947 was the year of independence in South Asia; it was also the year of the communal riots that to the outsider looked very much like civil war. The Lebanese Civil War, despite its nomenclature, has been variously periodized so as to become susceptible to a different taxonomy. The retrospective labeling of the 1975–1976 period as the Two-Year War allows the remaining decade and a half to be a revolution, urban guerilla warfare, or the theater of an interstate war. This expedient naming of wars, especially by political powers that may be interested in perpetuating and exploiting these conflicts, has made us wary of a chronological typology. Additionally, our reading of the women's texts from these discrete wars reveals that despite their political differences, these wars all implicate women equally and in multiple roles that extend beyond what might be expected of them.

Hence, and in keeping with our interest in uncovering and perhaps helping to construct a new mythology, we have organized this volume to reflect the different ways in which women intervene in wars: sometimes as recorders of violence but most often as wagers of peace. We wanted to provide relevant biographical information in each case. The unevenness of the selection headnotes represents a difficulty familiar to the feminist researcher: Because few women writers have enjoyed sufficient critical and historical attention, it is difficult to provide full documentation.

Hence, some of the writers who are well known have longer biographies than those whose works we and our translators chanced upon during the past five years.

In December 1992, we met in Durham, North Carolina, to go through the manuscript of this anthology for one last time to tidy up the loose ends and find a title. We had tried "Women Live War," "Women Live with War," "Women and War" and had rejected them all because they did not reflect why and how we had compiled this anthology. And then we ran across Laila al-Saih's poem "Intimations of Anxiety" and read the line "transfiguring blood into ink." We knew that this was the title of our anthology.

Blood into Ink is divided into two parts. The first part, "Remembering," is shorter than the second, "Waging Peace." As we compiled this anthology we discovered to our surprise that women's writings on war focus more on the process of the conflict and the individual's role in a potentially nonviolent resolution than on lamenting the horrors of war and the individual's helplessness in the face of an uncontrollable violence. Although this imbalance does reflect our own bias, it is in fact based on the availability of the texts. Our categories are not designed to be rigid but rather to stimulate reflection and discussion about the ways in which women transfigure blood into ink.

The works in the first part articulate experiences of anguish and despair as women and men witness the dismemberment of their land, their societies, their families, and their own lives and bodies. Women are expected to weep and they do. However, this mourning is not so much an elegiac salute to the heroic departed, a mirror to their greatness, a patriotic demand to "return victorious or dead" as it is a condemnation of the genocidal mentality of war, by whatever name it is called. Poets memorialize Auschwitz through the horror and violence of the war in Sri Lanka; women bathe in bloodied river water dazed by the desolation of war that surrounds them; children are massacred; mothers express anguish at the thought of giving birth to sons who will become killers or be killed. These poems and prose selections are also acts of faith and commitment to the re-membering of a fragmented past that is in danger of being lost. To write of the past as lost is the first step toward ensuring its survival. It may often also be a step toward acknowledging the stark senselessness of war and proposing a basis for actively waging peace.

Women may have always been in war; they have certainly always waged peace. However their participation in "combat" roles as women and not as men in disguise is a relatively recent phenomenon. Women may not necessarily wear uniforms or tote guns, but they are calling their daily gestures of defiance, their staying on the land and above all their surviving, Resistance.

A surprising number of works that appear in the second part, "Waging Peace," share a concern for the body and its clothes. An Afghani woman tears off her veil; an Iranian woman refuses the imposition of the revolutionary veil; Indian women working in indigo fields use their marriage saris as symbols of their revolution; a Bengali woman defiantly exposes through the rags of her torn clothes the blood and wounds on her tortured body. Some of the works in this section also show how women's families become their allies or enemies in times of war. Others demonstrate women's recognition of the humanity of the enemy, which complicates the perpetration of violence and leads to a hope for peace.

Children play a significant role in many of the pieces in the second part. For the Iraqi mother the only way out of giving birth to a future killer is to kill the baby. She illustrates vividly the paradoxical notion that in war conception entails death, contraception affirms life. Other writers imagine less violent counterprojects. If the young can paint peace or see a future beyond violence or turn war games into peace games, then the battles for power and control can be transformed into struggles for peace.

Blood into Ink reveals that in South Asia and the Middle East, women live battles and violence not as a constant state of alert and destruction but as a charged normality. Against the background of violence, both real and epistemic, life assumes a new rhythm. But the war is never forgotten. It must remain the constant, if often implicit, context, whether it be the young girl's stunned witness of her parents' death, the post–Indira Gandhi assassination riots when a Hindu mother tries to save the son of a Sikh mother, or the Lebanese Civil War for the client of a dress shop. The quotidian of war and the constant struggle for peace have not traditionally been part of most cultures' war myths, but they are as much a part of real life for many women in the twentieth century as they are central to women's war writings and mythology. These selections illustrate how survival is possible. More, it is transformative.

Unlike many anthologies whose purpose is to collate the best of the classics both old and new, our anthology is thematic. It questions embedded patterns of thought and behavior in connection with war and gender. *Blood into Ink* projects the unexpected: The norm becomes women coping with discord rather than women saluting and weeping for their men. Women's writings on war open up a level of difference that threatens the cohesion of male-dominated war myths. Using discursive distance, these women are looking in on their own societies in chaos and are rejecting traditional ascribed roles as silent and invisible helpmates. They are bringing to light the range of roles women have always played in war. They are refusing others' naming of their experiences.

They are making myths that others may recognize and use to validate their own experiences.

We have chosen individual pieces because we liked them and because they reflect what we are trying to do in this anthology. Are all of the selections equally "good"? What is good literature? Or is value contingent? As Barbara Herrnstein Smith asserts, literary value is not assessed through the survival or endurance of a text that generation after generation has been "objectively" judged to be great, a classic. The survival of a text is due to a "series of continuous interactions among a variously constituted object, emergent conditions, and mechanisms of cultural selection and transmission ... what are commonly taken to be *signs* of literary value are, in effect, also its *springs*."[3] Value is not an abstract, objective, ineffable quality generated by an object. Value is a concrete, subjective expression of the use to which an object can be put. This use value is then translated into less subjective language: importance, universality, truth. We have chosen each piece not only because we liked it, as we stated above, and felt that it fitted into the volume as a whole but also because we believed above all that that particular work had a role to play in the emerging mythology of women and war. Each piece is for each of us useful, important, universal, and perhaps "true."

Through poems, stories, and journals we share women's grief and anger and also their determination to keep the memories alive for themselves as well as for any who will listen. Writing makes the experiences real. Turning the blood and suffering of war into literature empowers a people to look at the experience, meditate on it, and, we hope, mobilize to end the violence.

Notes

1. Many have used the label West Asia to name the area the colonial powers designated as the Middle East. We would have preferred to use West Asia, but we decided to keep the more familiar nomenclature to ensure reader recognition. However, we have included only the Asian countries and have omitted all of North Africa, including Egypt.

2. For example, in Sally Hayton-Keeva's *Valiant Women in War and Exile: 38 True Stories* (San Francisco: City Lights Bookstore, 1987), only 30 percent of the selections come from outside the Euro-American sphere; in Daniela Gioseffi's *Women on War: Essential Voices for the Nuclear Age* (New York: Touchstone Books, 1988), only 16 percent of the selections are from outside the West; the Cambridge Women's Peace Collective's *My Country Is the Whole World* (Boston: Pandora, 1984), which spans over two millennia of women's writings on war, includes only 7 percent non-Western pieces; Jean Bethke Elshtain's *Women and War* (New York: Basic Books, 1987) omits all mention of women's experience in non-Western wars. In general, the more culturally inclusive works are: (1) collections of interviews (e.g., Bouthaina Shaaban's *Both Right and Left Handed* [Bloo-

mington: Indiana University Press, 1991]; Laurence Deonna's *The War with Two Voices* [Washington, D.C.: Three Continents Press, 1989], records the life histories of Palestinian and Israeli women; Tessa Cleave and Marion Wallace's *Namibia: Women in War* [London: Zed, 1989]; Beata Lipman's *Jewish and Palestinian Women Talk About Their Lives* [London: Pandora, 1988]), and (2) collections of analytical essays (e.g., Rosemary Ridd and Helen Callaway's *Women and Political Conflict* [New York: New York University Press, 1987] and Sharon Macdonald, Pat Holden and Shirley Ardener's *Images of Women in Peace and War* [London: Macmillan, 1987]). Only recently have monographs on women and conflict in Asia and Africa begun to appear. A few works deal with women's writings on war, but again the inclusion of non-Western writers is at best minimal (e.g., Helen Cooper, Adrienne Munich and Susan Squier's *Arms and the Woman: War, Gender and Literary Representation* [Chapel Hill: University of North Carolina Press, 1989] has only one essay on a non-Western war). The Lebanese Civil War is the only non-Western war whose women-authored literature has given rise to monographs. See Miriam Cooke's *War's Other Voices: Women Writers on the Lebanese Civil War* (London and New York: Cambridge University Press, 1988) and Evelyne Accad's *War and Sexuality: Literary Masks of the Middle East* (New York: New York University Press, 1990).

3. Barbara Herrnstein Smith, "Value" in Robert von Hallberg, ed., *Canons* (Chicago: University of Chicago Press, 1984), pp. 30, 34.

1

Remembering

Lament to the Spirit of War

You hack everything down in battle. …
You slice away the land and charge
disguised as a raging storm,
growl as a roaring hurricane,
yell like a tempest yells,
thunder, rage, roar, and drum,
expel evil winds!
Your feet are filled with anxiety!
Like a fiery monster you fill the land with poison.
As a rage from the sky,
you growl over the earth,
and trees and bushes collapse before you.
You're like blood rushing down a mountain,
Spirit of hate, greed and anger,
dominator of heaven and earth!
Your fire wafts over our tribe,
mounted on a beast,
with indomitable commands,
you decide all fate.
You triumph over all our rites.
Who can fathom you?

—Enheduanna
(Adapted to English by Daniela Gioseffi)

Amrita Pritam

(1919–   )

AMRITA PRITAM IS ONE of the most prolific and best-known Indian writers of the twentieth century. She began to publish in the 1930s and her poetry, short stories, novels, and novellas have been translated into nearly all the major languages of India and Europe. She was the first woman to win India's prestigious Sahitya Akademi Award for Literature in 1956.

Amrita Pritam was born in Punjab, India, and began writing before she was fifteen. In an interview with Carlo Coppola (*Mahfil* 1968), she discusses the beginning of her career, "My father was a writer and I was the only child. My mother died when I was eleven. I was absolutely alone, so out of loneliness, I started writing and my father encouraged me." Her father wrote devotional poetry but she quickly moved to more contemporary styles, claiming that she was "not a devotional person ... I love life too much." She has visited Russia and other (then) socialist countries several times since 1961. She has stated that although she admired some aspects of their society and many of their authors, she was dismayed by the lack of individual freedom and refused to identify herself as a Marxist.

Women struggling against injustice and oppression is the central theme of Pritam's writings, both fictional and autobiographical. Her horror and anger at the unmitigated violence committed against women of all the communities by Hindus, Muslims, and Sikhs during the partition years are revealed in many of her important works, such as her novel *The Skeleton* (1950) and the poem included here, "To Waris Shah" (translated from her collection *Lammiyaan Vaataan* 1948). In this poem she calls upon the eighteenth-century Punjabi poet Waris Shah, author of the Punjabi epic, *Heer,* which retells the sorrows of courageous Heer caught in the rules and manipulations of a patriarchal society. By asking the older poet to articulate the sorrows of twentieth-century Punjabi women made the victims of men involved in political violence, Pritam expresses the continuum between the personal and the public, the social and the political conflicts faced by women. She reminds us of the violence visited upon individual women in legend and history. By writing a poem about violence in which she calls upon another poet who has written about a woman's sorrow, she shows the importance of remembering and documenting different stories in order to break the chain of terror.

To Waris Shah
(waaris shaah nuuN)

Today I asked Waris Shah:
Speak from your grave;
Open a new chapter
In the Book of Love.

A daughter of the Punjab once wept;
You wrote her long story for her.
Today millions of daughters weep,
Waris Shah. They're calling you.

O Friend of sorrow,
Look at the Punjab.
The village square heaped with corpses,
The Chenab flooded with blood!

Someone mixed poison
In the five rivers;
Their flow
Watered the Punjab.

Poison has sprouted
From this fertile land.
Look, how far the red has spread.
Curse how far the red has spread!

Poisoned air
Floated into the jungles
Turning all bamboo flutes
To snakes

Waris Shah is the author of *hiir* ("Heer"), an epic in Punjabi written in the eighteenth century. Heer is the heroine; Ranjha, the hero; and Kaido, the villain.

Biting everyone's lips;
Their tongue tips rose up
And quickly all parts
Of the Punjab turned blue.

Song is crushed in every throat;
Every spinning wheel's thread is snapped;
Friends parted from one another;
The hum of spinning wheels fell silent.

Oars have left all boats
And float in the current;
Peepal branches with swings
Lie broken.

Where is the grove where love songs
Used to echo, where the flute?
All Ranjha's brothers
Have forgotten how to play the flute.

Blood keeps falling upon the earth,
Oozing out drop by drop from graves.
The queens of love
Weep in tombs.

It seems all people have become Kaidos,
Thieves of beauty and love—
Where should I search out
Another Waris Shah.

Waris Shah!
Open your grave;
Write a new page
In the Book of Love.

—Translated from the Punjabi
by Kiron Bajaj and Carlo Coppola

Laila al-Saih
(1936–   )

Laila al-Saih was born in Palestine. She studied psychology and philosophy at the Arab University in Beirut, Lebanon, and has worked as a freelance journalist in Kuwait. Her works deal with the Palestinian experience, love, and the liberation of women. Her collection of prose poems, *Rain Notebooks,* appeared in 1979. "Intimations of Anxiety," taken from her latest work, *Roots That Do Not Depart* (1984), is her poetic diary about the 1982 Israeli invasion of Beirut.

We selected our title, *Blood into Ink,* from this poem because the work exemplifies so well the focus of this anthology: war as one of the everyday realities of many women's lives. This is a love poem written at a time of war. A woman's anxiety about her love and her need to understand it at this time of upheaval and separation merge into the imagery of nature patiently waiting to renew itself. The poem articulates the poet's need to transfigure her life into a language that will document her experiences and thus transform anxiety and blood into love and ink.

Intimations of Anxiety

You do not know how hard it is,
transfiguring blood into ink—
emerging from one's secret dream
to voicing the dream.
Perhaps I need years to understand
what swirls within me when we meet.
Do you know that constellations of cities and paths tangle
restlessly in the sand?
I do not know the name
for such sweet incandescence.
Even now I have not discovered all the stars
fanning out in the soul and body
like eloquent shining symbols.

Under a mass of snow
a violet is patiently waiting.
Each opening rose partakes of
the patience of ages.
These are the things we must share,
and how the word takes shape within me.
Pulled between a world that created me
and a vaporous world I wish to create,
I begin again.
Each time you transform me
into a haze,
Wait for my anxiety
for this nameless creature thumping
in my breast.
I begin again
with your book,
from your book,
reading the first pages
over and over, dazzled, amazed,
enveloped by vast days and puzzling depths,
saying: The moment will come
in which I discover language,
voice of the sun's fruits,
dialect of waves engulfing my heart.
Maybe then I will be able to add
a single syllable to this existence—
this arduous impossible task.

—Translated from the Arabic
by May Jayyusi and Naomi Shihab Nye

Samira Azzam

(c. 1928–1967)

SAMIRA AZZAM WAS BORN in Jaffa, Palestine. In 1948, her family moved to Jordan. Like a number of young Palestinian women of the time, Samira Azzam decided to live by herself, and by 1950, she had moved to Beirut. She became editor-in-chief at Franklin House, an independent publishing company where writers like Taufiq Saigh and Badr Shakir al-Sayyab produced literary translations. She was active in Lebanese and Palestinian cultural life and was friends with Palestinian writer Ghassan al-Kanafani. She also produced her own works and published her short stories in a number of journals, including *Al-Adab*.

While living in Beirut, Azzam never forgot Palestine and its people. She helped Palestinians who came to Beirut in search of work. Kamal Boullata, a man aided by Azzam, recalled: "I remember she could always find a job. She found me two design jobs when I came to Beirut in 1965. She was a strong, assertive woman who had at the same time a great sense of gentleness and humor."

Finally, in June 1967, Azzam left Beirut to revisit Palestine. On June 7, she arrived at Allenby Bridge, where she learned of the fall of Jerusalem. She had a heart attack and died on that bridge.

Samira Azzam's short story collections include *The Clock and Humanity* (1963) and *The Feast from the Western Window*, published posthumously in 1971. "On the Road to Solomon's Pools" is taken from *And Other Stories* (1960).

On the Road to Solomon's Pools

He knew that the battle was uneven, and that his bullets despite their hatred would inflict little new damage. He knew that shooting was nonsense, and that his machine gun was merely a toy against the stream of shells. But he was trying to cover the retreat of families. They had begun to leave their village that afternoon, when they learnt that the ammunitions were exhausted. They realized that their remaining spelled suicide. He had agreed with some comrades from the national guard to cover this retreat. They had weighed their situation and knew that their ammunition would allow them to resist for a few hours only. Their village was on the slope of a hill overlooking a valley that separated them from the Jewish positions to the west. A train passed through its lands cutting off the school and some of the houses from the densely populated areas on the slope. He and his companions on the other roofs fired shots to make the Jews believe that their defenses were well supplied. It was a short game that would end as soon as he had shot his last bullet.

It was a bright, moonlit night which turned the almond and apricot blossoms in his garden and in others' orchards into tiny, white stars. These stars, whose innocent eyes looked on to a tragedy they scarcely suspected, turned the night into a poem.

In front of him beyond the railway line he saw the school distinguished by a desolateness that mocked the life he attempted to breathe into the souls of his young companions, and the stories that he told them before they began their morning exercises. He would stand in their midst and say: "Look, this is the mountain. The day will come when we will turn it into an Arab mountain." Eyes turned to the west to climb to the sun-drenched peaks.

His wife stood behind him reinforcing his steadfastness and trying to overcome her fear of the flashing shells.

He fired his last bullet. A cannon volley responded. He felt the stones of his house shake. He threw down his machine gun which without bullets was a mere toy.

He refused to believe that he had played out his role. At noon someone had told him that boxes of ammunition were on their way to Battir. Afternoon, sundown and evening had passed and nothing had appeared.

Had the ammunition arrived each one of his companions from the guard would have set himself up as a giant on each roof. Ahmad's searches through the neighboring villages had only produced guns with the ammunition that was already in them. A gun against a cannon. A dwarf against a giant.

He walked around the roof, his nails tearing into his hands. There was nothing weaker than masculinity under fire. He looked at his wife. She was weeping. This was the first time she had been afraid. It was as though the empty machine gun made her realize that Hasan's heroism was childish buffoonery, and that the battalions of young men he had tirelessly trained were mere puppets in the hands of a child. He had nothing to offer his wife, no guarantee to give her some peace of mind.

He felt that his empty machine gun, this useless piece of wood, was to blame for his miserable masculinity. Without bullets he would die in his house the death of a mouse.

He could not stand crying. When he looked at her in exasperation, she said three words: "Our son, Hasan? Umar?" He was fighting for the next generation. He taught during the day and bore arms at night. Yes, his son. The answer came from the barricades that needed fighters and the fighters who needed ammunition. The image of a gang celebrating a meager victory floated through his mind.

He looked at his wife. Should he die with her and Umar, or should they go to Solomon's Pools with the others. He would leave the boy with his mother and return to do something.

"Come on." He dragged her downstairs. He went to Umar's bed and picked him up. He was asleep. Perhaps he was dreaming of a beautiful new day when he could sleep peacefully in his mother's arms.

He saw his wife open the wardrobe and stuff some clothes into a case. Then she went to the small table and took their wedding photograph.

They set off, his wife carrying the case, he carrying Umar. He held him gently to his breast trying to make him feel secure. The boy was not afraid nor did he open his eyes on to the night of terror. The firing of the guns and the shelling of the cannons had quieted down. Maybe the Jews had finally realized the utter futility of shooting at this isolated village, and they had sat down to rest or to draw up a plan to facilitate their leaving the mountain. Battir was lying helpless on the slope to the valley.

Hasan looked at his house. It was still holding out with dignity. Its white walls, washed with the spring perfume of almond blossoms, drank in the silver of the moon. The stones of his house had been quarried from the mountain. His orchard was the fruit of an axe whose every blow was accompanied by a thousand promises.

He had planted an almond tree the day Umar was born. It had thrown down roots and produced leaves. He used to carry his son and, placing him near it, would say: "Let's measure. Which of you two is the taller, you or the almond tree?"

He saw his wife turn also. Their eyes met, and in an instant they recalled a history of emotions. They began when he met her as a student in Jerusalem. He fell in love with her and then took her to this house of his. Together they planted the orchard and filled it with flowers and trees. They built a house full of love. Yes, this was their house, their peaceful nest. Each stone told a different story.

Hasan sighed.

He tried to pull himself together and to garner courage from the warm, young body he was carrying.

They walked on. The road was empty and the houses quiet as though they were monuments in an ancient graveyard where the only living things were the trees.

Suddenly, some shots were fired again. He shouted to his wife to throw herself down. He bent also. They remained thus until the shooting stopped. Then they got up. Hasan looked around trying to work out from where the shooting was coming. Suddenly, a shell ripped through the quiet of the night. He shouted to his wife: "Run!"

They ran together and kept running for more than twenty minutes until he felt that his wife was exhausted and he slowed down. He lifted his left arm which was becoming stiff to calm her, when he felt something hot washing it.

Had it been hit?

He turned it over. There was no trace of a bullet and he felt no pain. He shuddered. Was it Umar? He suppressed his reaction. The slightest movement would paralyze his wife. So he was afraid to stop to check where the blood was coming from lest he raise her doubts.

He held the boy's body closer and started to walk so quickly that his wife could not keep up. The distance between them grew and he heard her call out. Her voice was sad and fearful. He responded in a muffled tone without turning around: "I'm here."

He waited for her to approach and then once again set off. He wanted to escape her however possible. Her voice reached him from behind: "You must be tired from carrying the little one. Give him to me."

He was crying and did not answer. He did not turn to her voice which was lashing his back: "It's getting cold. Take this blanket and wrap Umar in it."

He took the blanket without letting her see his face and wrapped the little one. He ran. He ran away from her voice that was calling him. Had she found out what had happened, she would have died on the spot. She should go alone with the streams of refugees.

He turned right and then down a side street. He stopped and lifted the blanket and turned the small body that was bleeding profusely. He collapsed under the weight of pain, anger and bitterness.

He put the child on the ground. The moon had waned and become red as though it were the sun rising in the west. The sky was filled with magical dawn colors and he caught sight of the square roofs of the houses at Solomon's Pools.

He bent down to kiss the smooth face. He called him until his voice was choked and his tears dried because of the burning in his eyes. He shook him again to bring back the miracle of life. The half-closed eyelid did not quiver with life. Because of him he had planted the almond tree and carried the gun.

He looked around him and then made his way toward the almond groves. He spent a long time trying to find a generous tree. He laid the child beneath it. Then he pulled at one of the branches and broke it off. He started to poke the ground with it in circular motions until he had made a little grave. When he had covered him with earth handful by handful, he stood up and shook the tree and it provided the grave with a cover of tiny white stars.

He recited no prayer. Hate had struck him dumb.

He tore himself away, and made his way through the streams of refugees. He tried to keep a hold on himself and to prevent himself from tripping over the stones. He folded the little, sticky blanket over his arm, knowing that two hours ago it had not been red.

—*Translated from the Arabic by Miriam Cooke*

Krishna Sobti

(1925–   )

BORN IN WEST PUNJAB, Krishna Sobti was directly affected by the partition of India, when West Punjab became a part of Pakistan. Her first novel, *Mitro Marjani,* established her as a leading Hindi writer. Her historical novel, *Zindginama,* has often been acclaimed as one of the most significant works on pre-Partition Punjab.

Writers of works about war often focus on children remembering and searching for their mothers. In this story by Sobti, a Muslim soldier and a Hindu child refugee are both victims of war. The soldier tries to redress the wrongs committed in the war he is fighting and to honor the memory of his sister lost in the conflict by attempting to protect the female child of the enemy. But to the child, the man is the terrifying, threatening enemy soldier, and even as he tries to comfort and reassure her, she screams for her lost mother and the only home she feels safe in, the refugee camp. One of the aspects of war that is consistently included in its mythology and literature is the continuing grief of victims and the often futile gestures by soldiers to restore normality during and after war.

Where Is My Mother?

When Yunus Khan of the Balauch Regiment scanned the sky, the moon had traversed half its nightly journey. He had found time to gaze at the sky and the stars after a good few days. Where was he all this while? Deep down in a cavernous ditch that had now started overflowing with blood. But he was no miscreant. He was fighting for the land of his dreams. One can sacrifice anything to gain one's goal. These four days he was all over—Gujaranwala, Wazirabad and Gujarat. He and his dashing truck. Far and distant. What for? For Pakistan. For the brotherhood of Islam. He had no selfish interest off his own.

Was it the fire raging in the far-off hills that Yunus Khan was seeing while standing on the roadside? The screaming of the helpless victims was nothing new to him. His ears were used to the sound of wailing women and crying children when he and his companions surrounded the villages and set them on fire. He had seen many a bonfire. Children roasted like piglets. Men and women burnt alive. He had witnessed charred bodies in hundreds after a street had blazed all night. He was not scared of dead bodies. Freedom cannot be had without bloodshed. Every revolution is accompanied by slaughter and incendiarism. And out of this holocaust an enchanting new nation was going to be born. He had to sweat for it day and night.

His eyes were sleepy. But he had to reach Lahore. He must ensure that not one kafir was left alive. There was a nip in the air but the thought of liquidation of the non-believers sent a wave of new vigour through his body. The truck was racing once again.

As the truck headed towards Lahore, Yunus Khan saw many villages ransacked and razed to the ground. He saw dead bodies strewn in the crop-laden fields. At times he heard the rioters shout 'Allah-ho-Akbar' followed by 'Har Har Mahadev.' Then there would be the panic-stricken cries of the helpless. Yunus Khan heard all this and remained undisturbed. He was visualising the birth of a new nation, greater than the Mughal Empire.

Now the moon appeared to be descending. The milk-white moonlight was acquiring a bluish tinge. Maybe the bloodshed on the earth was being reflected in the sky.

'Stop it, stop the truck,' Yunus asked the driver. There was a shadow of a sort on the roadside. A tiny shadow. No, it was a girl, a small child lying unconscious, covered by a blood-soaked scarf.

The Balauchi went towards her. Why did he stop his truck? He never bothered about dead bodies. It was a wounded child. So what? He had known mounds of massacred children. No, he must pick up the child. And if he could save her, he would do his best. But what for? Yunus Khan himself failed to understand it. He would not leave her alone. What if she was a kafir?

He picked up the frail unconscious body of the child in his strong arms. He brought her to the truck and laid her down on the front seat. The girl's eyes were shut. Her head was spattered with blood. And her face, a pale yellow patch, had blood stains all over.

Yunus Khan's fingers were moving through the child's hair, resting on the blood-soaked plaits. He was fondling the child. He had not known such sentiments before. Since when had he become so considerate? He failed to understand it. The girl lying unconscious did not know that the hands that had slaughtered her people were tending her in utter solicitude.

Yunus Khan no more saw a helpless girl lying unconscious before him. His half-shut eyes viewed his own sister, Nooran, back in his home town of Quetta. It was a chilly evening. His mother, a widow, had died leaving her an orphan. And then she, too, died soon after.

Yunus Khan suddenly realised that he was losing time. He must hurry. The child was wounded. The truck was speeding again. He must get her attended to immediately. Perhaps she could be saved. The truck was running as fast as it ever could. But why must he save this child when he had massacred hundreds of them? There was a strange conflict in his heart. He silenced it somehow. What had this innocent girl to do with their struggle? What had she to do with freedom and the birth of Pakistan?

Lahore was approaching. The Grand Trunk Road was running parallel to the railway line. It was Shahdara. He must not take the child to Sir Ganga Ram Hospital. In a Hindu hospital it would be like restoring her back to her own people. He would admit her in Mayo Medical Institute.

'Do whatever you can to save this child,' Yunus Khan pleaded again and again.

The doctor assured him that he would do his best.

The child was treated with the utmost care in the hospital. Yunus Khan continued performing his duties as a soldier, but he was restless. He was anxious and wanted to be by the child's bedside.

Lahore was still burning. He noticed a batch of Hindus, helpless and scared, rescued by a Muslim Military patrol. There were dead bodies dumped on a dung hill. There were naked women lying dead on the roadside. Yunus Khan who was most active till yesterday moved about listlessly today.

His footsteps suddenly became brisk in the evening. It would seem that it was his own home and not the hospital he was hastening to.

Why was he so anxious about this unknown child? She did not belong to this community. She was a Hindu—a kafir!

He imagined it was quite a distance from the hospital gate to her bed. He took long strides.

The girl lay on the bed, her head wrapped in bandages, her eyes still closed. The dreadful sight she had witnessed was still imprinted on her memory. She couldn't forget it.

How should he address her? His sister's name Nooran came to his lips. He stretched his hands and held her head in them.

Suddenly the girl moved and started shouting: 'It's camp … run, run for your life.'

'There is nothing. Open your eyes, child,' implored Yunus.

The girl opened her eyes. She saw the huge Balauchi standing close to her and she started screaming.

'Doctor, for God's sake do something to cure the child.'

The doctor gazed at her with his experienced looks. 'There's not much you can do. She is scared of you because she is a kafir.'

The word 'kafir' echoed and reached Yunus Khan's ears. A kafir! Why must he save her? No, he must. He would bring her up as his own sister.

Many days passed in this dilemma. Yunus Khan worked hard at his job during the day and in the evenings he walked the hospital corridors. He preferred seeing her when she was asleep or lying with her eyes closed.

And then she recovered completely. Yunus Khan came to the hospital in the evening to take her home.

The child looked at him with her big black eyes. There was terror and suspicion in them.

Yunus tried to coax her, but she remained mortally afraid. She feared he would choke her to death with his big brown hands. She was at her wits end. She closed her eyes. What did she see? She saw that dreadful night imprinted on her mind. The night and her brother. Her brother whose head was chopped off with one stroke of the sharp-edged weapon.

Yunus Khan called to her with all his tenderness. 'You are now all right. We shall go home.'

'No, no,' the child screamed. 'I have no home. I won't go with you— you'll kill me.'

'Me, child?' he asked. He wanted to reclaim his sister Nooran. But this child was no Nooran. She was a stranger, a Hindu child who was mortally afraid of him.

'I don't want to go home,' the girl pleaded. 'Take me to the refugee camp. I want to go to the camp.'

Yunus Khan dared not look into her eyes. He was at a loss to know what to do. He was helpless.

The soldier in him looked at the child with compassion and solicitude. He begged for understanding. 'Don't you bother,' he said, 'I am your own.'

'No, no,' she cried. Sitting beside the Balauchi in his truck, she was convinced that he would take her to a lonely spot and kill her. Maybe with a gun or a dagger. The child held his hand. 'Khan, you must not kill me. For God's sake do not kill me.'

Yunus Khan put his hand on the girl's head and vowed: 'You need not be afraid. You have nothing to fear. I am here to protect you.'

The child suddenly became violent. She tried to pounce upon him but he held her back. Thereafter she began screaming. 'Take me to the refugee camp. I only want to go to the camp. ... '

The Balauchi explained to her patiently, 'You need have no fear. You don't have to go to a camp now. You will live with me like my own sister ... in my house. You are like a little sister to me.'

'No, no,' the girl screamed and began beating the Balauchi on the chest with her small fists. 'You are a Muslim ... you'll kill me.'

She then started wailing, 'I want my mother. Where is my mother?'

—Translated from the Hindi by K.S. Duggal

Chitra Divakaruni

(1953–   )

CHITRA DIVAKARUNI WAS BORN in Calcutta, India, and educated at Calcutta University, Wright State University (Ohio), and the University of California (Berkeley). She lives in California and teaches creative writing at Foothill College in Los Altos Hills, California. Her poetry has appeared in journals, including *Calyx, International Poetry Review,* and *Woman of Power.* Her works have also appeared in anthologies, such as *The Forbidden Stitch* and *Home to Stay.* She has won numerous awards for her writings and has published three collections of her works: *Dark Like the River* (1987), *The Reason for Nasturtiums* (1990), and *Black Candle* (1991). She is also the editor of *Multitude: Cross-Cultural Readings for Writers* (1993). She is represented in this anthology as a poet ("Blackout" and "Indigo") and a translator ("The Sound of Leaves").

"Blackout: Calcutta 1971" deals with the events of 1971, when East Pakistan, now Bangladesh, fought a war of liberation against the overpowering domination of West Pakistan. India played a prominent and active supporting role for Bangladesh in the war. Once again, a woman in her role as a poet remembers and documents the war as it affected her life and that of her older sister. While describing childhood memories of that war, she includes the stories from legends and mythology that her older sister recounted to comfort her. But instead of comforting her, the ancient stories reinforce the continuity of war: "The Red Lotus prince ... I knew, wore khaki like the Mukti-Sena" (the freedom fighters). In this poem a woman documents not only her memory of a war she experienced but also the wars experienced in history and legend by other people at other times. In the final section of the poem, the writer tells of her older storyteller sister, hurt by a piece of glass, and raises an interesting question: Does the one who insists on remembering, recording, and telling the story of war stand in danger of being wounded because she herself stands so close to the theater of war?

Blackout: Calcutta 1971

i

All that year our windows
were crusted with thick inky paper
that smelled of soot, taped and retaped
as the glue evaporated
in Calcutta heat, and their edges
wilted and curled like love-letters
held to a flame. And still the war went on,

till those who could
left for hill towns with names like cool
running water, names you could believe in,
Mussoorie, Simla, Darjeeling. We stayed,
lay in sweat-sprouting dark, elder sister
and I, under a mosquito net
without a breeze to stir it, and listened
to the heavy insect whine of bombers.

I closed my eyes and saw them
above our city, stingers poised, releasing
from bloated bellies poison-silver eggs
that fell from the sky into the pictures
of elder sister's history book,
Nagasaki, Hiroshima, a fire
like a giant flower and the crisped-away
flesh of children's faces.

ii

The nights we couldn't sleep elder sister
told me stories. They weren't for real, she
said, but *I* knew. I heard them all the time,
the conch-snake whose shrill scream
could shatter eardrums, the fire-breathed monster
whose step shook the ground.
The Red Lotus prince who battles
the Demon Queen, I knew, wore khaki
like the Mukti-Sena and carried

a sten-gun. The walking skeletons
wailed each day outside
our blacked-out windows, *a bowl*
of rice-water, little mother, just one small bowl.

iii

In a dream, or a snapshot stapled to the brain,
it shudders the walls, that giant blast. Panes
shatter, a jag of glass nicks
elder sister's cheek and her hand
comes away wet, unbelieving. But I can't
stop. The moon is climbing
through the hole, a moon I haven't seen
in months, a huge, full moon. I reach
past shard-filled flooring. Color
and smell of fire, but cool,
like the night air now on my face. And in its center,
just as elder sister said, the old
moon-woman with her wheel, spin, spin,
spinning them out, like a long thread of blood,
all tangled up, our deaths.

Siham Daud

(1956–)

SIHAM DAUD, A PALESTINIAN, was born in Haifa eight years after the establishment of the state of Israel. In addition to working as a journalist, Daud is an assistant at the Arabesque publishing house run by Palestinian writer Emile Habiby. She is not a prolific writer, but her works have sporadically been published in Arabic-language newspapers in Israel. Sasson Somekh, an Israeli critic of Arabic literature, has translated some of her poems into Hebrew.

As in other works in this anthology, war has turned cities and nature into nightmares of gunpowder and smoke, and it is the children who suffer the most. Some of them cannot forget their memories of wars; others repress them. In "Do You Remember the Color of the Sea at Dair Yasin?" children are the main casualties of the war. Not only their bodies but also their minds and spirits are maimed as the children struggle to snatch up raindrops of hope. Again, the poet uses everyday images of food and making and drinking coffee to connect the memories and images of war and exile.

Do You Remember the Color
of the Sea at Dair Yasin?

About what shall we speak?
About Jaffa? About Acre? About al-Majdal? About Dair Yasin?
There is no sea in Dair Yasin!
What is the color of the sea in our country?!
Black, sometimes red (like Dair Yasin) and when rains torrent
It is merely the color of mud!
Sadness grows in it with the color of thyme
And the rains torrent
And it will produce gunpowder and palms and crushed workers
And children who love a lot
And eat a lot

And attack.
Their country was stones, shackles
Their country became smoke, arms
And they attack
Their camps were bigger than memory
Their camps became smaller than a ship and their olive pips
When they grow up they will be accused of weirdness and
    contentiousness
Memory glides to the ground to snatch up raindrops
This will be a celebration
The emergent dream tears the orchard and the prisoners' letters
We have been divided among camps and ships
We have made much coffee
The ship's stewards from Asia and Africa
Bring orders from their masters:
Search for the smell of coffee!
You will explain at length. They'll not understand the atmosphere of
    the camps and the ships
Beyond this sea young people were massacred
And they laugh
You keep talking so that your sweat may steam into coffee
They'll be sad, they'll revolt and they'll fear the downpour
And a child like Lina will bring them the proof:
Our blood has turned into coffee
And thyme remains, like mellowed grief, green, green!
And the sea in Dair Yasin is still huge!

           —Translated from the Arabic by Miriam Cooke

Hanan Mikhail Ashrawi

(1946–   )

HANAN MIKHAIL ASHRAWI WAS BORN in Nablus, Palestine. She attended the French Girls' School in Ramallah and earned her B.A. and M.A. in English at the American University in Beirut and her Ph.D. in Medieval English Literature at the University of Virginia, Charlottesville. She writes in English and has edited and translated poems from Arabic. Since 1973 she has chaired the English Department at Birzeit University, West Bank. She was chosen to be the Palestinian spokesperson at the Middle East peace talks that followed the Gulf War and culminated in the peace accords of September 1993.

"Night Patrol" was written in 1988, the year after the outbreak of the Intifada, or Palestinian Uprising, in Gaza and the West Bank. The poet enters the mind of an Israeli soldier as he contemplates his new enemy, stone-throwing children.

Night Patrol
(An Israeli Soldier on the West Bank)

It's not the sudden hail
of stones, nor the mocking of
their jeers, but this deliberate
quiet in their eyes that
threatens to wrap itself
around my well-armed uniformed
presence and drag me into
depths of confrontation I
never dared to probe.

Their stares bounce off stone,
walls and amateur barricades, and
I'm forced to listen
to the echo of my own

gun fire and tear gas
grenades in the midst of
a deafening silence which
I could almost touch, almost
But not quite. I refuse to be made
into a figment of my
own imagination. I catch
myself, at times, glimpsing
glimpsing the child I
was in one of them. That
same old recklessness, a daredevil
stance, a secret wisdom only
youth can impart as it hurtles
towards adulthood. Then I
begin to take substance before
my very eyes, and
shrink back in terror—as
an organism on its long
evolutionary trek recoils at the
touch of a human hand.

If I should once, just
once, grasp the elusive
end of the thread which
ties my being here with
their being there, I
could unravel the beginning ... no,
no, it was not an act
of will that brought me
here, and I shall wrap myself in
fabric woven by hands
other than mine, perhaps
lie down and take a nap.

Should I admit then into
my hapless dreams a thousand
eyes, a thousand hands, and allow
unknowingly the night's
silence to conceal me, I
would have done no

more or less than what
thousands have done before, turning
over in sleep clutching my
cocoon of army issue blankets,
and hope for a different posting
in the morning.

June 1988

Ghada Samman

(1942–   )

GHADA SAMMAN WAS BORN in al-Shamiya, Syria. In 1964, after earning her B.A. at the University of Damascus, she went to Lebanon to study for her M.A. at the American University in Beirut. She is a prolific writer of novels, short stories, and poetry that deal with the Arab nationalist struggle against imperialism as well as the role of women. She has been attacked by critics for her outspoken political and social commentary. Samman has written three novels on the Lebanese Civil War: *Beirut 1975* (1975) anticipates the war; *Beirut Nightmares* (1980) chronicles 206 nightmares of the war; and *The Billionaire's Night* (1986) begins with the Israeli invasion of 1982.

These selections are individual nightmares taken from the novel *Beirut Nightmares*, which records the mood of the November 1976 Hotels Battle in Beirut, during which opposing factions hunkered down in three hotels on the Corniche and kept up fire for several weeks. These fragments evoke the absurdity and horror of wars fought over religions that are not spiritual but ideological.

Beirut Nightmares

I shall make of my books a stage on which is acted out my struggle with existence.

Earth is not frightening if we die to construct a better life for our children ... what is frightening is to die for nothing.

I looked at my watch again. It really had no hands, nor even figures. It was just a small, white, closed circle with a black dot in the middle. I felt as though I, like the black dot, was a prisoner of a mysterious, desolate fate enclosed within some circle or another.

35

-ô   -ô   -ô

The new dead man, whose skeleton retained its grey-blue flesh said: "I also was a philanthropist. On the day that Beirut went crazy and started to kill people because of their identity cards at barricades—when people were killed because they were sons of Muslims or Christians—I came up with the idea of flower barricades. Whenever a guard stopped you at a barricade he would carry flowers, and instead of asking your religion and killing you if he felt like it, he would give you a flower for being alive and for being a compatriot. And they would plant flowers into the mouths of their guns hoping that they would turn into trees of goodness, and not into trees of fire. But I was killed by a tree of fire, even though I was innocent."

He was expecting to find sympathy among his dead companions, but he was still a stranger, and had not learned their laws. He was amazed that they turned away from him, and so he repeated his question: "By God, what did I do wrong? What was my crime?"

And the wise one among them answered: "Your crime was blindness. Did you really believe that you could cure the wound by sticking a rose in it?"

Nightmare 158

It is a luxury hotel and there's a party. The mountain air is blowing through the outskirts of a Lebanese tourist village. The snow is warm. The women are beautiful and empty, the men are shaking their paunches and calling this the New Dance.

It is Christmas Eve.

It is a luxury hotel and there's a party.

The woman has bared her breasts to celebrate the Messiahs' birthday. The woman has stuck on false eyelashes to celebrate the Messiah's birthday. That morning her husband bought a load of weapons which he distributed to the innocent urging them to kill in the name of the Messiah. Then he washed his hands quickly, bathing in Brut cologne he started to flirt with his neighbor's wife, pressing up against her body under cover of the dance in celebration of the Messiah's birthday. At that moment, one of the men's wounds were gushing blood from the holes the nails had driven through his bare hands and feet and from the crown of thorns plunged into his head and forehead and from his body bleeding from the vicious blows. The cross he was carrying on his back was heavy as he ran with it along the paths of the worlds through the ages.

Someone came up to him saying: "Wounded man, there are some people here celebrating your birthday. Why don't you go there and relax tonight."

He said: "I've forgotten the meaning of relaxation. I have washed the face of the earth with my blood. Wherever I went they drove another nail into my flesh. They keep on killing me under the mask of their love for me."

The man said to him: "They are waging a sacred war in your name and are dying for your sake. Go to them and you will refresh their hearts."

The man leaned his cross against an old oak tree. He washed his bleeding wounds in a clean stream. But the blood that had been flowing for about 2000 years did not stop. He decided to go to the party of those who were dying for his sake. His clothes were torn. But he decided that these were superficial details that would not upset people who were celebrating because of him. When he arrived at the door some armed elements met him and asked him:

"What do you want?"

He said "I've heard that they're holding a party to celebrate my birthday. So I decided to come to you myself."

One of the guards burst out laughing and said sarcastically: "He's crazy. He thinks he's the Messiah. Look at his rags!"

Another replied: "Why should he not be the Messiah? Is it just because his clothes are in tatters? Or because he has a strange accent?"

And then a large number of the armed elements knelt humbly near his wounds, and dropping their weapons they began to murmur their prayers.

But the adolescent son of the wealthy hotel owner rebuked them and shouted (a large silver cross glinted on his breast, and in his hand was a machine gun with an iron barrel): "Get up, you miserable idiots! Let me interrogate this humbug first."

And he turned to the Messiah, saying: "Are you armed?"

The Messiah replied: "I have never carried arms. Nay, throughout the ages I have turned the left cheek. But now it is my duty to bear arms in defense of humanity."

The adolescent armed element shouted: "What is your religion?"

The Messiah answered: "My religion is love."

The armed element shouted: "I've never heard of such a religion. Tell me in short: are you Muslim or Christian?"

The Messiah answered: "What do those words mean?"

The armed element started to shout again having been disconcerted by the poverty and calm of the stranger: "Are you from this area?"

The Messiah answered: "Yes and no ..."

The good, simple folk continued praying ... But the adolescent rich boy was whipping them and warning them of the misfortunes that might rain down on them and their families. So they got up and retrieved their arms unwillingly with dew-like tears in their eyes.

The hotelier's son continued his interrogation: "Your presence is dangerous for the hotel and the tourists and the pimps and the whores who visit it. What is your nationality, stranger? Your accent is not Lebanese."

The Messiah said: "I am Palestinian."

The adolescent armed element shouted in disgust: "Palestinian!! Horrors! You're an infiltrator, a saboteur, an informer, a colluder with the Marada offspring, a criminal, an enemy of the immortal Lebanese nation."

At that point a small group joined the adolescent, their weapons poised, and the Messiah replied: "But I'm the Messiah, you fools!"

They said: "The Messiah? Never mind that. What matters is that you're Palestinian. Palestinian!"

And they surrounded him and crucified him on the door of the luxury hotel, while most of the simple folk were weeping and some others had fallen victim to the adolescent's bullets. They drove nails into his hands and feet, exactly where those others had been about 2000 years ago. But no one inside heard the hammering as the nails were driven into his transparent body.

The music was loud, and the body of the neighbor's wife was supple and fresh, the dancing was exciting, and the wine strong and shameless.

When the party was over and everyone left, some of them saw a slim young man crucified over the luxury hotel. And they asked who he was and why he had been crucified this way. And one of the armed elements answered: "He was a Palestinian saboteur."

A drunken woman shouted: "I shall never light a candle for him!"; another cried: "I shall not pray for him!"; a third one cried out: "His clothes are dirty!" And they went home overcome by disgust. Palestinian? He deserved worse than the nails! And in their homes they continued to celebrate the Messiah's birthday!

Nightmare 64

They used to come out to him daily—family after family. He would shoot down entire families with the old and the young. And when they were hit by the bullets they would wave him their thanks and walk on a few steps toward the sea, where they would all fall down. Seconds later a wave would come and sweep them off the shore, clearing the spot for another family, and so on, forever. He must feel that as long as they keep coming in this way the Beirutis are committing conscious, collective suicide.

What madness has swept over this city? It has become difficult to have a sound, rational conversation with anyone. It is as though the civil war of these past months has affected everyone—as though all had drunk at the well of madness. Some of us are leaving, some of us are laughing and some of us are killing ourselves; some of us are dancing the dabke and some of us are still upset by the effect the war is having on the tourist industry.

Nightmare 94

An emigre tourist arrives in a luxury hotel overlooking the sea. He has been away for a long time. Before he had been told in his village school that he was of Marada stock and whenever he had asked his teacher why he was poor, the teacher had replied that the Marada never go hungry. But the stomach has a different logic and so the emigre had left. But he had never ceased to dream about his ancestors, the Marada.

When the Lebanese dance group came to the hotel he forgot how much money had been fleeced off him by the call-girl Tufaha and her musician. They sang to him of his fatherland, his glorious fatherland, and of the suns that grow in its vineyards and which are culled (some of them are fixed in the heavens, and some of them are squeezed and bottled and their nectar is drunk), and hang suspended in the stars riding ancient sun chariots, looking down on the earth and laughing at the smallness of the area occupied by the Arabs, and all the worlds occupied by other peoples. The dancer promised that she would be his guide and took the first payment in advance.

At the first light of dawn he arrived in the luxury hotel. By then he had decided to spend the month of the feasts in Lebanon. He noticed that parts of the building were covered in black dust, that some of the windows were burnt out, and that most of the glass seemed to be broken. The stairs of the marble entrance were cracked. He thought that this must be the latest fashion—isn't Beirut the first place to adopt all that is new? No one rushed to meet him. He was surprised, especially after the rapturous welcome he had received on his way from the airport to the hotel. People were lining the road and shooting bullets in the air in their joy at his arrival. True, he had not seen anyone, though he had heard the bullets. What a great and welcoming nation this is!

A sandbag approached from out of its barricade and said in English, smiling: "Welcome to Lebanon!" and the other sacks laughed. Do sacks walk and talk? How amazing! How impossible! Maybe he was still drunk from the whisky in the plane—it had not cost him anything, so he had kept asking the flight attendant for more. He had travelled first class, paying a lot so that Tufaha would see him come out of the first class exit when she came to meet him ... Why had she not come?

Another sack approached slowly and said to him: "Come quickly and let me show you to your room so that I can then get back to my post. The boys need me."

He followed the sack upstairs wearily. He tried to carry his heavy cases stuffed full of elegant clothes, and the sack said to him, "You won't need all that stuff here. ... "

He followed it. There was nothing in the hotel other than a few corpses, their eyes staring at him. He had reserved a room on the tenth floor so that he would have a good view of the sea. He had not known that the lift had broken down and that he would have to climb up a rope to get there. He climbed the rope, preceded by the sandbag who then showed him into his room. The bed was a coffin. He turned on the tap to wash his face and was amazed to find that these taps did not pour water, but blood. He looked at his face in the mirror and was amazed to see a man in it who shouted: "Go to sleep at once. When you wake up you'll start your sightseeing trip to other places."

He did not know if he had slept or not. He had not dared sleep in the coffin, so he had stretched out on the floor next to the table—a metal table used for operations.

A being with the body of a bird and the head of a human woke him, and the tourist said to him in terror: "Good morning. Bonjour." And the young "man-being" replied in Arabic: "Good morning." He asked for food and the young "man" brought him a pile of grass and he ate until he had had enough. He asked to be shaved, and the young "man" stretched out one of his claws (it was as sharp as a blade) and removed his beard in a flash. He asked for a car to go to the temples at Baalbek and the young "man," or rather the bird, asked him to close his eyes so that he might see better, and he picked him up and flew off with him. They went to many places of which he had never heard of before, and whose pictures he had never seen in brochures. Instead of flying to Baalbek first they went to a place called Karantina. He was amazed that people should live in tin huts, and that children should wallow in the mud and weep because of hunger and poverty. But he noticed that their eyes were red, or rather that there was a red gleam of determination and anger in them. After this visit the young "man" repeated his welcome to the only tourist in Lebanon on the first real, splendid sightseeing trip. And once more, he took him up on his shoulders like a hawk and in a flash the tourist found himself in a place of abject poverty, and the young "man" said: "Now we're in Tall az-Zaatar."

Nightmare 95

The armed "man" was still hovering around like a thunderbird, flapping his transparent wings, while the only tourist in Lebanon was grabbing hold of his thick hair that was like a lion's mane. In the valley he was able to see clearly the traces of a city eaten away by time and eroded by nature, and houses that had fallen into ruins.

The only tourist in Lebanon asked: "Are we still in Lebanon? These ruins don't look like Baalbek."

The armed "man" replied: "Didn't I tell you that we were in Tall az-Zaatar? It's in Lebanon, in Beirut in fact. It's not a tourist site, but a place where people live and reproduce and are not chess pieces to be moved about on a chessboard or to be removed at will."

The armed "man" alighted with the tourist, and they wandered around the place. The houses were older than the pictures of the temples at Baalbek, and there was a mist trying to cut off the sun from the exhausted people. But he noticed in their eyes that strange, red gleam full of vitality despite the pallour of their sick, tired faces.

The only tourist reiterated his question to his young guide: "Are we in Lebanon?" And he answered: "We're in Beirut itself. These houses, people, sighs of anger stretch a belt of fire around Beirut."

The only tourist in Lebanon said: "I beg of you, I'm exhausted. Take me to Hamra. I want to go somewhere familiar and pleasant." The young "man" flew with him awhile and then he alighted in a miserable street where poverty ruled. He ran along the pavements and jumped on to the decayed balconies and the sad shops. And the only tourist in Lebanon said: "Is this Hamra?" And the young "man" replied: "Yes. This is Hamra, and it is also in Beirut. The area is Burj al-Barajni."

And the tourist fainted. When he came to his senses, he asked the young "man" to take him to the cedars of the north, but he took him to the south. And the only tourist in Lebanon got tired, and he decided to enter one of the houses to drink something and wash his hands. And the pregnant woman who opened the door said to him: "We have no running water. Wait. I'll get you some water."

She went out to a swamp and filled a cup for him. He was horrified when he saw worms thrashing around in it. And he said to her: "I'm hungry. Do you have any bread?" And she gave him a loaf of thorns spattered with blood!

Nightmare 98

"Lady, o Lady, what did you do with your tresses?" said the old man to the woman he had known and loved so long.

She said: "I cut off my tresses and one by one strangled my children with them."

"Lady, o Lady, what did you do with your lover?"

"He deceived me, and his gallows are on the walls of my heart."

"Lady, o Lady, what did you do with the walls of your heart?"

"I hung them with the corpses of my days, and left them to the vultures to pick out their eyes and livers."

"Lady, o Lady, what did you do to your smooth, transparent skin?"

"I married it to the earth, I purified it with thorns and I perfumed it with gunpowder."

"Lady, o Lady, why are you not waiting for me on the platform of the night station as you have done every year?"

"Because I have lost the ability to become numb."

"But I am the feast."

"But you are a passer-by. I am sick of passers-by who are like harbour whores."

"Lady, o Lady, whose name is Beirut, have you lost your senses?"

"Maybe ... maybe not. Maybe for the first time I have come to my senses."

"Lady, o Lady, your lips are cracked like dried meat, your face is burnt like desert sand. Your neck is as thin as that of a bird whose nest has been destroyed. How do you keep going?"

The lady dragged him by the hand: "There is a hill of seven layers: the first is salt, the second corpses, the third blood, the fourth sin, the fifth remorse, the sixth penance, and the seventh conscience. And in the mysterious earth of this mixture is a green plant which makes its way through the darkness and the wind and the moans of the dying which mingle with the moans of those being born."

"Lady, o Lady, how do you spend your nights now?"

"I broke the cans of my nights on the seashore and I left them to rot like empty, rusty sardine cans."

"Lady, o Lady, I am afraid that this is the end, that you're no longer beautiful."

"I never was beautiful. There is no beauty without justice. I was a beautiful veil and now I am removing my veil and my jewelry and my furs and my gloves and am washing my face, if necessary with blood."

"Lady, o Lady, you no longer have a role to play."

"I have refused my role as the lead dancer in the cabaret of the Middle East. I have risen out of my ashes. I have purified myself in the river of blood. This is my only chance to be, to be saved. ... "

"Lady, o Lady, where is your hotel with its luxurious couches so that I may sleep?"

"The country is not a hotel. When you next visit us I hope that you'll become a citizen in the kingdom of joy—my kingdom."

"Lady, o Lady, where are you going?"

"To where I shall be saved, or to where I shall die. ... "

⁓ꝍ⁓   ⁓ꝍ⁓   ⁓ꝍ⁓

The old man gathered together his bags and his worn-out toys and his cheap pipes and returned to the station. In the dark, the green plant was glowing while the poor, the weak and the children were plunging its roots into their veins so that it might grow.

The gentle owl came and tried to make friends with the old man while he was waiting for the train: "This woman called Beirut, I wonder if she is going to commit suicide or if she is going to remove her veins so that phoenix-like she can rise out of her ashes?"

All this turmoil, all this violence, all this shouting: is someone dying, or is someone being born?

—Translated from the Arabic by Miriam Cooke

Meena Alexander

(1951–   )

BORN IN ALLAHABAD, INDIA, and educated in India, North Africa, and Great Britain, Meena Alexander has been highly acclaimed in India, the United States, and Great Britain for her work. She resides in New York and teaches at Hunter College. She is considered one of the most important contemporary South Asian American writers and is active in literary, social, and political groups throughout the United States and India. Her knowledge of life in India, North Africa, Great Britain, and the United States and her sociopolitical concerns form the core of her writings. Although she is known primarily as a poet, she has also published prose pieces, an important first novel, *Nampally Road* (1991), and a memoir, *Fault Lines* (1993). Her collections of poetry include *House of a Thousand Doors* (1988) and *The Storm* (1989).

"No Man's Land," a poem written by an Indian woman about the constant wars in the Middle East, bridges the two geographical areas covered in this anthology. It also reflects a theme that runs through Alexander's works—the effects of men's wars and injustices on women and children. In *House of a Thousand Doors*, Alexander portrays her two grandmothers. One grandmother slowly goes blind as a result of her imprisonment by the British; the other grandmother spends her life kneeling and praying at the doors of her house in order to gain her rightful place in a patriarchal society. Both women suffer, yet both women in their own way actively struggle against injustice: one grandmother as a freedom fighter, the other as a litigant at each door of her house. In "No Man's Land," the women, surrounded by the devastation of war and resting soldiers, watch their children trying to find nourishment in sticks covered with flesh and blood. Instead of offering lamentations or passive acceptance, these stunned women try to cleanse themselves in river water. Their gesture is an echo of ritual cleansing, but only bloodied water is available to them for their cleansing.

No Man's Land

The dogs are amazing
sweaty with light
they race past the
dungheaps

Infants crawl
sucking dirt from sticks
whose blunt ends
smack elder flesh
and ceaseless bloodiness

The soldiers though
are finally resting
by the river
berets over their noses.

Barges from the north
steam past nettles
cut stalks of blackthorn
and elder, olive trees
axed into bits

Women wash their thighs
in bloodied river water,
over and over
they wipe their flesh

In stunned
immaculate gestures
figures massed with light.

They do not hear
the men
or dogs or children.

Dahlia Ravikovitch
(1936–)

DAHLIA RAVIKOVITCH WAS BORN in Tel Aviv, Israel. After serving in the army, she studied English literature at Hebrew University in Jerusalem. Her first collection of poetry, *The Love of an Orange*, was published in 1959. She has edited several collections, including *All Thy Breakers and Waves* (1972), *A Dress of Fire* (1976), and *The Window* (1989). These books are collections of poems translated into English. She is the author of a collection of short stories titled *Death in the Family* (1970) and has also written two books of poetry for children. Ravikovitch has been awarded several prizes, including the Shlonsky, Brenner, and Bialik prizes. "One Cannot Kill a Baby Twice" was written in angry response to the 1982 massacre of Palestinians at the Sabra and Shatila camps in Beirut. The poem decries the senseless killing of children, whether the enemy's or one's own.

One Cannot Kill a Baby Twice

Upon sewage puddles in Sabra and Shatila
Where you delivered masses of people
Considerable masses
From the world of living to the world of truth.

Night after night.
First they shot
Then they hung
At last they slaughtered with knives.
Terrified women appeared in urgence
Above a sand hillock:
"They slaughter us there,
In Shatila."

A refined trail of a newborn moon was hung

Above the camps.
Our soldiers illuminated the place with lightening shells
Like daylight.
"Go back to the camp, march!" the soldier commanded
The yelling women from Sabra and Shatila.
He had orders to follow.
And the children were already laid in dung puddles
Their mouths wide open
Calm.

Nobody will hurt them anymore.
One cannot kill a baby twice.

And the moon's trail became bigger and bigger
Until it turned into a complete coin of gold.

Our sweet soldiers
They asked nothing for themselves,
How strong was their desire
To return home in peace.

Farkhanda Lodhi
(1937–   )

BORN IN SAHIWAL (then India, now Pakistan), Farkhanda Lodhi spent her childhood in East Punjab. She received an M.A. in Urdu literature from Punjab University (Lahore) in 1963 and an M.A. in library science from Punjab University in 1978. She is a lecturer in library science and a librarian in Lahore. She has written novels, short stories, and essays in Urdu and Punjabi.

"Parbati" was the first of Lodhi's works to be published. It appeared in the Urdu literary magazine *Aurg* (1966). It was then included in her first collection of stories, *Shehar Ke Log* (1975). Parbati/Parveen, the protagonist's name in the story, is also the name of an important Hindu mother goddess. It means "she who is of the mountain," the daughter of the mountain. Parbati/Parveen is the wife of Shiva, the god of destruction and regeneration. Her name when she is in Pakistan, Parveen, is from the Farsee and can mean either the Pleiades or pearls. Parbati, living in the time of the war between India and Pakistan in 1971, wishes to be an active participant instead of remaining a passive observer in this war where men fight across borders. She becomes a spy and in the process finds a new name and a new identity. The distinctions between war, duty, and love become painfully blurred when Parbati/Parveen becomes involved with an "enemy" soldier. Her voluntary, active participation in the war results in a child and terrible mental and emotional anguish, even after she returns to the safety of her own home and her own country. Political peace does not always mean personal peace, especially for women.

Parbati

"Kill!" Was it a voice or a returning echo?

"Kill!" And she was advancing.

Rifles thundered. From both sides, from all four sides, an echo, like a verse from a taped anthem, like a song sung by patriots.

"Kill!"

Guns, planes, sirens, whistles and the clanging of the heart, and then a silence. Creating turmoil within this silence, pitting the conscious and the unconscious against each other, a call.

"Kill!"

A bullet whizzed past her shoulder. Bending her head low, she continued walking. The border was only a few yards away and that is where she was headed. She couldn't hear anything. Her ears rang with the clamor of emotions, a storm raged in her soul. The earth's heart was being rent again. She tightened the clasp of both arms.

"Shooo!" Another bullet swished from that direction, then from here, from there again. Rain, noise, fire, heat, thirst …

Her ears covered with both hands, she slowly crawled forward on her stomach. She crossed the border long before sunrise. There had been no interruption in the unrelenting thunder of the guns; as a matter of fact, the sound was getting louder. All around her was the smell of gunpowder and the early rays of the sun were momentarily blanketed by black smoke.

Hiding in the bushes she straightened her body and breathed heavily. There was no chance of anyone coming this way. 'If I hear footsteps or see someone approaching I'll immediately jump into the stream on my left,' she told herself confidentially. Then, for a long time afterward, she bit her swollen lips and pondered over her situation. She was faced with so many hurdles. The wound on her knee was bleeding again while the wounds on her chest had stiffened from the mud that clung to them as she dragged herself. 'Where can I go in this condition?' Over and over again her mind pondered the same question.

The morning birds were not singing. Why were they silent? Fire and thunder had swallowed their happiness. The earth suddenly appeared as a barren place. That the face of the universe would become so melancholy so rapidly, surprised her. She felt her heart stifling with fear and hatred; a wave of hatred for her own, for those she did not know, for herself as well, gripped her whole being and the world inside her grew darker and darker. And sunrise was nowhere near happening. Yes, there were bombs going off and flames of light blazed momentarily, then disappeared. She stumbled on. Further on it seemed as if cries of despair had rent the breast of silence. Screams, as if women were being widowed, as if children were becoming orphans and the rare treasures of chastity were being looted. The roar of tanks and trucks, slogans rising and falling noise … people were awake, people who had been asleep were awake and had begun the struggle for living, but her brain had gone to sleep. It was numb. 'How can she go to these people? She who is nearly naked, covered with blood, a few tatters covering her breasts.' She felt reviled by her own person and she stopped. In the next instant she was walking again with a new determination.

She continued walking. The village was now only a few yards in the distance. The village dogs barked in fright. 'Where are all the people?' Once again silence reigned. Now she was close to the outer wall of the village. She couldn't see anyone behind the crumbling wall; perhaps there was no one there. She wanted to weep, weep at the desolation of the village, at the helplessness of man. Or she should go back where she had come from and never return.

"Kill!"

She saw jeeps coming toward her. A cloud of dust and smoke, flames leaping among small, dry bushes. The remaining sheafs of wheat had burnt to a cinder and the branches, the bones of the old oak tree were crackling in the fire. She wet her lips with her tongue. She was so thirsty, there were thorns raking her throat. She did not rise from the mound of debris where she had fallen half-dead. Then she heard footsteps, closer, closer still, and someone was saying, "Kill!"

Quickly she lifted herself and made an attempt, unsuccessfully, to cover her body. Standing in front of her, staring at her meaningfully, were two armed soldiers. Their groping glances, those looks that seemed to be searching for something under the tatters, beyond the flesh, in the mind, in the heart. Fear and a sense of danger made her body numb. She could not speak; it was as if she had lost her power of speech, as if there were stones in her eyes instead of pupils.

"Why didn't you leave with the other villagers? You are in very bad shape."

She found this tone of voice encouraging. Her eyes filled with tears. "I … what can I tell you. I've been running away from the wild animals in the other village. You are my brother, please finish me off, do me this one favor."

She spoke without restraint and the soldiers wondered if they should shut her up or let her die by herself along with her story. One of the men dashed off and returned with a blanket from somewhere which he threw over her. The soldiers were nervous; they were reluctant to make her young, full body a target and fire rained all around them, the atmosphere burned.

"Do you have any relatives?"

"Let her be, I say, don't waste your time."

"Life or death?" the first one asked her.

"Whatever you can give," she replied. There was a challenge in her tone now and her voice rang clear.

"That's in the hands of God," the soldier said. He turned his head and saw that his companion had already left. He too walked away, without saying anything else. She was saved. Shells and gunpowder kept pouring around her and she stayed where she was. No one came that way either to save her or to kill her.

In the afternoon, when she was completely enervated from hunger and exhaustion, a small caravan came to the place where she had been lying, and set up camp. There were only a few men. The women and children, with ashen, frightened faces, stood under a sheesham tree; babies screeched in their mother's laps, the mothers' lips were dry and colorless. Then jeeps and trucks appeared on the scene. A small group of soldiers herded the people together like goats and began putting them on the trucks. One of the men, who looked like an officer, was giving the soldiers instructions in undertones. There was no sign of anxiety on his face. He inspected the area around them with confidence. The soldiers were working very fast. Their lighthearted conversation and their jokes helped allay the mood of sadness that prevailed.

"Mother, are you running away from death? Well, in that case you stay behind and let us take someone more useful instead." He laughed.

"Ahh, no, my child!" she screamed. "I'll go and drown myself in the stream."

"Mother, you love life, don't you?"

"Yes son. But death has to come someday, it's just that I don't want to die at the hands of the *kafirs*."

"Mother, you have an opportunity to become a martyr," the soldier said to the old woman.

"Martyrdom comes from actions, son, not just like that. And what have I, unfortunate woman that I am, done to deserve martyrdom?"

Everyone was laughing. Work continued amidst laughter. As if nothing had happened. As if people had risen from sleep and the morning had brought in its wake a new age, a new world, as if people suffered exhaustion simply because of the interest and panic resulting from the thought of exploring this new world. The women were silent and shadows of perturbation darkened their eyes. Behind this temporary lightheartedness and joy was a deep anxiety which forced the officer to look again and again at the eastern horizon, which compelled him to herd the people like goats and sheep.

She was wounded. She was put on a stretcher in one of the jeeps. Her face was awash with the yellowness of death and she was being taken to a hospital so she could be brought back to life. She became hysterical.

"Kill me ... no, no, kill me. How can I go back to my people ... no, no ... I've been defiled. My brother will kill himself when he sees my condition, how will my mother face the world? I beg you, I beg you on the honor of your virgins, on the loyalty and dignity of your wives, leave me here. I have been ravaged by wild men, let the dogs devour my flesh. I have no one any more, not even my own self."

She kept babbling on and on and the jeep kept going. The men in the front paid no attention to her ramblings, treating her as if she were luggage that they had to transport to its proper destination. Once the jeep stopped, one of the men got off and his seat was stacked with empty boxes, bundles and other miscellaneous items. The roadside teemed with people, their emotions betrayed by their cries. Young boys peeked at her through the window of the jeep and she thought irately, 'Why doesn't the jeep move on? Am I on display?'

"I'm on display," she exclaimed loudly. The indifference of the officer in the front enraged her; why didn't he pay any attention to what she was saying? Everyone had turned into stone. What had happened to people? They were like puppets, puppets in the hands of politics and time.

"Are you deaf?" she screamed at the man in the driver's seat.

"I don't have time," was the reply she received.

She got up and leaned over the front seat.

"You don't have time? You don't even have time to throw me somewhere?"

The officer turned to look at her. He felt her breath at his temples.

"I'm not going to throw you anywhere," he said after a pause, "because you're young and you're not bad looking."

Then he changed the subject. "Why don't you lie down? Come on, don't make more work for me."

She had come to find something out and she was brushed off. The jeep continued to move along at a steady pace. Gusts of fresh air began to make her feel better.

"What will you do with me?"

"Pickle you!"

She assumed silence. There was no room for further conversation.

Finally the jeep entered the gates leading to a large building and stopped. Several bearers ran toward them with a stretcher, but she got down from the jeep without any help.

"Well, salaam."

"Walekum-as-salaam." The officer looked at her through his dark glasses. A woman wrapped in a blanket, covered with mud, hair awry and tears lost in the dust on her face; she looked like a mad woman.

"What's your name?" The man's heart softened with compassion and sympathy for the helpless, lonely woman.

"Nothing."

"Nothing isn't a name, you know."

"Parveen." She gave a short reply and became lost in thought.

"Parveen?" The man repeated and added, "Peena."

She smiled. A question floated in her eyes: 'What is my destination now?'

The man took off his sunglasses and looked at her closely.

"My name is Hasan. Is there anything I can do for you?"

"No!" Parveen retorted angrily. She felt disappointed with Hasan, strangely disappointed.

"God be with you then."

"And with you." Parveen's hand hung in the air for a long time. Her heart was beginning to soften.

Once she recovered she was sent to a camp from the hospital. When people inquired about her relatives she became angry, she ranted and raved as if her being had been pillaged and wounded by an experience of cruelty and devastation; she became hysterical. Gradually people stopped asking her.

In the camp Parveen lived with a widow who came to love her as her own daughter. All day long she tutored the women and children in the camp and earned the respect of the camp residents. Soon she was everyone's *Apa*. It was customary for her to have classes for children in the mornings and evenings; the children seemed happy in her tutelage. To the homeless, anxious mothers, this was a source of much needed relief and, finding a moment's respite from presentiment, they sat down and ruminated about her fate.

"Ahh, what a nice girl she is. What will become of her?"

One of the women, feeling particularly bitter about Parveen's fate, beat her breast and exclaimed: "Ahh, why did the *kafirs* ravage her?"

Young girls were being married off with great urgency in the camp. Women who worried unceasingly about all the world's young girls anxiously sought a groom for Parveen. But you needed heart to marry her, not just eyes. As a matter of fact, youthful eyes pursued her all day and to escape them Parveen finished her work before sundown and then went to the fields and sat alone on the gleanings of corn left there. Who knows what she did there, why her gaze lost itself in the horizon. And finally she returned, her steps slow and faltering, like that of a holy man's who leaves the solitude of his temple to go to the village.

Parveen belonged to everyone; all the people in the camp worried about her, mothers and fathers fretted about her.

Everyone worried about her because she always wore her dupatta down to her forehead and kept here eyes lowered. This was why she attracted the attention of simple folks. Men who were sensible showed her deference by getting out of her way when she was walking about in the camp. She now commanded everyone's respect.

She didn't want to become too well-known in the small community of the camp. Avoiding the company of older people, she spent most of her time with children. Others in the camp understood her reasons for this isolation; those who harbored broken hearts and had been injured recently did not have the courage to rake her wounds.

On her way to the camp one evening she ran into Zenab. She had met and befriended Zenab in this camp. This eighteen-year-old village girl's father was missing. She resided in the camp with her small family and was often seen roaming on the outskirts of the camp; her eyes and her feet ran endlessly over the small paths and trails in search of her father. If her father returned, her mother and her brother and sister could find a home and then they could find a husband for Zenab. These were bad times. Mothers worried incessantly and Zenab and many other young unmarried women waited anxiously, with pounding hearts, for fathers, brothers, and bridegrooms with whom they could spend the rest of their lives. The daughters of Eve want nothing more; the young women of the villages are not equipped to desire more than this. When news arrived of those who had died, they cried, when they received tidings of life and victory, they blossomed. This constituted the limits of their feelings and their lives.

Zenab blocked Parveen's way.

"Apa, you think if you don't tell anyone about yourself, no one will be looking for you? Come with me, there's someone asking for you."

Parveen hesitated. A wave of fear and panic swept across her somber face.

"Come on, why are you stopping?"

Parveen began walking with faltering steps. She did not say anything to Zenab.

"Apa, why are you afraid? Your relatives won't devour you. Whatever happened was not your fault." Zenab thought she had guessed the reason for Parveen's dread.

As soon as Parveen saw Hasan standing before her, the earth and sky seemed to whirl around her. The universe appeared to be saying, "No! No!" There was only one question in her mind. Why has he come? Why has he come? Why has he come? Without lifting her eyes, without responding to Hasan's greeting, she stood rooted to the ground, trembling. That her will power would abandon her in this manner and she would prove to be so weak, was something she could not believe. Slowly she raised her eyes, gradually her lips moved.

"Salaam … "

"Why are you so nervous?"

"I'm all right."

Then Hasan started talking without waiting for her to say anything further.

"I went to the hospital one day, on an errand, and found out that you had been sent to this camp. Today, by chance I was going this way, and I've met you. That's just as well." His speech was choppy.

"Yes, I'm glad to see you." Parveen spoke formally. Zenab had left.

"You've recognized me, haven't you?" Hasan asked. "Do you remember my name?"

"Yes, very well."

Hasan was silent for a few moments. Then he said, "I don't know why I have this feeling that you're the personification of a secret. Why do I want to know this secret? I know I have no right, but … "

Parveen smiled at him. His eyes were questioning her.

"For a man every woman is the personification of a secret. Let's talk about something else." Parveen's tone was polite.

"Parveen, I want to talk to you about something. Not war, that's God's wrath. No, I want to talk about His love. I want to dream about peace and love." Hasan was quiet again. Parveen was also silent. Silence continued to speak and they listened.

"I'll be going now. I'll come again, God willing." He walked away. Shocked and perturbed, Parveen watched him without moving.

Hasan came often after that. They would sit under a tree and talk about themselves and listen. Parveen recounted stories about her shortcomings and her failures, trying to convince Hasan. She was very concerned about Hasan's interest in her. What was he looking for? she often asked herself. But there was a joy hidden deep inside her which occasionally spilled from her eyes and which Hasan recognized. However, Parveen's mind did not accept this joy; she would not be convinced.

One day Hasan began telling her about an incident in his childhood. "You know, Peena, one remains a child where certain things are concerned. I think I'm still a child—when I was seven I used to play in the street outside our house. Sometimes one gets hold of wonderful things during play, isn't that true?" Whenever he narrated a story he wanted the listeners to show they were paying attention and Parveen had forgotten to say "Hun, hun."

"God protects man's innocence. So, this is what happened. One day I discovered a pearl lying in the mud. It was so beautiful, or at least it seemed beautiful to me. I spat on it and wiped it with my shirt front. It looked brighter than ever. I put it in my mouth and continued playing. Peena, to this day I don't understand why it is that when we like something very much we want to devour it. A child's desire is impulsive; adults learn to curb it, but the desire never goes away. I remember my mother scolded me and slapped me; she said 'God knows what dirty things you pick up and put in your mouth.' With the pearl clutched tightly in my fist, I cried for hours afterward. Why didn't my mother respect my wish? My infantile brain registered that idea for the first time that day. The shock of this realization made my heart bleed all day long. Later, I begged my sister to stitch the pearl to my shirt collar where I wore it proudly for many days. It may have bothered people around me, but it made me happy. I still remember that pearl vividly."

Parveen smiled and laughed at the recounting of this unimportant event and Hasan continued to be delighted by her femininity.

Disregarding ethical boundaries and political contracts, the neighboring country suddenly attacked under cover of darkness. Several fronts opened at once. Hasan was forced to run from one front to the other. Their army was small and they were in a confrontation with a formidable enemy. One man had to do the work of four. Hasan was a lieutenant. There were many officers who were killed in battle and Parveen was worried about Hasan, although he was nothing to her. When he came she was filled with dread, when he left she thought of him endlessly and prayed: "May Hasan come back safe and sound, he must come back safe and sound." Sometimes she felt Hasan was her destination and nothing existed beyond that destination. Whenever he came to visit her he told her innumerable stories. His army is routing the enemy at every front, the enemy is being defeated, this is happening, that will happen. Completely unaware of the consequences, Parveen would sit quietly, staring at the sky. She didn't think of anything except Hasan's voice.

Hasan was wounded in the arm. He got leave for fifteen days and took Parveen home. Hasan was breathing in an atmosphere of love and war at the same time, impervious to what was right or wrong. Retreat in love and war is death; he was not ready to accept either the death of his body or his love. His country was winning the war and winning the battle of his heart was his own personal responsibility. Hasan was married a few days later.

On the day of the wedding Parveen was sunk in silence. Despite Hasan's insistence she wouldn't tell him what she was feeling. Then, gradually, a change appeared in her. She focused her entire attention on the house. She laughed and chirped. This was Hasan's house; this was her house. When Hasan left for the office, she sat on the prayer rug and recited something all day long. On the walls of the house she hung framed verses from the Quran and Hadith and when Hasan returned from work he found her absorbed more and more in religion. He wondered how a simple woman with little education and from a small town could think and do all of this, why she would be so involved with religious and literary works, why, at this age, at this time, she was so obsessed with religion. With each passing day Parveen's complexion blossomed, the expression of purity on her face brightened. Peace had come. Mother earth's countenance bloomed.

During evening tea Hasan saw something on Parveen's face that made him stare at her. She blushed. Hasan gathered her in his arms. Her head nestled on his chest, Parveen's breath came fast and the whole world seemed to have become embodied in their warm breaths. Lit with the pure light of emotion a look, shining, magical. Hasan asked suddenly, "Peena, why've you become so religious? I'm surprised."

"I'm trying to thank my creator who has given me so much," Parveen said. "So much," she whispered under her breath, "gave me so much, so much … "

Hasan peered into her eyes and smiled.

"What has He given you?" he asked mischievously.

Parveen averted his gaze bashfully, then lowered her eyes.

"Oh, I see." He kissed her eyelids and engulfed her with love.

There was one word that beamed in Parveen's mind like the morning star—victory, victory, victory—

Good weather brings clear skies and fresh breezes. Hasan received two promotions one after another. He attributed his success to the good luck he thought Parveen had brought him. He felt that this lucky woman had provided the first step toward a glorious future. Hasan began to adore Parveen; that delicate woman with a wheat-colored complexion ruled over his heart, his mind and his house. Her behavior and her attitude toward him wooed Hasan so that he forgot everything else. Parveen symbolized the complete woman; she knew how to scold like a mother and tease and adore like a sister, and she could also be coquettish and make sacrifices like a wife.

Hasan moved to another town after his promotion. With Parveen at his side he shifted into a new house in a place where she was not known at all. They were both happy and content with this change; their lives took on a new meaning. A flower was to blossom in their garden soon, who could be more fortunate than Hasan? Days of peace—there was life all around them, surging and sweeping.

At the breakfast table one morning Parveen saw that Hasan was not his usual cheerful self. She became nervous. After their marriage he had not been able to sit quietly for one moment. Parveen looked at him closely. He seemed engrossed in drinking his tea. His eyelids were puffy. Parveen's heart lurched.

"Hasan, what's wrong with your eyes? They look puffy."

Hasan placed the cup of tea on the table and remained silent. He wasn't looking at Parveen. She shook him by the arms and became tearful.

"Why are you quiet? Why don't you tell me … "

"I couldn't sleep all night," Hasan said in a tired, enervated voice.

"Why?" Parveen asked anxiously. "Why didn't you wake me up?"

"I wasn't really awake myself. I can't describe what kind of a state I was in. I was having a horrible dream and I kept weeping, I wept a lot." Hasan leaned his head against the back of the chair and stared at the ceiling. His eyes became wet. Hasan and tears? Parveen was astounded. Could this man who had played holi* with blood in the battlefield, who encountered formidable armies before him and who leaped heroically over them in victory, a brave and gallant soldier, could this man have such a weak, soft heart?

"Tell me what the dream was. You'll feel better after you've shared it with me."

---

*Holi is the Hindu festival of Spring when people sprinkle and spray bright colors on one another.

"Why do you want to hear about the dream? It will only make you feel sad."

"You have to tell me," Parveen insisted.

Hasan began haltingly.

"There's a garden in which spring arrives ... " He spoke slowly, deliberately, as if he were trying to paste pictures on the album of his imagination.

"There were two birds, lost. I built them a nest and they started living there happily. Then, I don't know how, the nest caught fire ... their babies were in that nest too, Peena ... " He paused. "Then the fire flared up and I kept weeping. When I awoke my pillow was wet and my heart was heavy with a feeling that seemed to suggest that I was the one who had set fire to the nest, I was the criminal, I burnt everything, offered everything to the flames. And after that I couldn't go back to sleep."

Parveen became lost in thought as she listened. Shadows of apprehension floated across her face. She was silent and she trembled. The previous night, while she slipped in and out of sleep, she had heard the sound of Hasan's footsteps and felt his face leaning over hers. Then she fell asleep and now Hasan was telling her the story and everything in the house had become somber and mute.

They did not speak to each other all morning. Their hearts were shrouded in heavy curtains of dread through which neither of them could see the other's face. Can people suddenly become strangers to each other? Like two fluttering shadows without faces which had left light behind, somewhere far behind, and were now just two helpless shadows quivering unsteadily on the slate of time.

Before leaving for the office Hasan said, "Get ready in the evening, we'll go for a long drive. I don't want to suffer through the same horrible dream again tonight and I think a drive will calm my spirits. You also look tired." Then he bent down to kiss her forehead but didn't kiss her and left. There was an air of resolution in his gait that hadn't been there earlier. Parveen felt an ache, an inexplicable wave of hope and despair.

They left early in the evening. The moon was slowly slipping toward the west. Clasping the locket tightly in her hand, Parveen sat quietly, lost in thought. That evening Hasan had brought her a locket to make her happy, a locket with "Allah" inscribed on it. God's name in Parveen's hand, her heart invaded by a world teeming with fearful dangers and difficulties, the harrowing stillness that reigned about them, and Hasan's silence.

"Where are we going?" she asked again.

"You know I've always managed to startle you." Hasan was not very talkative today.

"Yes, you've always surprised me." Hasan's answer proved satisfactory to Parveen. She was so accustomed to his habits that she didn't think it was necessary to ask for further details.

"Go to sleep," Hasan said, bringing her head to rest on his shoulder. The jeep continued on. Parveen shut her eyes and pretended to be asleep. All of a sudden the jeep came to a halt. Hasan lifted Parveen out of the vehicle gingerly, as if she were a glass bottle, and, with an arm around her for support, began walking with her. Perhaps they had arrived at their destination.

It was dark and chilly. They walked on. Beneath their feet sand slithered and every once in a while they stumbled.

"Where are you taking me, Hasan?" Parveen asked again in a tearful voice. Her feet felt heavy, she was walking with great difficulty. Her steps dragged in the sand. But Hasan was pulling her along. There was no sound in the desert except that of the sibilation of the sand and the wind rustling through the bushes. A field of stars extended over the sky as far as the eye could see.

Hasan stopped. He embraced Parveen tightly, kissed her, then stood away from her. The journey had been long and cumbersome; he was out of breath.

"Parbati, go. God be with you." He walked away from her.

Parbati screamed. Because of the darkness they could not read the expressions on each other's faces.

"Parbati, remember you have something of mine," he stopped for a moment and said. Then his shadow disappeared quickly behind the bushes.

"Hasan! Hasan!" Parbati ran after him and fell. She waved her arms in the air and continued to cry his name; she tried to stifle her screams with her hands for fear that her voice might cut through the silence. Hasan was gone.

Shiva abandoned Parbati, Adam pushed Eve to the other side of Paradise and left her there alone. At this time she was neither Parbati nor Parveen, she was only a woman, she was the earth filled with love, with fecundity. She lay on the sand and wept. Her locket, inscribed with "Allah" rolled about in the sand, the trinity disintegrated in the desert, Allah, Adam and Eve scattered in the face of politics.

"Hasan, Hasan, Hasan." Parbati's golden dream had ended. Night was coming to a close, the light of the new day slowly spread across the horizon. Bending over her was a man.

He was saying, "Let's kill her now, my man."

And she announced in a tone of conciliation: "I'm Parbati. Colonel Mehta's wife." She didn't want to die.

On this side of the border she was Mrs. Mehta once again. Shrimati Parbati Mehta, Colonel Mehta's wife. Complexion wheatish, of medium height, a serious expression on the face, a mole over the left cheekbone, an old scar on the right eyebrow; her description had been printed in newspapers and posters. During the war she had gone behind enemy lines as a spy. For a while she kept sending them reports of her activities. Then her life changed. All her passion and her ardor were directed elsewhere. Her new, entrancing life became accustomed to another path like a stream changing its course. This was the path to which Hasan led her. Hasan had nurtured her garden, he was the father of her unborn child. The knowledge that she was to become a mother had elevated Parbati's position in her own eyes; she felt as though she had come into her own, as if she had only just become aware of her abilities and talents. She was an actuality that people had denied, calling her a sterile woman, infertile earth. She was one whose bosom was filled with treasures.

How young and carefree she was when she married Mehta. He gave her everything, but he couldn't endow her with self-confidence. She was sure that her home would not be threatened by the absence of a child. As for Mehta, tall, burly Mehta, she was justly proud of him. Because she was his wife she had obtained a special place in society. But despite all this people viewed her with hostility. To this day anyone and everyone was ready to wed their daughters to him. Ten years of domesticity passed. She was a twenty-eight-year-old, experienced woman when she realized that she could do a great deal more than just be a mother. There was one thought that preoccupied her incessantly: 'I'll do something special before I die, I'll definitely do something special before I die.'

War broke out with the neighboring country. Mothers sent out their beloved sons to make history with their blood. Borders demanded blood for their safety, fresh, young blood, cast in a mold of flesh and skin which mothers gave birth to, raised and nurtured, so they could sacrifice it at the altars of their country. They see it spill with tears in their eyes and then their heads are held high with pride.

They say, "I too have a share in this country's soil, I have nurtured it with my blood, this fecund earth is my being—I am the earth, I give birth to sons and I devour them as well."

Parbati became more and more restless. Blood rushed through her veins, blood that was passionate and vigorous. She was increasingly conscious of her inadequacies. She realized that today and tomorrow, always, she would be deprived of this one blessing. She too wanted to contribute a drop to that flowing river; a drop that claimed its existence from her blood. But this was not possible. True she could sacrifice her husband and obtain this blessing, but that was also difficult. What would she do if she lost him? She thought, at this time when there was a fire raging in all directions, life had been reduced to an uncertainty, she could get news of Mehta's death any moment. And how would she continue her life without Mehta? There were no awards, no ribbons. She decided she would do something that would give her life meaning. If a woman couldn't be a mother she would want much more out of life.

Her life with Mehta had reached an impasse. But along came war and imbued life with change and new standards. Mehta suggested Parbati train as a nurse, but Parbati didn't want to heal wounds, she wanted to suffer her own wounds; she was driven by a desire to run into the battle-field and stand alongside the soldiers, fight and vanquish the enemy. She pleaded with Mehta to find something for her and finally he came up with the idea that she spy for them behind enemy lines. Using her intelligence and good looks she could serve her nation and lay her life down for her country if the need arose, and thus she would become immortal.

With help from shots of morphine she had wounds inflicted on her body and, for the sake of her country, crossed the border in the dark of night. She played her role expertly and for a long time the chain of messages continued. But then her life took a new course. Gradually Hasan's face descended into her heart, Hasan who won her heart and melted her spirit with his soft speech and his actions. After she found Hasan, Parbati forgot about her earlier life. It was as if what she had once had was not life but a period of imprisonment which she spent in anticipation of freedom. Hasan became the final goal for which her soul had struggled so long, or was he just a man who had blessed her with confidence? She who had felt guilty in the presence of all those around her, now felt proud. She could now proclaim that she was no less than anybody, that she too had a special place in life.

↦   ↦   ↦

Like a delicate flower she was transported from the border to Colonel Mehta. He treated her with genuine affection and care, but Parbati was uneasy. She was troubled by the thought that if Mehta discovered the truth he would not treat her well at all. And he was sure to find out. Parbati didn't tell her husband anything, but he guessed. His eyes blazed with anger, he turned on her like an enraged wolf.

"I never expected this from you ... " He paused for a moment. "For the sake of your country, I suppose, well ... you had no choice, you were forced." His tone softened. He recalled Parbati's many sacrifices. He put his head on her shoulder. Parbati was lying on the bed quietly, watching Mehta's face change with each new emotion. She was silent and felt as if she had made a stop at a serai to rest after a long journey. Despite Mehta's accusation she didn't feel as if she had committed a crime. She knew she hadn't committed a crime, she was satisfied.

"Don't worry," Mehta said in a comforting tone, "we'll take care of it."

"We were childless, we'll raise it," Parbati suggested.

"Pernicious seed! The offspring of an outcast! I won't keep it in my house. Parbati, listen carefully, you too have been made impure and I've only taken you back because of your love and your loyalty. We have to destroy it, now, today or tomorrow."

In one breath Mehta delivered his demand, his condemnation and his threat. He was aware not only that his wife's honor had been defiled, but he was also conscious of his own failing. From across the border Parbati had brought back something for which they had both longed and yearned. But Mehta had no share in this, and Parbati, this low woman, was determined to prove him inadequate. He could defeat her with a show of force. He leapt toward her.

"You won't do this, I won't let you!"

"I'll kill you!" He advanced toward her with his hands raised.

"Kill me then."

Mehta's fist fell on her chest and she recoiled in pain. Crouching, with her legs protecting her stomach, she submitted to his beating, to on-slaughts from his hands and his legs. Her bones and the blood that coursed through her veins received a beating to save the life that existed within her for safety, she continued to protect that which was hers, to which she was mother. She was a mother and she was the earth. 'No, no, I won't let this happen.'

Mehta lost, he lost on all fronts. After this incident the tension be-tween them grew. Her time came nearer. He was absent from home for many weeks at a time. In his absence Parbati felt at peace, she didn't ex-perience the pressure his presence induced and she could wait calmly for the day when her life's earnings would be placed into her lap and she would be fulfilled.

Parbati left for the hospital without waiting for Mehta. She informed neither her in-laws nor her parents. However, she did write Mehta a short note in which she said he could make peace with her if he wanted to or break all bonds if that was his desire, but she didn't expect anything from him. She had nothing to do with anyone anymore. The whole world had disappointed her, even Hasan. Parbati had also decided to sunder all links. What she was going to do eventually and how she would do it, she didn't know as yet. Only after her dream became reality would she be able to make real decisions. She waited. Time passed. Tick, tick, tick, tick.

The morning was bathed in fresh dew. A new day in spring had dawned, a new day for Parbati.

The bearer informed her that Colonel Mehta was here. Parbati looked up with confidence. Mehta could not break all links with her. She ex-pected him to ask for a reconciliation. He was here. She clasped the baby to her bosom. Mehta entered her room smiling, but instead of gazing at her with softness and affection, his eyes blazed with a fire, a fire that sparkled. Parbati returned his smile and remained silent.

"Let's go," Mehta ordered her.

"Where?"

"Home, where else. I've brought the car."

"Are you mad? Can't you see the baby is too ... "

Mehta interrupted her. "You're driving me out of my mind Parbati." He came closer. "I beg you, please, kill these emotions, start a new life, learn to live with me again, you've disgraced your country, your faith, your husband—you're a murderer."

Parbati said nothing. Her head was empty. She wasn't thinking anything. Quietly, like a weak little goat, she followed him out of the hospital. What would the people in the hospital say if she created a ruckus, so she decided to accompany him. During the ride home Mehta was aloof and he grumbled and rambled as if he were intoxicated.

"Parbati, you are a woman, a *nari*—the Muslims call fire *nar*, they're right. You're fire, you enflamed everything, reduced everything to ashes. I can't even let you go, what shall I do? Parbati, Parbati, you've weakened Shiva, you've disgraced him ... "

When she got home Parbati got a comfortable bed. She wondered where the servants were. Mehta cooked supper himself and gave her hot milk and biscuits. Parbati didn't feel the need to talk about the change that she saw around her. She was tired of playing roles and now she wanted to simply observe. There was a certain delight in being only an observer and she was experiencing that delight. She felt satisfied, at peace. What will be, will be. She abandoned the boat to the care of the waves. She wanted to see what was going to happen next.

Evening came and then night, and then the signs of early morning crept in. She kept her eyes open all night, staring in anticipation of the hand that would advance toward the light of her life and try to blow it out, any minute, any minute. She dozed, slumber, dear slumber, curtains, heavy curtains, oblivion, she was dreaming. Mehta is here, he's standing next to her looking for something, feeling with his hands, the baby begins to cry. This was no dream.

Snatch, push, pull—a struggle between life and death—tears and entreaties, jealousy—envy and suffocation—defeat and a sense of sin.

"I want to kill him!" Mehta roared like a wild tomcat which kills its young in order to possess its female.

"No, no," she cried in anguish, and clasping the child to her breast, bent low. She would do anything for him, her body would withstand any attack to save the child. "I'll leave in the morning, I'll go away, far away." She spoke impassionately, with determination, with anger. Her breath was hot with emotion. What she did and said after that even she couldn't remember. She left the house.

She neared the border before the evening shadows lengthened. A storm of emotions had completely engulfed her senses. A crazed woman traversed the bosom of the earth, the earth that is mother, that is one-ness, that is human.

She had forgotten that on this earth were countries and countries had borders and standing on borders were guards. She kept walking.

The sun was slowly sinking into the west. The sky and earth were bathed in the crimson blood of the setting sun. On and on she advanced, slowly, slowly, closer, closer. A bullet whizzed past her, grazing her shoulder. She clasped the child tightly to her breast and covered his face with her head. Another bullet, then another—she had come very far. Shouts could be heard around her. "Kill! Kill!" The sound of gunshots filled the air. A storm—she, alone, and all these bullets—smoke, swelling and growing darkness—rising and falling voices—the earth of the border—her blood, red, hot, young and fresh—and then stillness, silence and an echo.

"Kill!"

—Translated from the Urdu by Tahira Naqvi

Anne Ranasinghe

(1925–   )

ANNE RANASINGHE WAS BORN in Essen, Germany. At the outbreak of World War II, her parents, who later died in Nazi concentration camps, sent her to England. She did not return to Germany until 1983. In England she studied nursing and journalism, before moving to Sri Lanka in 1950. She is seen as synthesizing three cultures, German, British, and Sri Lankan, in her life and writings. She has published collections of poetry, including *Plead Mercy* (1975) and *Against Eternity and Dos Kness* (1985), and anthologies of short stories, including *With Words We Write Our Lives Past Present and Future* (1973). She was awarded the Sri Lanka Arts Council Prize for poetry in 1985.

Having fled Nazi Germany as a child, she again experienced the horrors of war in Sri Lanka when she was caught in the ethnic and communal conflicts of the last two decades. "Auschwitz from Colombo" is from her first collection of poetry, *And a Sun That Sucks the Earth* (1971). The poem reflects one of the central themes of Ranasinghe's works—the need to remember atrocities committed in war and to assume responsibility for its survivors by documenting the events of wars.

Auschwitz from Colombo

Colombo. March. The city white fire
That pours through vehement trees burst into flame,
And only a faint but searing wind
Stirring the dust
From relics of foreign invaders, thrown
On this far littoral by chance or greed,
Their stray memorial the odd word mispronounced,
A book of laws
A pile of stones
Or maybe some vile deed.

Once there was another city; but there
It was cold—the tree leafless
And already thin ice on the lake.
It was that winter
Snow hard upon the early morning street
And frost flowers carved in hostile window panes

It was that winter.

Yet only yesterday
Half a world away and twenty-five years later
I learn of a narrow corridor
And at the end a hole, four feet by four,
Through which they pushed them all—the children too—
Straight down a shaft of steel thirteen feet long
And dark and icy cold
Onto the concrete floor of what they called
The strangling room. Dear God, the strangling room,
Where they were stunned—the children too—
By heavy wooden mallets,

Garroted, and then impaled
On pointed iron hooks.

I am glad of the unechoing street
Burnt white in the heat of many tropical years.
For the mind, no longer sharp,
Seared by the tropical sun
Skims over the surface of things
Like the wind
That stirs but slightly the ancient dust.

Emily Nasrallah

(1938–)

EMILY NASRALLAH WAS BORN in Kfeir, South Lebanon. When she was nine years old, she asked an uncle who had emigrated to the United States to send her to boarding school in Shwaifat. She studied for her B.A. at the American University at Beirut and Beirut College for Women (now, Beirut University College) and worked her way through the university by writing as a journalist. In 1962, she published her first novel, *September Birds.* Her other novels include: *The Oleander Tree* (1968), *The Pawn* (1973), and *Those Memories* (1980). She considers her most recent novel, *Flight Against Time* (1981), to be the sequel to *September Birds. Flight Against Time* was translated into English in 1987. Her collections of short stories include *The Island of Illusion* (1973) and *The Source* (1978). She has written two short story collections on the Lebanese Civil War: *Woman in 17 Stories* (1983) and *The Lost Mill* (1985). Between 1981 and 1987, she contributed a regular column on famous women's lives to the women's magazine, *Fairuz.* Of all the Beirut Decentrists, she is one of the very few who throughout the sixteen years of the Lebanese Civil War, attempted to remain in Beirut, the city she calls "the only place I can write."

"Our Daily Bread" is the title story of a 1985 collection of short stories (translated and published in 1990) that she wrote after the Israeli invasion. At the beginning of the story two women converse about the presence of war in their everyday lives. The miracle of survival is celebrated only to be revealed as a charade. Deliverance from death is no assurance that destruction is not lurking around the very next corner.

Our Daily Bread

We would sit together and talk about the war, Sana' and I. Sometimes pessimism and hopelessness descended upon us, covering us like a tent. Then we would grow silent, as though cement blocks and sand bags had blocked the way for words. Our words sank and hid within the depths of our throats.

But in untroubled times of tranquillity, we would sit around and ana-
lyze the situation, in our simple way that depended on theories.

At the end of one of our sessions, Sana' stood up, and with a mocking smile on her face and a sigh from the depth of her heart, she said,
"And now that we've put to rest all the unresolved matters of the world
and put an end to the war, I have to go back home and cook for my
family."

And with a wink she added sarcastically, "You do know, of course,
that a woman's role is not restricted to theorizing and finding political
solutions and discussing philosophical matters. We have to cook and
clean and take care of everything in order to deserve our title of real
women!"

She threw out her words in a funny, endearing way, and took her leave
of me in a loving manner. The war had not changed her, nor hardened
her, as it had so many people.

Sana' had her own unique way of welcoming friends or bidding them
farewell. She hugged warmly and affectionately. Without reservations,
she poured all her love into them, and coated their hearts with her ever-
present joy of life. She gave everyone around her a feeling of warmth and
well being; a promise of better things to come in spite of the darkness of
war, in spite of the walls of anger, hatred and resentment erected around
us. She made us feel that the world she inhabited, and us with it, would
always be alright.

Some time ago she came to visit me, after a forced absence that had
lasted months. I hugged her, my heart soaring with the joy of seeing her
again safe and sound, with the relief that she had—that we all had—
made it out of our basement prisons, out of our damp and smelly shel-
ters.

"I was afraid we would not meet again," I said to her, looking at the
changes the war had wrought on her already slim figure. "I ... was ... " I
choked on my tears.

She realized my words would drag us into the tragedy of what had
happened. She jumped out of her seat and with a laugh she twirled
around in a little dance to show she was still the same, then returned to
her place, and laughed ... She laughed until her eyes filled with tears.
That was Sana'. Always using laughter to mask the tears in every delicate situation, holding her smile up like a shield in the face of tragedy.
And she often cried with laughter, but she never cried with pain or sadness.

That was Sana', sweet and unique and funny.

Then she and I sat and talked, just like we had always done in the days
of peace and good living.

It was the first time we had seen each other after the invasion of Beirut. We did not talk much, for the sound of rockets and explosions still

deafened us; the smell of fire and smoke burned our nostrils; and the names of victims filled the distance between us. After awhile we sat in silence—she smoking her cigarette and sipping her bitter coffee and I looking out at the remnants and rubble of the homes around us.

I tried to interrupt our silence and bring her back to the present. "Where to from here … ?"

She looked at me at length and said nothing.

I repeated my question, "When will salvation finally come our way, Sana'? Do you think we have reached the limit, that this is the beginning of the end?"

Again she looked at me, silently, and the silence filled more empty moments. I respected her feelings and withdrew into the hidden pockets of myself. There I saw a pencil moving of its own volition in the distance between us, drawing a caricature of our little session.

I shuddered. Then I started laughing out loud, bringing her out of her silence. She looked towards me and said, "I hope to God that only good things are making you laugh. What is so funny?"

Actually, I did not really know why I was laughing, for the situation was rather sad. Or was I crying, hiding my tears with laughter? I still do not know the meaning of my laughter at that time. I do not want to dwell on that confusing moment when everything around us had collapsed, and we were trying to reconnect the broken lines of friendship and human relations.

Yesterday she appeared anew, after a long absence outside the country. Her presence reminded me of a saying by an Indian philosopher, "Sometimes we see the face of God in the presence of our friends."

I was cooped up inside my house, walking through rooms empty save for the holes in the walls made by the flying shrapnel of continuous war. They were like slap marks on the face of memory. I no longer remembered what corner would provide me with some semblance of peace and tranquillity, in which to remember friends now scattered around the globe, who only yesterday had taken refuge in each others' hearts.

I lived in a circle of anxiety, the sounds of distant artillery fire echoing around me. They coincided with sounds of sirens, speaking of yet more victims falling on every front, until the very earth groaned with the burden and the rocks crumbled from the weight. The radio stations still competed to get the terrible news out to their listeners.

Suddenly, Sana' arrived. She looked healthier than I had seen her before, her face had regained its colour. But when we embraced I could feel her tremble against me.

"Congratulate me on my narrow escape … " she said, before I had a chance to ask her anything. "You could have been walking in your friend's funeral procession … this morning."

:ed away from her and whispered, "May God send nothing but

ٮ٠٠, no, it's only good," she said, mocking me. "A small explosion, is all. A booby-trapped car and it nearly ended my life."

"You?"

"Yes, me. What's so strange about it being me? How am I different from anyone else? Why not me … "

"Tell me. Calmly tell me what happened," I interrupted.

"The explosion at the bank," she said. "Didn't you hear about it?"

"Of course, I heard about it. Once and twice and ten times."

"I was there!" she said quietly.

I cried out in disbelief, "There, there? At the bank, or on the road?"

"I was on the road, and I had just entered the building next to the bank. I heard the explosion as I was getting into the elevator. My ears still ring with the sound of it."

I had little to say, except to murmur the prayers that come automatically, as though they were my only salvation and my last shelter. "Thank God for your escape … "

"It was luck," she said calmly, "I escaped injury, others did not. It was just their turn and not mine. Next time might be my turn, who knows? We cannot afford to forget that for a single minute."

I tried to pull her out of the cloud of pessimism that had enveloped her. "Every day brings its own provisions. It is enough to deal with the evils one day at a time."

She watched me for a while. Then without saying a word she walked to the front door. Quietly she opened the door and stood on the threshold for a few seconds. Then she disappeared out the door, leaving me with that strange confusion, the mysterious sensation one has when confronted with someone who "nearly left the land of the living." Someone who will never again be able to take life for granted; someone for whom the incident becomes an obsession, feeding on the mind and nurtured by the heart. It is as if that person had received a sign and the sign had been drawn invisibly on his forehead.

I do not remember what farewell she bade me. Except that she had murmured something about having work to do, having an important rendezvous to go to.

I prayed for her and followed the prayers with a thousand "God be with you's." And I returned to the nucleus of my home, my office. But before I opened my book and took up my pen, I turned on the radio. The news-flash music was on, the tune that makes hearts jump in a panic: "Here is the latest news flash on the situation." My blood turned to ice as I listened to the voice pant at the enormity of the news it was

delivering: "A huge car bomb exploded a few minutes ag͞
a large number of casualties. We will keep you posted as ͺ
comes in … "

A few minutes ago! In that district? That's the same neighbourhoo͞
where Sana' lives. Did she go home? No, no … she said she was going to
an important rendezvous. She said she was busy.

I reached for the phone to dial her home number. It was impossible.
The hotter the war situation, the colder the telephones become. No sign
of life, no dial tone. Dead. Below zero temperature.

But *Sana'*! How do I get to her? Could she be among the wounded? Or
one of the d … No … no …

The radio announcer again. With numbers and the names of victims
this time. More than twenty killed and tens more injured. I listened carefully; an endless list of names. None of them Sana'. Maybe she had already passed that area before the explosion. Or maybe she took another
route. She must have taken another route if she was going to that meeting of hers. But where … ? Where was that meeting taking place? Why
hadn't I asked her? What if she went home to change her clothes before
going to the meeting? I should have asked her. Maybe … What if … ?

Doubt is a vicious killer. It always attacks when you're down. And once
your defences have gone down you can only sink further into despair.

I spent the next few minutes in the shadow of my doubts, guessing.
My only contact with the explosion was the needle on my radio moving
from one station to the next, all of them delivering the same news to
their listeners.

I was still in that state when my phone gave a strangled ring. I jumped
on it, took up the receiver with trembling hands.

A stranger's voice on the other end said, "Mrs. Muna al-Ghazal?"

"Are you Mrs. Muna?" asked the voice again and only my lips answered that indeed I was, while in my head a devil rampaged.

"Yes, yes, that's me. And you are … ?" He did not give me a chance to
finish the question.

"I am Dr. Nouman, from the University Hospital … "

"Dr. Nouman, yes. What is it? Why are you calling me?"

"I would like you to come to the hospital immediately. Your friend indicated—before she—well, that her family was out of the country and
that you are the person closest to her. Come immediately."

"No … I don't know you, Doctor. You must have the wrong number.
You know how the phones are these days. Besides, my phone is not even
working, you couldn't have called me. You don't know me and everything is so mixed up, the telephone lines, the names, the numbers, the
faces … You dialled the wrong number, Doctor!"

✵   ✵   ✵

No ... no ... I won't believe it. Only a little while ago she left here, in perfect health and spirit. She told me she had escaped an explosion by a miracle. She came to tell me that.

She left saying she had an appointment. An important appointment. And I know her: she never breaks a promise. She never misses a rendez-vous.

—Translated from the Arabic by Thuraya Khalil-Khouri

Jean Arasanayagam

JEAN ARASANAYAGAM WAS BORN in a "Dutch Burgher" family, a term often employed in reference to Sri Lankans descended from Dutch colonizers and Sri Lankan women. Arasanayagam says her inheritance comes from having "suckled on a breast shaped by the genetics of history." She is a graduate of the University of Ceylon and the University of Strathclyde, Glasgow. She was already a well-known painter and batik designer when her first collection of poems, *Kindura,* was published in 1973. She has published several volumes of poetry, the latest being *Reddened Water Flows Clear* (1991). One collection of short stories, *The Cry of the Kite,* was published in 1983, and another, *Fragments of a Journey,* was published in 1992. She has won two Sri Lankan National Awards for her nonfiction and poetry. She won the Triton College International Poetry Award in 1990 and participated in the University of Iowa International Writers Program in the 1980s.

Jean Arasanayagam's techniques as a painter can be seen in the strong visual imagery in her short stories and in poems like "Genocide." Her works speak not only of her colonial inheritance but also of her experience of being married to a man of the minority Tamil community. The communal violence that has torn Sri Lanka apart figures prominently in her works. The antagonism between the Sinhalese majority and the Tamils erupted into savage attacks in July 1983. Arasanayagam and her family had to flee their home in Kandy and face the horrors of living in mortal danger in the land they consider home. The horrors of communal and economic wars, the chaos and grief that come from losing one's home, and the need to accept and understand herself as a woman of different ethnic identities are all portrayed in "Genocide"; in the poem the author sees nothing but destruction and finds no home for herself or her family, those "of alien breed."

Genocide

Gutted houses
Gutted lives
Charred wood

Charred flesh
Shattered brick
Shattered glass
Hammer blows of fists
Iron rods
Breaking walls
Breaking doors
Club poles
pulped flesh smoke choked breath
slashed limbs stab wounds human
torches blazing in the streets
eyes wild frenzied of the mob brutal
cries bloodcurdling screams human
bloodhounds scenting alien blood
marauding gangs stalking the innocent,
                    blood wells up flows disgorged
                        from gashed fountains and springs
                    in charred gardens
                    wine-dark blood streams
                in sunlit air crimson buds
                newly open swiftly crumple
            pervasive odor of scorched
        flesh charred and blackened
    stumps like broken statuary
strewn on burnt-out lawns

flames soar licking hot with pulsing tongue
each edifice consumed by fire of hate
lust for death make rabid panthers
springing from dark lairs
flanks freshly steaming with the heat
of hunt the unarmed defeated
skulk in jungles fleeing from
the orgiastic love for death
        hiding among the manna grasses, thorn
                thickets tea bushes or seeking
            covey in homes that grant temporary
                asylum to those who crossed
        a borderline to this brief safety
    we are prisoners of fear

crouching in dark locked rooms
drawing each breath of blood
heart leaping at each
closer murderous cry,

some fall at doorsteps as they flee
stabbed to the heart, axed down
and poled frail birds whose wings
foiled in their flight were crushed
melted like wax in mounting fires.

yet whom do they destroy?
those who to each other are unknown
who know not nor will ever know
each other's histories or personal
loves and hates, no longer equate
a child's toy with a human life
as cradles burn
as beds of lovers go up in flames
the only ecstasy is death
bathed in the blood of the murderer
even the guilty now absolved
of every sin, becomes a saint
yet whom do they destroy?
wrenching apart like broken fingers
fractured bones unclasped from palm
They go back to their lairs and dens
piled with loot, clothe themselves in
others' skins
they have destroyed themselves
yet do not know it
waiting for the next call to stream
into the streets with burning brands
and bombs and clubs and poles they
make their gleeful bed on carnage
In each man who is alien
to their tongue and speech
they see both enemy and prey
The patriot loots and burns and
        murders

goes back into his lair and spawns
more criminals who have no hope
of either life or death or any life
      hereafter

Within the flames of burning cities
write and twist their purgatorial
      souls
Within the fire great monsters rise.
Hulks of dark giants bruited
against the fearful midget kind
diminished by fear, who make no
stand no gesture of defense
gestation from the womb of hell
      brings forth more of their breed
      begotten of hatred and lust to
      kill.

What chance what hope
When all is wrecked
Dead bodies float beside the Temple
      of the Tooth
in the calm waters of the lake-beaten
and mutilated,
      Beggars still hold out their
      empty palms to all who pass,
      They alone in poverty can see
      no difference
Perished in pyres with rituals of
      hate
or immolated within the walls of
      burning rooms
A few survivors hold their hands
corpses of husbands, wives, and
      children
pieces of charred and broken brick
Here there is no longer any home
for those of alien breed.

B. Sugathakumari

(1934–   )

A WELL-KNOWN SOUTH INDIAN poet, B. Sugathakumari has been a teacher and an educational administrator in Trivandrum, Kerala.

In this poem, "Colossus," the anguish of mothers who give birth to men who become killers is placed in the context of the mythology of war, which begins with brother killing brother. As the mothers watch, a warrior grows in violence until he threatens to devour the earth herself. But the women who observe this violence do not sit back passively, either in this poem or in other works in this anthology. In this poem, the poet calls upon the god Vishnu to repeat his deed of another time and to rescue the earth from the monstrous force of destruction. In other works, such as Amrita Pritam's "To Waris Shah," the poet calls upon the aid of another poet to put a stop to the violence. And in Mridula Garg's short story "The Morning After," a mother tries to save the son of another woman.

Colossus

Long ago, beyond the memory of man,
In a blind night eclipsing sun and moon,
Writhing in pain,
Mother gave birth to a child.

In the dark moment
When the first brother slew the first brother
And buried him,
The child woke up and cried.

Then, as murders raged
In seething darkness,
As lies surged up in triumph,
As deceits stole close

With daggers hidden behind smiles,
The child grew strong and smart.

His mother's milk not relishing,
He searched for battlefields and blood
And laughed in glee at sight of them.

He began to run about,
He grew dark as night,
His fiery eyes grew round
And teeth and nails grew long.

And once he saw
The agony at Calvary;
Sucking it in,
Another six feet he grew.

Thus he grew up
And stood a terrible figure, tall and straight,
Our forefathers fed him well.

They fed him with famine,
On the tortures of war,
On the pain of the deserts
Through which came slaves
Writhing under whips
And groaning under loads of stone.

Life crawled into night
Burdened with centuries' pain and sin.
And now the colossal Terror's
Hunger shakes the earth.

We, yes, we too fed him well
With suffering piled high hill-high,
With the blood of the world wars,
With the ever-burning smoky flame of Hiroshima,
With the greedy hatred of empires
Swallowing each other,
With the debris of broken ideals.

The more, the more we give,
The fiercer the monster grows;
His hunger rages;
He grows taller than the sky;
Towards us his arms come lengthening.
His mouth gapes wider;
We pour into it the tears of dharma
And again the blood of Truth.

No, not enough!
Shaking with laughter
The monster bends down,
Takes our earth in his hands
And stands up straight and huge.
His wriggling tongue likes every corner of the earth;
He has begun munching it.

The sky fills with the poison of his breath;
My heart is faint;
I have only a lute in my hand
To face this giant!

Whom do I call through my lute?
Whom do I search for?
I search for a mighty one,
Mighty as the Varaha*
That rescued our Mother
from the depths of the sea.

> —*Translated from the Malayalam by B. Hrdayakumari*

---

*The boar incarnation of Vishnu, who rescued the Earth from the depths of the sea

Aliya Talib
(?)

IN FEBRUARY 1990, Miriam Cooke received a package from the Iraqi Embassy in Washington, D.C., that contained dozens of novels, short story collections, and books of criticism. All of these publications were part of the War and Culture Series sponsored by the Iraqi government during the Iran-Iraq War of 1980–1988. Among them was a collection of short stories by Aliya Talib, titled *Corridors* (1988), from which both these selections were taken. We know nothing of her life and circumstances. We assume that she was born in Iraq and has continued to live there. Most of the writers whose works were published in the series are not known outside Iraq. The Baath regime seems to have paid artists, architects, and writers to celebrate their victory over Iran, sometimes even before such a victory was in sight. Some of these creative artists were able to produce critical works that were not censored. This is the first such story to be published in the West.

Torn between reality and imagination, between her old and new selves, between her missing husband and her soldier-to-be son, a woman pastes together a fragile facade of normality. The deliberate ambiguity of the language compels a careful reading: War imagery serves to link this woman's story on the home front with men's experiences at the war front.

A New Wait

The ponderous pendulum swings without tiring. Glazed eyes follow it in a circling motion, confusing a head already heavy with thoughts. Right, left. The circle is never complete. It approaches the middle, then returns to the east without taking leave of the west. She felt a raging storm surge within her exhausted heaviness. Heavy thoughts. Her head had no more room for them. She pushed sharply. With trembling hands, she raised him, feeling the mercilessness of his weight on her arms. Her delicate fingers weakened and dropped him on her breast.

What had happened? Was she sick? She scarcely knew. She might even have begun to fear herself. She was a stranger to the rage mired in her depths. "It's very late." It had to arrive even if after a few days, because he needed new supplies to annihilate the raging gaps caused by his absence.

Was she confused because it was late? She didn't know and the specter of the woman she had once been pursues her. She hides her face. She must not see her even if she is not the one to have imagined her, because she must not once again see the features of her weakness.

She feels her rage. She frightens her. She rebels mercilessly, violently until she is closer than ever to what she had invented. Suddenly, she collides into a hot look and is immediately despondent. It had become very painful. This unstoppable hemorrhage of feelings. She kept on bandaging it until the weight of the bandages threatened to choke her. She closed her eyes on his image imprinted on her pupils.

It had to come now. Not a few days hence. Now. Now. She had to hear with her own ears the echo of letters. But what would happen if it didn't come. Ah! I don't want these thoughts. Go away. Go away. Leave me alone. I've become very strong. I can dig you out with my fingernails.

I'm no longer me. I closed the door of return years ago. I struggled against weakness throughout the hours of loneliness that his absence brought. I never let them stand in my way.

Suddenly, a feeling of peace came over her as she imagined the glow of a reassuring smile radiate from the edges of the picture's small frame.

She screamed: "I need you!"

She closed her mouth quickly. The echo of her scream bounced against the head of her child. He had begun to fidget and roll around in the wide bed in one of whose corners she was sitting alone and confused.

She was roused by a continuous ringing from the machine that sat deafly outside. She moved quickly while keeping her eye on his turbulent movement. Then she ran barefoot toward the noise.

"Yes."

"Is that the residence of Jihad Muhammad?"

"Yes. Go ahead."

"There's a letter for you. Please collect it."

"Thank you very much. I'll be right there."

The short words exploded into a euphoria that bombarded her feelings. "I was waiting for you." She no longer knew what to do. She flies around in different directions going nowhere. She grabbed hold of a cloak of indeterminate color. The buttons at the back that refused to close exactly in the middle infuriated her.

"You always hurried to close them when they were stuck exactly in that spot."

She let her body down. She stretched her arm angrily to close them before her feverish thoughts once again forced her to slow down. She went to the kitchen and then back to the bedroom. He was still deep in a beautifully relaxed sleep. She gazed at his face, touched his skin. Softness, a slow walk, many movements of the head as he spoke. How could he have his movements when he had not even seen him?

She shook her head. This was not the moment for comparisons. She had to hurry. Had she noticed that in his latest picture? "I've not received the reply. I write to you about one thing and you reply about something else. Our times conflict. They're not allowing you to answer me quickly. Weeks and days pass before I get any news. So much happens only to get wasted and destroyed in the gaps between letters. I want them to be full to the last possible line. I want to take my fill of the sight of your hand print on the last white page. Did you leave me a clear trace this time? Last time, there was none even though the drawer was full of images that swim through every instant of my day."

She shook herself suddenly when the grandfather clock chimed and then addressed the child:

"Ah, you've got a tough life. Get up, please."

The words had no effect, so she changed him. He was clearly annoyed. She whispered, "There's another letter." Impatiently, she carried him as he dozed. She closed the door behind her with her other hand.

Six quick years had passed since he had first seen the light. She had never before felt his weight. He had been like a soft sponge that she had liked to carry, she had never used a stroller to ease the weight, he had been a treasure she delighted in embracing. But now he made her short of breath, unable to speak coherently and her eyes looked around for his strong arms.

They told her that he had probably been taken prisoner; some of his companions even believed that he had been killed. The battle had been so fierce and its light so bright that the sun had not woken early that day; it had found a substitute in the exchange of fire that had been so intense they had used up all the ammunition in the gun barrel and the battle could not wait for it to be refilled.

How could the storming feet do anything but advance, since the way was very clear? Many said that they had seen him, they had rubbed shoulders more than once as he shouted and jumped after the enemy. However, he suddenly insisted on chasing a black beard who had disabled his friend's foot.

"You have no more ammunition."

"Where is my bayonet?"

That was the last thing he uttered. But that image stayed in his companions' minds after all those years. He had not let him escape before planting his bayonet in his prey. He never stopped going east. East toward all the dark fleeing faces until he disappeared out of sight of his companions, and they never again saw his rushing feet.

"He shouldn't have rushed on like that?"

"What do you mean?"

"I mean ... maybe he should've waited for us."

She could not answer. She had to remain controlled in the presence of this companion who was so upset while telling the story.

"I know him. When he attacks he becomes blind to all but his target which becomes a giant he must overcome. Did you know that you took up long hours of our conversation?" He felt embarrassed. She understood his dilemma. He had exposed his fear for her. Yes, he was afraid for her weakness.

"She doesn't fear anything when she's alone."

"Aren't you exaggerating?"

Then his thoughts would take him far away. He imagined her sitting in concentration in a small room with her family who kept asking her over to stay with them while he was away. She waited for things to be offered to her. When the gift was late she did not ask. She'd keep on waiting even if they forgot her.

Her fingers trembled as she tore open the new letter. With a wild yearning, she devoured the lines, often bringing them close to her face. In the breaths of the sheets she searched for his smell which she had sensed before her fingers touched the paper.

A few, miserly lines. They did not quench her thirst. But she smiled with pleasure as she read the words.

"I would never have believed that it was you who was telling these stories. Have you really become like that? Tell me more. I am happy about your latest news. Kisses to Ghazwan,* to yourself and to everyone."

She was overcome by a feeling of pride; she felt as though a small medal had been hung on her chest. His hands almost touched her long hair as she swept it away from her blouse.

She slowed down. Her thoughts calmed down. She closed the door behind her. The little hand escaped from hers, and happy feet ran toward the green garden filled with flowers which he loves: "I planted them for him. He'll be so happy when he returns."

Now she knew all the answers which he had considered trifling. She had not gone with him to inspect the frame of their new house. She had thought that he was extraordinary, a giant. Had he not been how could

---

Ghazwan is the emphatic of *ghazwa*, which means one who attacks insistently. The association with the impetuous father is clear.

he have erected this entire building on land that had been empty for many years?

In vain, he had tried to make her understand that he was nothing special and that they could do things together, if only she could find the strength. But she was dismayed when she heard him say such things.

Then he went away. She felt as though she had assumed a huge burden of which she would never be rid and about which she could never complain. She had to move but a belt of ice squeezed her. For years she had pushed aside her worries and problems; she was completely dependent. She had to … she had to …

She took many steps. They seemed weak at first and became stronger as she continued. She must have looked strange, kicking up white clouds as she passed by before her shining white house was complete.

She must have looked funny with flecks of white paint in her hair as she painted the window frames.

Whenever her baby fell into the piles of materials scattered all over the place and started to howl, she'd hurry over to hug him, and she'd point to the rooms that were done. "That's your room. We'll play together here, just as he had always hoped we would. We'll be happy waiting for him to come home. We'll make the most of our time as we await the return. Help me carry the watering can so that we can water the flowers he loves so much. Make them glow even more. Don't let them wilt. He deserves all this and more. We'll remain here and, as he wished, we'll take care of the house just as his letters take care of us."

"Aren't you thinking about working?"

"Who? Me?"

"Yes. Otherwise what's the use of your degree?"

She would stammer. Were she to work, she'd have to face people she didn't know and establish relationships and have conversations with them. She'd be able to go out alone and not in his shadow. She'd return home at the end of the day exhausted. She'd have to sleep during part of the day. Should she do this?

For days he did not return to the subject. When he did she was evasive lest he discover even more of the weakness she was trying to hide.

She ceased to get up at ten in the morning and began to wake with him in the grey light of dawn. She'd kiss her baby who was snuggled in her womb on the day that the echo of his father's voice ceased to resound throughout the house. He settled in her feelings piercing, calm, melodious, constant.

He pulls the edge of her garment, almost tripping her. She turns angrily and when she sees his image, she puts her arms around him and repressed laughs erupt toward and then out of her lips.

"What's up?"

"Read me Daddy's letter."

His fingers play with the little drawer to take out the previous letters. She reads them to him and keeps the new letter calmly in her bosom in anticipation of the next one.

"Will he come home soon?"

"Yes, but not now."

"So, when?"

"Not before I make you exactly like him."

She picks up her pen to script confident words.

"We're fine. You are always with us. People are noticing me at work. The carnations are all out. I am no longer afraid to be alone. Ghazwan is a new man who holds the seat next to me for when you return. Kisses ..."

—Translated from the Arabic by Miriam Cooke and Rkia Cornell

Aliya Shuaib
(1964–   )

ALIYA SHUAIB WAS BORN in Kuwait. In 1992, she earned her M.A. in literature and philosophy from the University of Birmingham, England, where she is now working toward her doctorate on the concept of the bodily identity of Muslim women. In 1989, she wrote a collection of short stories entitled *A Woman Marries the Sea.* Her second short story collection, *Faceless,* was published in 1992. She is also an artist, and her first exhibition of collages took place in Kuwait in 1989. Subsequently, she had exhibitions in England. This short story was inspired by the death of a blind old man in Kuwait during the Gulf War of 1991 and is dedicated to "the soul of the blind man and his wife, Lulua,* who were murdered on Monday, August 17, 1992, in Kaifan, Kuwait."

The Sea Is There

She told him that she would come the following morning, she would take him to the sea. Ah! He would walk on the warm sand, his feet would sink into the beach, and he would open wide the windows of his soul to the salty breeze.

Afterwards he would return to the familiar darkness which had become a coat of thick feathers behind which he hid from the world. The more he hears Kuwait, the more he loves it. He can only hear: the groaning of the tarmack in front of the house every night, the whispering of the pavement which embraces his steps and his prayers ever since Kuwait opened her black eyes to the blue of the sky. He hears the laughter of the clouds travelling to further horizons, and the stars calling to him, and the moon asking him to play the Fairuz tape over again and to sing with her: "Give me a flute." She told him she would come the following morning.

---

*Lulua is the Arabic for "pearl."

She is his beloved daughter. As for the others, they had not asked for a long time, not since independence. He no longer cared or needed to curb his feelings whenever his wife said to him: "The children have forgotten us." He would just smile.

She was enough for him.

He was enough for her.

She supported him whenever he got up and he supported her when night lowered its heavy curtains and her head sought its pillow on his right shoulder.

She was his staff and he was hers.

10 P.M. Lulua was asleep and he was alone.

The servant girl had asked him at 9:30 whether he wanted anything. He had laughingly replied that he knew his way around the house, that the stones that he had placed with his own hands and the walls that he had built with his own sweat would guide him should he lose or forget his way.

She wished him a good night under her breath.

He remained alone.

He listened to Lulua's uneven breathing. Her perfume that he knew in his heart where she had planted her lilies and jasmine. His love for her was more than his old heart could bear. For 90 years he had loved her, before she was born, before he knew her, before he had met her. Ninety years he had felt his heart beat at her approach and when she passed her hands over his white eyes.

Tonight, a strange feeling overwhelmed him, then something fluttered within him uneasily like the wings of frightened birds.

He said to her: "Sleep, my spirit is with you." He remained alone. After completing the evening prayer, he felt a light shudder shake his weak body. He didn't say anything to her.

He felt light, as though he weighed nothing. He went out, groping along the walls. He wanted to see the sky. The servant did not ask him how—she led him out. He stopped briefly, and trembling said: "I'm cold." She ran to fetch a wool wrap to put on his shoulders, even though the night was warm. She said nothing. He said: "Go in. Leave me alone." He breathed in the air that he loved, the air that blew in from the sea of Kuwait as she was getting ready to sleep. He was shivering. Everything was white and God was close.

Kuwait is a pearl hidden in the heart. It is the love whose whiteness no smoke or doubt can contaminate. The whiteness is a tune played by angels who surround him without his knowing. Lulua was sleeping and his

beloved daughter was sleeping in another house and dreaming of tomorrow. She was dreaming of the sea laughing when it saw him approach, even though he had abandoned it since the occupation. He
would say to her: "I'm afraid I shan't find the sea." And she would tease
him, saying: "The sea is there waiting for you and asking about you."

He thought that he should tell her that he was missing his children
and wanted to see them. He would ask about them even if they did not
ask about him. Yes, he would ask. He was overcome by joy at the thought
of the encounter and of the feel of the little ones' heads and of their running towards him and of their sweet smell.

⊸   ⊸   ⊸

He wept throughout the occupation.

"Let them take everything, but not the sea. Let them take my soul, my
children, my house and my money. Anything but not the sea. The sea is
Kuwait. Should the sea go so will Kuwait."

After the liberation, he was happy and silent. He did not go out.

Lulua said: "The sea is there. It hasn't gone. I saw it." He was silent and
did not go out. He remained alone and she slept.

The whiteness pressed its thin, soft fingers on his heart. Their perfume and sweetness flowed over his soul, and his soul opened up to
their touch. He felt that he was light, that he was rising up off the
ground. He felt nothing. He was seeing for the first time, seeing a pale
whiteness. He was rising. He saw Lulua sleeping and he remembered
that she had fallen on his chest, weeping: "The sea is there, Kuwait has
not gone." He kept rising. The angels were lifting him with their glowing
faces and their little wings, smiling at him. He saw them clearly. She was
crying: "The sea is there. It is." He was silent, wiping away her tears and
breathing in her scent.

The whiteness is like a shining pearl. He was happy. He knew that the
sea was really there.

—Translated from the Arabic by Miriam Cooke

Bibliographic Notes to Part One

Alexander, Meena. *Fault Lines.* New York: Feminist Press, 1993.
_____. *House of a Thousand Doors.* Washington, D.C.: Three Continents Press, 1988.
_____. *Nampally Road.* San Francisco: Mercury House, 1991.
_____. *The Storm.* New York: Red Dust, 1989.
al-Saih, Laila. *Rain Notebooks.* Beirut, 1979.
_____. *Roots That Do Not Depart.* Beirut, 1984.
Arasanayagam, Jean. *The Cry of the Kite.* N.P., 1983.
_____. *Fragments of a Journey.* Kandy, Women's Education and Research Center Publication, no. 33/E (1992): 15–92.
_____. *Kindura.* Kandy, 1973.
_____. *Reddened Water Flows Clear.* London: Forest Books, 1991.
Azzam, Samira. *The Clock and Humanity.* Beirut, 1963.
_____. *The Feast from the Western Window.* Beirut, 1971.
_____. *And Other Stories.* Beirut, 1960.
Divakaruni, Chitra. *Black Candle.* Corvallis: Calyx Books, 1991.
_____. *Dark Like the River.* Calcutta: Writers Workshop, 1987.
_____. *The Reason for Nasturtiums.* Berkeley: Berkeley Poet's Press, 1990.
_____, ed. *Multitude: Cross-Cultural Readings for Writers.* New York: McGraw-Hill, Inc., 1993.
Lodhi, Farkhanda. *People of the City.* Lahore: Seher Publication, 1975.
_____. *Shehar Ke Log.* Lahore: Seher Publication, 1975.
Mahfil. Michigan State University Publication, vol. 5, no. 3 (1968–1969):5–26.
Nasrallah, Emily. *Flight Against Time.* Beirut, 1981.
_____. *The Island of Illusion.* Beirut, 1973.
_____. *The Lost Mill.* Beirut, 1985.
_____. *The Oleander Tree.* Beirut, 1968.
_____. *Our Daily Bread.* Beirut, 1990.
_____. *The Pawn.* Beirut, 1973.
_____. *September Birds.* Beirut, 1962.
_____. *The Source.* Beirut, 1978.
_____. *Those Memories.* Beirut, 1980.
_____. *Women in 17 Stories.* Beirut, 1983.
Pritam, Amrita. *Loamiyaan Vaataan.* Delhi, 1948.
_____. *Long Journey.* Delhi, 1948.
_____. *The Skeleton and Other Stories.* Delhi: Hind Pocket Books, 1950.
Ranasinghe, Anne. *Against Eternity and Dos Kness.* N.P., 1985.
_____. *Plead Mercy.* N.P., 1975.
_____. *And a Sun That Sucks the Earth.* N.P., 1971.
_____. *With Words We Write Our Lives Past Present and Future.* N.P., 1973.

Ravikovitch, Dahlia. *All Thy Breakers and Waves.* Tel Aviv, 1972.
_____. *A Dress of Fire.* Tel Aviv, 1976.
_____. *The Love of an Orange.* Tel Aviv, 1959.
_____. *The Window.* Tel Aviv, 1989.
Samman, Ghada. *Beirut Nightmares.* Beirut: Ghada Samman Publishing, 1980.
_____. *Beirut 1975.* Beirut: Ghada Samman Publishing, 1975.
_____. *The Billionaire's Night.* Beirut: Ghada Samman Publishing, 1986.
Shuaib, Aliya. *Faceless.* Kuwait, 1992.
_____. *A Woman Marries the Sea.* Kuwait, 1989.
Talib, Aliya. *Corridors.* Baghdad, 1988.

2

Waging Peace

Meditation of Mahakali

*I resort to Mahakali, who has ten faces, ten legs
and holds in her hands the sword, discus, mace,
arrows, bow, club, spear, missile, human head and
conch, who is three-eyed, adorned with ornaments
on all her limbs, and luminous like a blue jewel,
and whom Brahmā extolled in order to destroy
Madhu and Kaitabha, when Viṣṇu was in (mystic)
sleep.*

—Translated by Swami Jagadīśvarānanda

For Her Brother

Weep! Weep! Weep!
These tears are for my brother,
Henceforth that veil which lies between us,
That recent earth,
Shall not be lifted again.
You have gone down to the bitter water
Which all must taste,
And you went pure, saying:
"Life is a buzz of hornets about a lance point."
But my heart remembers, O son of my father and mother,
I wither like summer grass,
I shut myself in the tent of consternation.

He is dead, who was the buckler of our tribe
And the foundation of our house,
He has departed in calamity.

He is dead, who was the lighthouse of courageous men,
As fires lighted upon the mountains.
He is dead, who rode costly horses,
Shining in his garments.
The hero of the long shoulder belt is dead,
The young man of valiance and beauty breathes no more;
The right hand of generosity is withered,
And the beardless king of our tribe shall breathe no more.

Let the stars go out,
Let the sun withdraw his rays,
He was our star and sun.

Who now will gather in the strangers at dusk
When the sad North whistles with her winds?

While you have tears, O daughters of the Solamides,
Weep! Weep! Weep!

—**Al-Khansa**

Chitra Divakaruni

(1953–)

IN "INDIGO," THE SECOND selection by this author included in this anthology, Divakaruni is no longer threatened by a war raging around her; she is not reliving her own childhood memories nor is she listening to someone else narrating the memories of a legendary battle as she is in her poem "Blackout: Calcutta 1971." In "Indigo" the poet takes on the persona of women in another century who decide to actively participate in the war against their British colonizers, the masters who own the labor of their bodies. As in most of the works in this anthology, the war is fought not in a far-off place but right in the fields and homes where the women live and work. And once again, women use their own bodies and clothes—their wedding saris and wedding emblems—as symbols of their weapons in the battle they have joined. After more than eighty years of increasing oppression, the Peasant Revolt of 1860 succeeded in destroying the British indigo plantations in India.

Indigo (Bengal: 1779–1860)

The fields flame with it, endless, blue
as cobra poison. It has entered
our blood and pulses
up our veins like night. There is
no other color. The planter's whip
splits open the flesh of our faces,
a blue liquid light trickles
through the fingers. Blue dyes the lungs
when we breathe. Only the obstinate eyes
refuse to forget where once the rice
parted the earth's moist skin
and pushed up reed by reed,
green, then rippled gold
like the Arhiyal's waves. Stitched

into our eyelids, the broken dark,
the torches of the planter's men,
fire walling like a tidal wave
that picked up speed as it came,
flattened the ripe grain with a smell
like charred flesh, broke
on our huts. And the wind
screaming like the women
dragged to the plantation,
feet, hair, torn breasts.

In the factory, we dip our hands,
their violet forever blue,
in the dye, pack it
in great embossed chests
for the East India Company.
Our ankles gleam thin blue
from the chains. After,
many of the women killed
themselves. Drowning
was the easiest.
Sometimes the Arhiyal gave us back
the naked, bloated bodies, the faces
eaten by fish. We hold on

to red, the color
of the saris, the marriage mark
on their foreheads,
we hold it carefully inside
our blue skulls, like a man
in the cold Paush night
holds in his cupped palms
a spark, its welcome scorch,
feeds in his foggy breath
till he can set it down
in the right place,
to blaze up and burst
like the hot heart of a star
over the whole horizon,
a burning so beautiful you want it
to never end.

Kamaladevi Chattopadhyay
(1903–1990)

IN HER MEMOIR, *Inner Recesses Outer Spaces,* Kamaladevi Chattopadhyay speaks of being educated at home by her mother and family before she went to school in England. She also discusses her active participation in India's struggle for independence and her work on behalf of women, refugees, and India's cottage industries. After independence (1947), she left the Indian Congress Party and refused to join the government because she did not think it was necessary or even helpful to join in order to change society. She then took on the daunting task of rehabilitating the people who had come to India as refugees after the partition of the subcontinent in 1947. She established the Indian Cooperative Union in order to mobilize the refugees to rebuild their lives through their own work. She also participated in reviving the traditions of Indian theater and handicrafts, which had suffered neglect and disrespect under centuries of British rule, and continuously lobbied for social legislation and educational reforms for women. Because of her activities, she was imprisoned for a total of five years along with other women active in the independence movement; nevertheless, she and her colleagues persisted in their efforts even while in prison.

The following selection reveals Kamaladevi Chattopadhyay's commitment to Mahatma Gandhi's ideal of satyagraha and techniques of nonviolent civil disobedience. This Indian woman's memoir bears out our belief that women involved in conflicts and wars need to document their struggles since no one else will. The participants must constantly remind themselves and their audience of women's active roles in war and peace.

Inner Recesses Outer Spaces

After a brief visit to Pune I took an overnight train back to Bombay. From Borivili station I started jogging in an ancient Victoria towards the camp when the first glimmer of dawn seeped across the horizon. Within minutes I was under arrest. At the station prominent posters had announced

95

arrests of Gandhiji and Vallabhai. That had been the Viceroy's rebuff to Gandhiji's request for a talk.

In the lock up I met the Seva Dal Sevikas from the Borivili camp which had been subjected to a pre-dawn raid and a round up of the inmates. We were put up for a make believe trial. One incident made mine significant. I was asked for my Bombay residence address. I naturally named the Borivili camp. 'That does not exist', replied the magistrate impatiently as though I was wasting his precious time. 'Where were you arrested'? came the next question. 'On the road', was my factual reply. 'So you have no residence, you were picked up on the road. You are a vagrant.' So when I was sentenced, I was evidently brought under the Vagrants' Act (S. 109 Criminal Procedure Code) as a person who was 'without any ostensible means of livelihood and a source of danger to Society' and therefore logically placed in C class in prison! I later recalled that the Satyagrahis in the Nagpur Flag Satyagraha too were arrested under the Vagrants' Act.

The Arthur Road women's quarters where I was now lodged was a long way from the Yerrawada private barrack consisting of only two rooms. They were already overcrowded. Large crowds of Satyagrahis poured in all the time. We were physically crowded in with the ordinary criminals, some of whom were obviously far from healthy. This ill-assorted mingling was not an ethical issue but one of health hazards. Our repeated requests for segregation were ignored. Perin Captain, a prominent political worker of Bombay, was both vocal and very determined. Though she was among the exceptional few in class 'B', here we were all huddled together. She took charge and decided that we refuse to go in at lock up time. So we stood on the verandah as though our feet were caught in the cement floor, and challenged the women warders to use force. They were physically unequal to the task as we could overwhelm them by sheer numbers. So we won our point.

As convicts we had to wear prison clothes which consisted of very thick, rough, heavy sarees. To those of us who had become accustomed to heavy Khadi, this was not too much of a hardship. The large majority, newcomers to politics, were still in the delicate Bombay mill sarees. They were horrified at the very sight of the prison uniform. They absolutely revolted when they were forbidden underwear. True this would mean permitting use of their own garments, not allowed under the jail rules, for there was no provision for underwear in the prison manual. A battle ensued.

With the whole country aflame, the authorities were in no mood for concessions. For them, the movement had to be crushed at any cost. Fresh arrivals elated us with exciting tales of the big struggle on. We remained unyielding.

In the midst of this the Prison Visitors' Committee arrived. We submitted a list of our legitimate grievances, top priority being given to the underwear apparel. It was known that I had drafted the memorandum. Next day the jail superintendent asked me if I was the spokeswoman for the political prisoners. 'If you mean did I draft the memo, Yes', I replied. 'What all of you did is wrong. You cannot do this', was his emphatic comment. 'What is the Jail Visitors' Committee for, if we cannot submit our problems for its consideration', I queried. 'It can only function within the jail manual, it cannot go beyond, and you know that you are only fanning a revolt which must end in regret for you. I warn you', stating this with an angry snort he walked away. He was a very angry Irishman.

A little later, the jail matron asked me to pick up my belongings and go with her. Being the work hour there was no one around. I was asked not to go to the work room and take leave of the others. The black prison van took a quick round and within minutes I was in a barrack at the back of where I had left. I now entered a quiet and what seemed like an empty barrack, when on the threshold stood a tall white figure, holding out both hands and a warm smile on the face saying: 'So it is you, I could not guess though when I was asked to share the barrack'. I really rubbed my eyes. It was Miraben, her eyes as gentle as ever, as she warmly folded me in her arms. I felt like a storm-wrecked boat being docked in a secure cove. I explained I was there really because I was in disgrace. 'What, more disgrace?' she exclaimed and we both laughed.

I realised she would be a state prisoner like Gandhiji. She described her daily rote. She cooked her own food which I was welcome to share with her. I gladly agreed. She let me share her books, her *charka,* join in her prayers. What unbelievable good luck. I rejoiced though I was only too well aware this was a swift transitory stage. However, I decided to make the best of it while it lasted. We enjoyed each other's company. We had so much to say to each other, we read together, sang bhajans. And then it all ended abruptly. I was to be moved to Belgaum. I arranged for my son to see me off at the train. For the first time I saw him look very forlorn and depressed. No doubt he was one of thousands of his age going through this trauma. Unlike the earlier Satyagraha jail-going, this was grim, bleak. Quite a crowd was at the station with loads of food, flowers, assorted gifts hurriedly put together. All along the route, at many stops, people came anxiously looking for us, with food, flowers, gifts. It was not possible to sleep. We would have to be callous not to respond to them. It was their way of expressing their identification with the national cause.

Hindalga Women's jail at Belgaum was spacious by normal standards but much too small for our contingent. The single barrack, though large, got jam packed. Two small barracks were for the 'B' class.

Belgaum was rather cold for me, for winter was at its height. We had two *Kamblis* (thick rough blankets) supposed to be standard for shepherds. We slept on one and covered our bodies with the other. It did not fortify me and I shivered all night. A young Sevika, Vidya, who had shared several training periods with me in the camps, became concerned. She slept beside me and when the temperature dropped she crept closer, pulling her blanket over me too.

To make matters worse within days of my arrival I developed acute jaundice. All I could now get was sago conji, thrice a day, streaked with milk. The worse my condition grew, the angrier the jail doctor became. He convinced himself I had thought this up to harass him. 'Those with delicate digestive organs should stay at home, not come to jail and harass us', he was never tired of admonishing me.

I had been ill a long time, almost endlessly it seemed until I was losing all count of time. The days flitted past like grey shadows that formed a kind of monotonous moving curtain. It was as though everything was receding further and further behind this shadowy curtain. Even people around me became unreal figures moving over a screen. The only consciousness was the throbbing pain which dulled in the morning and sharpened from afternoon onwards. Nobody knew for quite a while what exactly was the matter with me, the authorities whose business it was to find out, were indifferent. It was all in the day's work for them.

Having always enjoyed good health, I am very impatient of ill health. I hate the sense of helplessness with its compelling dependence on others, and now more then ever. As sympathetic souls kept coming to me I felt terribly exposed, like a body laid out on view. All the defenses I had with such effort built up were shattered. Even familiar faces became strange as they peered down at me. I could not shut them out, like a house which without the sheltering roof lies exposed in the glare of the sun. I would close my eyes and feign sleep whenever approaching footsteps sounded. Inwardly I shrank and curled up inside myself every time a hand was laid on my forehead. I often felt the need to be taken out of myself. I needed work that would be strenuous, keep me busy where my physical self would have to labour. My entire upbringing had been to make me soft but the life I had adopted was one of enduring toughness. It was familiarity with the rough and tumble that I felt was needed to round my life off.

The thing that did get me down was my diet, a fact that enraged the jail authorities. Sago Conji (porridge) with an invisible streak of milk was my sustenance morning, noon and evening for months, with no sign of recovery in sight.

News of my deteriorating health went out. The daughter of Shri Kamaksha Natarajan, Editor of the Social Reformer and a valued colleague of mine in the Social Reform Movement, Kamakoti, was with us

but in 'B' class. When he learnt of my condition through her, he was enraged and pressed the higher officials to depute a senior doctor to report
on me. I was by then in my third month of jaundice and naturally very
weak. The doctor found out what my diet was. 'What would you like to
eat?' he asked. His visit somehow annoyed me, for just at that moment a
young sevika had just been admitted into the prison and on seeing me
she began to sob. She thought I was on my death bed. So I replied rather
abruptly to the doctor that no useful purpose could be served by indulg-
ing in polite conversation, that I had been a prisoner long enough to
know prison rules. He seemed undaunted. 'I am going to prescribe a few
items outside the jail manual. I would like to know your preference.' I
said I would like some fruit, even the minimum I felt would correct my
digestion. 'That is insufficient. Instead of sago, I am suggesting two
slices of bread with butter.' He seemed to have calmed the agitated
Natarajan by telling him that all I needed was feeding up.

My prolonged sojourn in bed made me realise with a shock the complete absence of even an elementary clinic for the inmates. While I was
recovering I began to collect a few pre-requisites for setting up a hospital. Mridula Sarabhai, who happened to be one of the inmates, assured
me she would donate for my hospital some of the more expensive items,
once she was released,which she did. As a brief description of my adventures with this hospital has been recorded earlier, I refrain from further
dilation on it.

Running the hospital meant a lot of physical labour. I took on the
maximum until it wore me out. I revelled in it. At last I got the chance to
wade through the rough and tumble my life had hitherto lacked. I was
being moulded into a tough fighter. My richest and most abiding experience in Hindalga jail, came through the close relationship I cultivated
with the women from the remote corners of Karnataka, mostly Sirsri-
Siddhapur and Ankola of Uttar Kannada district where a powerful no-
tax campaign had led to severe repression and large scale arrests. These
were the poorest women I had occasion to live in close contact with and
get glimpses of their everyday life of want and hunger. My knowledge of
rural living was of Mangalore, in Dakshina Kannada. Though the two
districts were single once, almost a half century earlier, a spontaneous
no-tax campaign which almost frustrated the administrators, had led to
the extreme step of tearing the district into two slices, attaching the
northern piece to the then Bombay Presidency, the southern to the Madras Presidency. Bombay city rapidly blew up into a modern metropolis,
this prosperity touching little of the tail end of the presidency, i.e. Uttar
Kannada. On the other hand in the Madras Presidency all parts developed, educationally, industrially, socially. My own district of Mangalore
never had the dynastic landlords owning vast tracts, fields or plantations. There was a much fairer distribution, with small landowners,

modest coffee plantations and small industries. We never knew the abject poverty which large concentration of possessions in few hands breeds, as they did in Uttar Kannada.

My prison mates hailing from there were an eye opener to me. Their description of their life made my hair stand on end. A full meal was a rare luxury, they simply had to make do with what they could get. They covered their bodies with pieces of cloth. On a rare occasion like a marriage they got a full sari. Their horizon seemed non-existent. Did they ever dream of a different life? The question held no meaning. According to them for generations it had been so. There were no schools in their region, whereas I was used to at least one school in every village. Illiteracy was unknown to us. Their life was a far cry from what I had been familiar with.

How and why were these women here? I was overpowered by a million questions struggling to spill out of me. Quietly over the long evenings they told me stories. Since Gandhiji's call reached them, they had become aware of their own inadequacies, that they did not live as humans, in dignity, in self-respect. Their concepts of what they wanted was not just mere food, better houses, proper clothes, etc. Yes, they needed these but it was more than that, they explained. They wanted freedom, not only for them, but all who were today in bondage like themselves. As the great leader had called upon everyone of them to get free they must refuse to be in bondage. The heavy dues they were called upon to pay now seemed to them like the wages of slavery. They worked hard, they did not shirk but were not treated as humans. They repeated in a kind of anguish: 'No one should be in bondage.' Now they felt they were free for did they not prefer going to jail rather than be content to be slaves? 'Had they seen the Mahatma?' I asked. No, but they brushed that aside—never mind—his call had reached them. It needed much more *punya* (merit) to have his Darshan. He too was in prison to bring freedom for all. He too suffered like them, did not only ask others to suffer. He was a true leader—'Were you not afraid of the consequences when you broke the law?' I asked. Came an emphatic reply: 'No! We understand now that it is fear that makes us slaves. Our life circle was set that way from the moment of our birth. Our dharma, we were made to believe, was to drudge and live on the leavings. The Mahatma has made us free so we are not afraid. His care for us gives us respect. We are asked to serve, not slave.'

Such intimate communication was largely facilitated through my familiarity with their language Kannada. But it had limitations. Their words and phrases sketched but the outline. The intensity of their passion and the depth of their sincerity which was the core and had stirred my inmost being seemed to elude my vocabulary to give appropriate shape to it in concrete phrases.

Sahar Khalifa

(1941–   )

ONE OF THE FOREMOST Palestinian novelists, Sahar Khalifa was born in Nablus. As a very young woman, she entered into a traditionally arranged marriage; then, after thirteen years of frustrations and disappointments, she divorced her husband and decided to dedicate herself to writing. In 1988, she earned her Ph.D. in women's studies and American literature from the University of Iowa. She now works as director of the Women's Affairs Center in Nablus.

Sahar Khalifa has written five novels. Her early novel, *We Are No Longer Your Slave Girls* (1974), made quite an impact because of its advocacy of feminist freedom. But it was after the appearance of her third novel, *Wild Thorns*, in 1976 that she received literary recognition and acclaim. That novel has been translated into Hebrew, French, German, Dutch, and English.

In her work, Sahar Khalifa expresses her deep belief that feminist consciousness is an integral part of political consciousness and that the struggle and tribulations of Palestinian women are part of the general political Palestinian struggle for liberation. Although she writes in modern Arabic, her language is deeply rooted in the Palestinian vernacular.

The following excerpt is from her fourth novel, *Memoirs of an Unrealistic Woman* (1986), a book that has been translated into Italian and German. When the narrator, the daughter of an inspector of schools and the merchant's wife, learns about the struggle for freedom in Ireland, Vietnam, Cuba, India, and other countries, she changes her mind about trying to be a good wife and staying out of the national conflict. She decides to join the revolution to liberate her land, women and herself.

Memoirs of an Unrealistic Woman

I am and continued to be the inspector's daughter until I married and became a merchant's wife. Sometimes I am both. When the husband is sarcastic, he'll call me "the inspector's daughter." When the father's angry, he'll call me "the merchant's wife." In fact, I was happy to be the inspector's daughter. The inspector has knowledge, prestige and authority over other educators. When my father walked through the streets, many hands would be raised in greeting, "Good morning, Professor," "Good evening, Professor," "Good bye, Professor," "Hello, Professor." The father perfected the behavior of a professor in the classroom, at home, everywhere. So that is how people treated him. They would nod as he expounded some point, saying, "That's right, Professor." The father must have loved this title, for he'd go on and on, and the people would nod and nod, and I kept getting prouder and prouder. The prouder I became the more I demanded. I was anxious not to seem stupid, so I hid my questions and reactions and my twisting lips. I would affect a heavy step and a calm demeanor until I got bored and exploded. Then my father would say, "This girl is airheaded!" So as not to seem stupid, I didn't ask the meaning of the word. Secretly, I looked the word up in a dictionary and found that it had a definite connection with "air," and I felt better. Air refreshes, it is light and essential to life. But the father interpreted it differently, claiming that airheadedness meant the opposite of respectability. I panicked and did nothing that would not be praised until I got bored and exploded. Whenever I breathed freely, others choked.

I am and continued to be the inspector's daughter until I married and became a merchant's wife. I felt doubly proud to be the daughter of the inspector professor and to be part of an established family, since my father was proud of who we were. His job brought him respect, his family brought him respect, so it was obvious that he should be respectable and that I, the daughter of a respectable man, should consider myself also to be respectable. Yet my airheadedness, my holding my breath, my deliberate and heavy gait, my mask of innocence over my devil's face as I stopped my lips from twisting made them call me shameless. With time, I realized that I was respectably shameless or shamelessly respectable; that my identity was and always had been confused. I was a girl, yet because of my fear of their fears I acted like a boy, and became half-half. I wanted more respect, so I rejected who I was to become an "androgyn," neither male nor female. That's what I heard the wise old women say as they smiled and frowned, encouraged and warned. I preferred to have people talk about me than to have them say nothing. My identity became more confused. At school, I became aware that the poor girls were stronger, nicer and more truthful. I earnestly tried to emulate them in their speech and in their sincerity. But everyone rejected me: the rich girls looked down on me; the poor girls didn't see me. I was lost between them as I had previously been lost between male and female. But I did remain the inspector's daughter and I did become the merchant's wife. I was lost between the past, the present and the indistinct signposts to the future. I wavered and was unsure about what had previously been instinct. I owned only that which others chose for me; I was connected to them only through their commands to me, confusing commands. I executed them poorly and was a poor rebel. So it's not surprising that my step was cautious and my hand shaky. I dropped glass whose scattered splinters scratched my thigh. And I stumbled. I heard my mother scream and curse, so I gathered up the splinters and my hands bled. I saw the blood and was afraid and wanted to run away but could not. I froze to the spot, my legs bumped into the ground but into the air also.

That's how it was that I stopped work. One leg on the ground, the other in the air. For years, I slept like that. Then, one day I awoke and found myself married to the merchant, and I was wretched. I remembered the glory to which I had been accustomed in the inspector's house and I was in despair. I became convinced that wretchedness was my lot. It was only in dreams and deceits that I tried to change things, but dreams and deceits are not practical. So I stopped turning. Woe to her who turns and to her who does not turn. When I turned it was against the wind, and when the wind changed direction so did I. I hummed the tune of "airheadedness" and again consulted the dictionary to reassure myself about the word's connection with the core of life; air is refreshing, sweet and light. I, too, must be light with a light shadow.

[In a later chapter, Afaf begins to move out of her domestic prison. She discusses women's role in the Palestinian revolution with her activist friend Nawal.] My friend told me about Ireland, and I told her that Palestine was enough of a problem for me. I had even had enough of Palestine. What's to be done, Nawal? My mind is small and so is my heart. I am selfish and airheaded. Whatever you say, I don't have time to think about it. Pity me so that I may have pity. How can I have pity when I am not pitied? I know nothing. Tell me what to do.

After agonizing through it all, I had decided to stay where I was with my all-consuming job. I cook, wash, tidy, dust, wash dishes and suffer insults when the husband has drunk too much whisky. God is witness that he has never stinted in payment, the refrigerator is always full. She stared at me angrily and called me a "defeatist."

We quarrelled and made up. In the interests of peace, I asked her to tell me all about revolutionaries who had fought for their independence. Vietnam, Cuba, India, Sind, South Yemen and today it was Palestine's turn. Finally, I asked her, "When will it be Afaf's turn?" She replied, "Afaf is part of the Palestinian women's revolution which is part of the Palestinian revolution which is part of the world revolution." Suddenly, I felt a great longing and tenderness for my husband, and I wept.

By the end of the meeting, we had concluded two things: first, the women's revolution was necessary for the success of the total revolution; second, revolutionary men had to mobilize the women.

"How will they mobilize the women? Do they say to her, 'Rebel, reb-el'?"

She just looked at me without saying anything. Finally, we agreed that it was both simple and impossible, yet possible if I found work. I kissed her in front of the others who seemed relieved, and I promised to look for any kind of work. As I walked through the streets, I didn't see the lights, I didn't hear the car horns, I didn't feel the presence of others, I didn't know my name. Then, I remembered that I was Afaf and that I was staying in a hotel. I sat in the lounge among strangers and drank beer. I was on the road to the revolution and to the homeland, but the bridge was closed.

—Translated from the Arabic by Miriam Cooke

Nessia Shafran

(1940s–   )

Nessia Shafran was born in Israel and now lives in the United States. The following selections are from her memoir, entitled *Farewell Communism,* that was published in 1981. In these excerpts, a female child discovers that people she considered to be her enemies are no different from other people. As an adult, the woman looks at the history of her country and the land she lives in and works for the rights of others. "Long live Jewish-Arab friendship" was a slogan shouted during Communist demonstrations in the early days of the new state of Israel.

"Long Live Jewish-Arab Friendship!"

> *Falaheen will come with their warm smiles*
> *And our suntanned solid guys*
> *And they will dip their bread in the oil of offering*
> *For the blood feud is over.*
>
> —Haya Kadmon, "We Were Born Twins in This Land"
> (Haya Kadmon is a poetess of the Communist party in Israel.)

One night my father came home from the *club* accompanied by two men with mustaches. I was seven. The comrades, who came from out of town, spent the night with us. Before I fell asleep, Mother whispered in my ear: "They're probably Iraqi Jews." You can imagine how my mother felt the next morning, after the two comrades had politely thanked us and left, and my father had told us they were Arabs from a village in the Meshulash.* They were the first Arabs I had ever met. They had slept in our beds and eaten breakfast at our table. They were no different from other people I had known.

Six years later, soon after becoming members of Banki, the Israeli Communist Youth Movement, we visited several Arab villages in the

---

*Meshulash: An area in the center of Israel with a large concentration of Arab villages.

Meshulash area. In Taibe, we were invited for lunch by a family of comrades. I was shocked by their poverty. There was no running water and no electricity in the house. A mat covered with cushions took up most of the room. In the corner were some sooted kerosene burners. Kfar Kassem, the next village we visited, was even more pitiful. After paying a visit to the graves of the forty-nine,* killed two years earlier by the Israeli army, we walked through the narrow streets. The filthy streets, the dozens of dirty children following us, and the women carrying water buckets on their heads, all these confirmed again and again what we had already heard in the Communist youth movement about the terrible conditions in which the Arabs in Israel were living.

Two months later we visited Nazareth. It was a solidarity visit with the families of the detainees. On May 1, 1958, the Communist party had decided to stage a May Day demonstration without permission, and afterwards dozens of party members were detained. As members of the Israeli Communist Youth Movement, we went to Nazareth to visit their families.

When my friend Mina and I entered the home of our host family, I was astonished. The rooms were full of elegant furniture, heavy rugs covered the floors, bright chandeliers hung from the high ceilings, and the beautiful young hostess was sitting in a large armchair with a small poodle in her lap. It was straight out of Hollywood. In the predominantly East-European neighborhood of the fifties where I grew up I had never seen anything like it.

Had I not recorded this visit in my diary I would have probably forgotten all these details. The next day we visited some villages in the Nazareth area and saw again the poor huts, mats, sooty kerosene burners, poverty. These were the Arabs about whom we had read in "Kol Haam".† These descriptions roused in us feelings of rage against the oppression of the Arab population, but it also made it difficult for us to see those poor miserable Arabs as our equals.

In later years, I learned that our comrades in Haifa got to know another kind of Arab. These were Arabs who lived in beautiful houses full of Damascene furniture and antique copper vessels; Arabs who were born into aristocratic families and who had been educated in the best universities.

This class of Arabs did not come to our club in Petah-Tikva. Most of the Arab youth we knew were scarcely educated and they came from villages in the Galilee looking for work in the big city. Several young Arabs

---

*Kfar Kassem: On October 1956, 49 villagers were shot by border police.
†Kol Haam: The Communist daily in Hebrew. Now defunct.

visited our club, but only with two of them did we establish a long-last-ing relationship. The first was Ahmad, a thin quiet youth, who came from a village in the Galilee and worked as a cotton picker. Now I assume he did not understand much of our discussions about the progress of socialism from utopia to science, or about imperialism as the culmina-tion of capitalism. We tried to raise his "political consciousness", and got him to organize Arab youth with the help of an Arabic-speaking party member. Although he never became a full member, he participated in all of our activities and was often invited into our homes. After two years he disappeared from our club, and returned to his village.

Mustafa joined us later and our relationship with him was closer. He introduced himself as Yossef—a common occurrence among many Ar-abs who came to work in the big cities and gave themselves Hebrew names. But we urged him to use his real name—Mustafa. He partici-pated in all our activities, including illegal slogan writing on walls, to which the police put a stop. He, too, did not become a full member. Again, his "political consciousness" was not sufficiently developed. I tried to teach him Hebrew and gave him some revolutionary books I hoped he would read. In those days, I had the naive belief that if one knew how to read one could read and understand anything.

We accepted him despite his different education and cultural back-ground, but the wider Jewish society did not accept him. For a while he had a Jewish girlfriend of Iraqi extraction. He even talked about marry-ing her. But the girl's brothers threatened to kill him if he would not leave her alone.

A short while later he went back to his village to an arranged marriage. We were all invited to the wedding. It was one of the most fascinating weddings I can remember. The whole village participated in the celebra-tion, and we, the only Jews present, were greeted gracefully by all. The bridegroom rode a noble mare through the narrow streets of the pictur-esque village Jassar El Zarka on the Mediterranean. The bride was wait-ing for him surrounded by her girlfriends.

Rumor had it that the bride was not among the sought-after girls in the village, and that the marriage had been forced on him by his family. For those of us who had known him for years, it was hard to grasp how our comrade Mustafa could return to his remote village and marry a vil-lage girl whom he probably did not love.

It started to dawn on us that deep down there are unknown currents which are much stronger than all the theories we believed in; that our comrade Mustafa was torn between Marx and Muhammad, and that Muhammad had won.

During all these years there was only one Arab youth who came to our club who was different. Jamal was handsome with blue eyes and wavy hair; he was a student at the teachers' college in our town. I was fifteen when he came to our club, and I fell in love with him at first sight. Unfortunately, he disappeared a few weeks later. He probably never realized how many dreams were woven around him by a comradeship-seeking Jewish girl.

Marriage, or at least dating, between Arab men and Jewish women, was then a romantic ideal for a lot of the girls who had grown up in Banki. There were some living examples, and the most famous of them were Arna and Saliva Hamis. Arna, a striking blond, was the daughter of Gideon Mer, a pioneer, who first isolated the malaria virus. The handsome Saliva Hamis was a member of the Central Committee and one of the most activist Arabs. Other Arab leaders, all of them Christian, were also married to Jewish women. Emil Thoma, one of the party's ideologues, was married to a Jewish woman named Haya, who choreographed many party events. George Toubi, a member of the central committee of Banki, was married to a blond woman named Zippora. Even a girl our age from Haifa was dating Mahmud Darwish—then one of the rising young poets in the party.

Jabra Nicola, one of the old timers, was the first Arab leader who married a Jewish woman. His son Eli, whom we met frequently in the general gatherings of Banki, was a good friend of ours. In the 30's, when Arabization of the party began, many Arabs came to meet Jewish women. It was at that time that romances between Arab men and Jewish women started.

Refuge, a novel which was published in 1977, describes in detail the complex and delicate texture of such a marriage. Sammy Michael, the author, was born in Bagdad where he was active in the leftist underground. Like many other Iraqi Jews, he joined the Communist party upon arriving in Israel. Being a member of the party in Haifa, and being versed in Arabic culture, he got to know the Arab members, especially the more educated members, in a way few other party members could. For a rank and file member like my father, who was born in Poland at the beginning of the century, the Arabs were comrades in struggle, but he could never really understand them beyond the stereotype, a positive one of course, of an alien.

Sammy Michael draws the portrait of a mixed couple. Shoshana was born in Yessod Hamala, one of the first settlements established in Israel. She is a typical sharp-tongued Sabra. Her family ostracizes her after she marries Fuad, an educated Christian Arab and one of the party leaders. The Jewish neighbors reject her too. "Get out, you convert whore, you traitor," the grocer shouts, threatening her with a can of pickles. Shoshana moves to her husband's village in the Galilee. Doors are opened, but not hearts. The Arabs in the village expect her, as a woman who "left them and came to us", to hate the Jews. Shoshana chooses the third option, the one chosen by most mixed couples in the party—to live in Haifa, the only place where Jews and Arabs could live together.

The Yom Kippur War brings to the surface the latent conflict. Amir, the oldest son, sees himself as Jewish and wants to join the army, although it is clear to him that "he'll get a kick on the Arab part of his ass." The two younger brothers listen to Egyptian radio and pray for a great Arab victory. Fuad, the father, is a proud Arab, but he also understands the Jewish fears. The young Muslim intellectuals in the party, those who identify openly with the terrorist organizations, despise him: "Those Christian intellectuals are like the Jews. They stink from sitting so much with Jews."

The younger Arab generation, represented by the poet Fathi, disturbs Fuad. Fathi writes about the oppressed Arab, persecuted by the barbarian Israeli army, and trembling with fear at his nightmares. Fuad is disgusted by the excesses in Fathi's poetry. He is looking for the proud Arab in poetry. Fathi is pursued by many Jewish girls. Dafna is the closest of them. But he won't marry a Jewish woman, like the Christian intellectuals. He is engaged to a simple girl who is waiting for him in his village. He could have married a more educated Arab girl, but regardless of the superficial polish he acquired on his trips to Moscow, he prefers "a simple girl, whose soul has not been dirtied by high school education, and whose foot has never crossed the club threshold."

At the beginning of the Yom Kippur war, Fathi, who is afraid of arrest, takes refuge in the home of Shula, a party member whose husband has been recruited. Unlike the older Fuad—Fathi has no doubts. He wants "to break the legs of an Israeli soldier. To cut the arms of an Israeli soldier before he can reach his weapon." But he himself is hiding in the home of an Israeli soldier. And the soldier's wife, whom secretly he would have liked to conquer, treats him more and more coldly. He feels humiliated and finally leaves her house, giving up the refuge she has provided.

Shimon Balas, a party member since his youth in Iraq, also deals with a love affair between an Arab man and a Jewish woman in his book *A Locked Room*, Said is a young Arab from the Meshulash who works as a night guard in the communist daily "Kol Haam." There he meets Semadar, a beautiful Banki member, and the two fall in love. It is a long, complex and painful relationship. Despite their love for each other, and the slogans of friendship between Jews and Arabs on which they have been nurtured, they decide to go their different ways. This is a typical ending to many other love affairs between Jews and Arabs in the party.

Whatever one's attitude may be, intermarriages may be accounted among the main achievements of the party in its attempts to build a bridge of friendship between Arabs and Jews. However, its importance should not be exaggerated. Such intermarriages occurred between men and women unrelated to the party as well. Moreover, the party did not even change the pattern of such marriages. I don't know of any marriage between a Jewish man and an Arab woman in the party. The only difference, perhaps, between couples in the party and those outside, was that the latter usually chose one side, and defined themselves as Arabs or as Jews, while couples in the party attempted to raise their children in defiance of national differences—not Jewish and not Arab, yet also simultaneously Jewish and Arab.

The children did not always agree with their parents' noble intentions. Some chose their own identity when they grew up (two of the three sons of Arna and Saliva Hamis, for example, joined the Israeli army). Others escaped the confusion into which they were born by marrying a foreign woman, or by choosing exile. [...]

The decisive factor for the Arabs' support of the Communist party resulted from the fact that this was the only party which the Arabs did not identify with the national interests of Israel. Therefore it was the only channel through which the Israeli Arabs could express their national aspirations. [...]

The Knesset elections in 1959 marked an important juncture in the relationship between the Communist party and Israeli Arabs. It was the first time in the history of the Knesset that the Communist party dropped from second place, behind Mapai, the ruling party, to third place in the Arab sector. The reason, as expected, is related to new developments in Arab countries. At that time there was a dispute between Gamal Abdul Nasser of Egypt and Abdul Karim Kassem, president of Iraq. The Soviet Union supported Iraq, but most Israeli Arabs enthusiastically supported the pan-Arab ambitions of Gamal Abdul Nasser. The party attempted to underscore this conflict in its propaganda and to emphasize a popular issue like the massacre in Kfar Kassem. Nevertheless it lost 33% of its Arab votes, and the number of Knesset members dropped from six to three. Israeli Arabs proved in no uncertain way that their support is not guaranteed under any circumstances. If the main condition—identity of interests between the Soviet Union and the Arabs—does not exist—they will not choose the Communist party above any other.

This augured ill for the saga of Jewish-Arab relationships in the party. It was proof—the significance of which most Jewish members were not yet aware—that the traditional politics of a Communist party, which emphasized class struggle, would not work among the Arab population. In order to gain Arab support, the Communist party would have to become an Arab national party.

Beginning with the elections of 1961, after Nasser and the Soviet Union made peace, the support the Communist party got from the Arabs continually increased. This support culminated after the 6 Days War, when Arab and Soviet interests became almost identical. The influence of the party among the Arabs increased to levels unknown before, and the

Communist party became for the first time a mass party among the Arabs—an old dream of Moscow since the 20's.

Above and beyond the interests of the "great powers" involved in the relationship between Jews and Arabs in the party, the rank and file members, at any rate the Jews, passionately believed in the possibility of Jewish-Arab friendship.

True, the Communist party was marginal, but it was the only organization in Israel which accepted Jewish and Arab members on equal terms, at a time that such an idea seemed almost impossible. Thus the party proved to be a unique testing ground where Arabs and Jews could together think through the unique complexity of their lives in this country.

The status of the Arabs in the Israeli Communist party resembled in certain ways the position of American blacks in the American Communist party. Reading memoirs of Black Americans, including Richard Wright, I was struck that all, including those who later left Communism bitterly disappointed, repeated the assertion that the party was the only place where Blacks could be accepted as equal among equals. All over "great" America there was no other organization which would accept Blacks as equal. And every Black American, who got to know the Communist party closely, could not forget this outstanding moving experience: a Black person, in the first part of this century, being accepted as equal by white people.

However, the relations between Jews and Arabs in the party were not simple, just as the relations between Blacks and whites in the American Communist party were never simple. These were complex and delicate relations, which despite much sincere efforts often looked as though they were suspended over a chasm.

Formally there was absolute equality among Jews and Arabs in the party, but on the moral level such equality never existed—the Arabs were more equal. The Arabs had an advantage over us. The Jewish members also grasped the Arabs' moral right as absolute and incontrovertible, needing no apology nor guilt. They had lived in this country for centuries and their belonging to this country was obvious, beyond any doubt. They did not take any part in the destruction of European Jews. The holocaust did not happen on their land. True, the Jews who lived in the Arab countries did not have equal rights, but their situation was much better than that of most European Jews.

The Arabs did not owe us any moral debt. They settled in this country hundreds of years after it was abandoned by most of its Jewish inhabitants. Only a fool could have expected them to believe in the divine promise given to Abraham. The story of the special relationship between the Jews and the land of Israel was not their story in any way. They were the victims of an old mystical episode which was not related to them at all.

The source of the problem was the fact that the Jewish people, against any known historical logic, survived for thousands of years without a territory of its own. Subsequently, when the Jews were looking again for a territory to settle, there was only one small piece of land that could be considered. This land, tragically, was inhabited by another people. The conflict indeed seemed as if it had no solution.

Historically, the Arabs had the moral and legal right. The only thing we had on our side was this existential no-choice, based on an old mystic attachment, which is hardly a current coin in the sober world of the 20th century.

The birth of the Jewish settlement was in sin—the old sin of Zionism. This old sin even the Communists could not escape at the very personal level. The suburb where we lived still carried its Arabic name. Among other suburbs built around Petah Tikva, which carried fancy Hebrew names, the name of our suburb stood out as foreign. It was built right after the War of Independence, but almost nothing survived of the life which was lived there before.

An old Arab house, where a Yemenite family settled, and some scattered fig trees, were the only traces of the past. My mother would sometimes tease my Communist father, a man who believed in the right of the Arab refugees to return to their land, himself living on the ruins of an Arab village. My father would answer that our house was not built on the site of the village, but of the orange groves. As if it mattered. For Jewish Communists, perhaps for others as well, it was a tragic conflict they had to live with. It was perhaps the biggest sacrifice Jews had to make—even if they regarded themselves as non-Zionists—for the sake of Zionism. [...]

The party encouraged emotional involvement in the sufferings of the Arabs, but never encouraged similar involvement in the sufferings of the Jews. The Arabs who knew us well perceived us one-dimensionally. The uneducated Arabs, like Ahmad and Mustafa, who spent a few years around us, did not know anything about the history of our families. I don't remember if we ever told them, despite the fact that each one of our families embodied, in its own way, the Jewish tragedy. The educated Arabs built a wall between their feelings and knowledge about Jews. The position of the party strengthened this impregnable wall. As far as we could see the Arab comrades never doubted their view of the Jewish-Arab conflict.

Israeli Arab Communists have said little about their personal feelings. The only books written so far about relationships between Arabs and Jews in the party, *Refuge* by Sammy Michael and *A Locked Room* by Shimon Balas, were written by Jews who knew the Arabs intimately, probably better than any other Jewish member in the party, but nevertheless Jews. Said, the Arab intellectual protagonist in the novel *A Locked Room*, talks about wanting to write an introspective novel. But this has remained nothing more than a wishful thinking of a Jewish author.

There have been no first-hand testimonies. The only source left is the general atmosphere which prevailed in the party. And the feeling was that the Arabs never perceived us as we really were. Above all they did not grasp the impact of the holocaust on our lives. We were the conquerors, the rulers, the strong ones. What could they know about lives which were hanging on a cliff; about a whole generation without grandparents; a generation that carried the names of murdered family relatives; a whole generation whose history was hidden in yellowing picture albums. The Arab comrades chose not to invest any emotional energy in the Jewish tragedy. It was an understandable position, as they were not to blame for this tragedy, but this position, as understandable as it was, could only come to a dead end in the new reality of the Middle East.

This has been one of the major failures of the Israeli Communist party. The party did an excellent job among its Jewish members in introducing the sufferings of the Arab population. But a similar preparation of hearts has not been achieved in the Arab quarter. The party has not tried to prepare its Arab members to reconcile with the real-politic of the region, which has been transformed completely, with no more possibility of turning back the clock.

Not only the Arabs had the wrong image of the Jewish Israeli. Our self-image was shaped by the Arab images of us. We, refugees from all corners of the globe, who were saved at the last minute from all kinds of deaths, never viewed ourselves as refugees. We believed that the Arabs had the right to return to their land or to accept reparations, but we never stopped to think that we too had some refugee rights. The Communist party never mentioned the property Jews abandoned in the Arab countries. They also never mentioned the property my father's murdered family, as well as thousands and thousands of other families, left in Poland and in other East European countries. And the Communist party, with all the connections it had with those countries, could have done something. If justice—why not justice for all?

We, the Jewish Communists, were torn between two poles. The one-dimensional self-image which ruled the party allowed us to grow neither as Israelis nor as Jews. This was also true for other political parties. The injustice done to the Arabs stood in sharp contradiction with what we perceived as "Jewish sensitivity", and a Jew without such moral sensitivity was not perceived as a complete Jew.

It was a vicious circle. And there was no way a Communist Jew could get out.

Today, so many years after the split in the party, there is still a great sense of frustration, disappointment and failure among those who were once party members. Even the disappointment with the myth of the Soviet Union does not arouse as much emotional rage as does the relationship between Arabs and Jews in the party. It is also not accidental that the only two novels written so far about the Israeli Communist party deal with this subject. [...]

Disappointment prevailed when it became clear that everything we believed in was an illusion. Members at all levels passionately believed in the dream of friendship between Jews and Arabs. Most did not even suspect that the facts contradicted the image of friendship that was so diligently cultivated by the party. And those who knew developed defense mechanisms, which protected the ideals and trivialized the facts.

The main problem was rooted in the fact that the party fulfilled different functions, sometimes contradictory, among the Jews and among the Arabs. For the Jews socialism was the main thing. For the Arabs—the national question. The struggle against military rule was a strong unifying force among Jews and Arabs, and its urgency concealed less urgent disagreements. But when the military rule was abolished there was no other urgent goal to unify Jews and Arabs. The disagreements became more and more pronounced.

Whoever read "Al-Ittihad", the Communist daily in Arabic, could clearly see that the party had a different policy in the Arab quarter. But most Jewish party members did not read Arabic. The party did not encourage its members to learn Arabic. There were quite a few Russian classes, but I don't remember any Arabic classes. The Iraqi-born Jewish party members were the only ones who could read "Al-Ittihad," and some of them warned the leadership about the contradictions between "Kol Haam" and "Al-Ittihad". But the defense mechanisms people developed in the party, including the leadership, blurred and then ignored the differences.

The policy of the party in the Arab quarter occasionally embarrassed Jewish members sent by the party to lecture in Arab towns. A member of the central committee told me about a visit of his to Taibe a short while before the split in the party. He was told that one of the Arab leaders had spoken recently in the village, and that he had told the party members that the party opposes the law of return, and immigration into Israel in general. He could not believe his ears. Yet this was not unusual: Jewish members did not know the party's policy in the Arab quarter; Arab members did not always know the party's policy in the Jewish quarter. Most of the rank and file Arab members never read "Kol Haam".

The party never published any information which could damage the image of friendship between Jews and Arabs in the international Communist movement. We never knew that Arab Communist leaders refused to sit next to our leaders in international meetings. If there were problems, they were kept secret. These were internal problems of the party which should not be shared with the rank and file members.

The party had different cells for its Jewish and Arab members. One would have thought the party would encourage mixed cells, at least in mixed cities like Haifa. But the Arab leaders resisted mixed cells on the pretext of different languages. Our group was an exception. I don't know about other youth groups where Arab youth participated, though there may have been some. And I have to admit that in our group the Arabs who participated were marginal, passive, incidental.

There were problems in personal relationships as well. There is no doubt that some honest sincere friendships were formed between Jews and Arabs in the party. But in many cases these were unnatural and compulsive relationships, formed under little understood psychological pressures. There is hardly anyone, from leaders on down to young Banki members, who does not carry some embarrassing memory about such relationships.

One of the old timers in the party, who was a member of the central committee before the split, told me: "At a party in honor of the Soviet writer Semionov who was visiting Israel, I was sitting next to S., an Arab member of the central committee. S. drank a lot during the evening. Suddenly he got close to me and asked in a drunken voice: 'Tell me, why do you need this state of Israel? Tell me, why do you need it?' The old saying came to my mind: in vino veritas."

A member of kibbutz Yad Hana, the only Communist kibbutz in Israel, told me: "We once caught an Arab gang who stole from the kibbutz fields. We wanted to turn them over to the police. But the party's Arab leaders asked us not to. We gave in. Today I regret it. I believed all my life in friendship between Arabs and Jews. But I could not understand why an Arab thief should be treated any different from a Jewish thief."

A party member who frequently visited the villages of the Meshulash area told me: "At a certain point it became difficult to visit Arab homes. I have an ulcer and I hate to eat lamb. But I wanted to show solidarity with them—so I ate it. In addition, it was difficult for me to watch how they treat their wives as work and baby machines. I could never accept this kind of treatment from a Jewish party member. But here I had to keep my mouth shut, and pretend they were my equals. I could not help but look at them from above. With friendship and kindness—but from above."

A girl who grew up with me in the youth movement told me many years later: "To this day I remember with embarrassment how humiliating it was that the Arab guys from Nazareth would flirt with us during Banki picnics. We were sitting around the campfire, in the Red Army Forest or in one of the camps, singing along or listening to a talk. There was a joyous feeling of comradery. We often sang the Arabic song, "Milli milli ya sanabel". The atmosphere was great. Suddenly I'd notice that someone was moving too close to me. I'd try to move away. But pretty soon he'd get very close again, and sometimes even touch. If a Jewish guy treated me like that, I'd simply move, and if he was especially rude I'd slap him. But they were Arabs. So I pretended nothing ever happened."

Unfortunately, many of the Jewish-Arab relationships in the party were based on inequality. The Arabs were often treated with a leniency bordering on hypocrisy and servility. The status of Arab women, for example, was an issue which bothered many of us. We all believed in the power of Communism to educate, and we thought the party should exert its influence to improve the conditions of Arab women. But it did not, probably to avoid confrontation with deeply-rooted prejudices in Arab tradition.

At a certain point the burden of Arabophilia became too heavy to carry. There was an annoying feeling that something was going wrong. The desired friendship between Jews and Arabs became a ritual with little substance. Although the political claims of the party could still be accepted, the emotional repulsion could no longer be hidden. The soul of a party is not expressed only in its political platform. It is also manifested in the delicate balance of its different components. And here many members began to feel as if they were taking part in a deceiving game.

There was no greater frustration than the one we experienced when it became clear—as it did in 1965—that even the most noble intentions could not withstand the competing national feelings. I don't know how the Arab members felt when the dream of Jewish-Arab friendship was shattered. Perhaps they were more realistic from the beginning about the possible limits of such friendship. And they still had those old scapegoats which could be blamed for everything: Zionism, Chauvinism, and of course, Its Highness Imperialism.

I, and many others like me, could no longer hang on to them. The holy cows began to be butchered one after the other.

—*Translated from the Hebrew by Nessia Shafran*

Suraiya Qasim

(1945–   )

SURAIYA QASIM HAS AN M.A. in journalism and is a free-lance writer. She has worked as a stringer for *Asiaweek* (Hong Kong), and her poem "Singing Silence" was included in *Lyrical Voices: An International Poetry Anthology* (1979).

Women have been unwilling trophies and victims of war throughout the ages. The protagonist of "Where Did She Belong?" becomes doubly homeless due to a war. Munni Bai is born between a temple and a mosque. As a prostitute, she is used by both a Muslim man and a Hindu man. After making love to her they both speak of their hatred for the men of the other community. Neither man protects her when she is forced to leave the city where she works because of the division of land between Hindus and Muslims. And once again, in the new city she has a Muslim client and a Hindu client. Both have homes and money. She only has her body, which she has to keep on selling, and her generic name, Munni Bai. She has no home of her own. War and political violence seldom offer peace or even solutions for women's personal problems of everyday violence.

Where Did She Belong?

Munni Bai was her name. Was it her cradle name? She did not know. Indeed she did not know if she had a cradle at all in the first instance. She hoped she had had one. After all, her parents could not have carried her about all the time.

But parents! Who were they? She did not know. All that she did know was that she must have had them. How else could she be in this world? But who on earth were her parents? She did not remember either of them.

What could her mother have been like? Was she beautiful or a repulsive creature? To go by her own looks, her mother, whoever she was, must have been at least attractive. Beauty rarely, if ever, comes out of an ugly womb.

But what about her father? What did he look like? What did he do for a living? And, come to think of it, to which community did he belong?

These were the questions Munni Bai never tired of asking herself. Not that she wanted to be prepared to answer them should someone ask them. In the world in which she lived, parentage did not matter; looks and youth alone did. And Munni Bai was a ravishing beauty at a mere seventeen!

With her Venus-like face, conical breasts, slim waist, she was acknowledged throughout not only Hira Mandi but the city of Lahore as the girl to be possessed. And possessing her was not difficult—anyone who could pay could possess her. She lived to be possessed—of course at a price. Her wares were for sale.

This acknowledged princess of Hira Mandi did not like what she did. But there was nothing else she could do. Besides, what would 'Ma' say if she refused to do what she was bidden?

Ma was a matronly figure who ran the brothel whose chief attraction was Munni Bai. Ma was alternately brutal and kind to her wards. There were six of them, including Munni Bai—the youngest and the loveliest of them all.

Ma treated Munni Bai with greater affection—real or simulated, for she was the chief source of her income—than she did anyone else. The birch was so sparingly used on Munni Bai that it seemed as though it was reserved for the others.

Munni Bai could recall only one occasion when Ma had thrashed her. That was when the girl had the audacity to ask forbidden questions. Finding Ma in a genial mood one day, Munni Bai had asked: 'Ma, who are my parents? How did I come to be where I am? Why do I have to do what I do?'

Ma's face suddenly turned red. In a jiffy she picked up the birch which had lain hidden behind her and used it mercilessly on her 'darling daughter'—as she herself used to address Munni Bai.

As the victim writhed in pain, Ma went on: 'The answer to your first question, you bitch, is that I don't know who your parents are. You're a foundling. I found you crying and lying unattended on the road, the main road, mind you, equidistant from a mosque and a temple. Traffic was flowing by you, but no one had the heart to stop and attend to you, let alone pick you up, feed and fondle you.

'Fortunately for you, and unfortunately for me, I happened to be passing that way at that time. I took pity on you that winter evening, picked you up, wrapped you in my shawl and brought you home where you still find yourself.

'Since your parents, pox on them whoever they were, had left you half-way between a mosque and a temple I could not decide whether you were a Hindu or a Muslim, whether to give you a Hindu name or a Muslim name. Therefore I gave you a name used by both Hindus and Muslims in our world.

'That, anyway, has always been immaterial in our house. On Divali, as you know, we all burn earthen lamps and worship the Goddess Lakshmi with greater piety and gusto than most Hindus. And throughout the month of Ramzan, all inmates of this house observe the fast. So what difference does it make whether you are a Hindu or a Muslim? You are, in fact, better than both because you combine both in you.'

Despite her bulk and stern exterior, Ma knew that age had begun to take its toll on her. No, she was not exactly old. Middle aged, yes; but not old. She was just past fifty, but considering the sort of life she had led, had had to lead, she looked old and, worse, felt it.

Ma paused for breath before she could atone for her heartlessness by answering the other questions. 'I have answered, you bitch, your second question also in the process of answering your first: the question how you came to be where you are? Your third question is why you have to do what you do. That is more easily answered. You eat during the day what you earn at night, and you've got to have something to eat if you want to stay alive.'

Having thus explained everything, Ma strode back to her room and shut herself in. When one of the girls took food to her room, Ma refused to open the door from within, saying she was not hungry.

That night Munni Bai could not sleep. She lay tossing in her bed. She could not lie on her back which still ached. Now suppose some 'customer' called! What would she do? What could she do?

She was the first choice of every customer, and her refusal to oblige might turn him away for ever if he was a regular. After all, there were other Kothas in Hira Mandi! Competition was stiff.

And Munni Bai could not afford to lose customers. No woman in this profession could. Plainly, it was a question of making hay while youth shone; and youth somehow did not seem to last even as long as the sun did. If the sun went down in the evening, it arose the next morning. But once youth sank into age it was never to come out of it again.

Munni Bai hated even to think of it. Hadn't Ma said that she had to eat during the day what she earned at night? Munni Bai knew that a time was bound to come when the night would yield nothing to see her through the day.

Contemplating the bleak prospects between the spasms of pain resulting from the caning she had received, Munni Bai switched off the light and lay in darkness. Suddenly she developed a feeling that the door of her room was being opened surreptitiously as though by a burglar.

Now she could distinctly hear advancing footfalls as someone entered her room. Who could it be? A burglar? What was there in the room for a burglar? Indeed, she herself had nothing which could be stolen. The elite of the society had already robbed her of the only precious thing she had ever possessed.

The soft tread sounded familiar. Yet Munni Bai did not move in her bed and kept her eyes closed. A figure approached her cot and sat down on the vacant side, adjacent to Munni Bai's back. A hand which was muscular enough to be masculine touched and then slowly lifted her unbuttoned blouse, unstrapped the loosely hung bodice and with the utmost care went over the lacerated back. An instant later Munni Bai, with her eyes still shut, felt the sensation of some ointment being applied softly to bruises and spread to the rest of her back. The ointment smelled of sandalwood.

Munni Bai felt so relieved and so touched that she sat up, embraced Ma and cried like a child.

Days passed, and with each day Ma's establishment attracted more clients than any other in the whole of Hira Mandi. Everybody wanted Munni Bai and only Munni Bai. She on her part made herself available to as many of her customers as she could.

However, Munni Bai's heart was not in her profession. But she had to keep her heart beating, and the only way to do so was by overcoming the feeling of disgust and revulsion that often suffused her heart.

In the privacy of a closed room she was totally at the mercy of the master of the moment. Some dealt with her brutally and she suffered in silence. With the passage of time her body became inured to every kind of treatment. But her soul still squirmed.

As she kept busy the best part of every night, Munni Bai had more hours to herself during the day than anyone else in the establishment. With nothing to do in those idle hours, she would lose herself in thought.

She would think in particular about two of her customers who also called themselves her lovers. They had come to her at different times, but they spoke the same language. They made love and talked hate. As she lay in the bed totally spent, Munni Bai would suddenly start hating them—hating them for the innate hatred they divulged so soon after making love to her.

Raj Kamal was about twenty-five and extremely virile. But since he had a wife at home, and a rich one at that, without whose benefactions he would be out on the streets begging, he had to divide his passions between Munni Bai and his wife. Thus he could not inject full ardour into his love-making with Munni Bai. So he made up vocally for what he lacked sexually.

He would often tell Munni Bai, in the gentle flow of amiability induced by satisfied lust, 'These good-for-nothing fellows, the Muslims, who cannot live for a day without loans from us, have already started living in a fool's paradise. They are already dreaming dreams of a country of their own from which non-Muslims like you and me would be expelled!

Munni Bai would invariably interrupt him: 'What do you mean by saying "non-Muslims like you and me"? How do you know that I am not a Muslim? And what if I am?'

'But that's impossible! A beauty like you can only be a Hindu,' Raj Kamal would assure her with considerable vehemence.

His outbursts would amuse Munni Bai. She would tease him: 'Still, what if I turn out to have been the child of Muslim parents? Would you have desisted from making love to me?'

'Don't talk rot,' he would shout at that. 'I have been making love to you because you are such a ravishing beauty, and a ravishing beauty can never be anything but a Hindu. I am convinced of it.' But it was clear every time that he was a bit nettled.

'Raj, tell me one thing honestly. Suppose, for the sake of argument, that a Muslim country comes into being. Suppose also that I am then adjudged a Hindu and expelled from it as you too would be. Would you abide by me in whatever country we both happen to be?' Munni Bai could not keep count of the number of times she had asked this question, but every time the answer was the same.

'What a silly question, Munni Bai!' Raj Kamal would scoff. 'No force on earth can drive us from our homes and hearths. Lahore—Hira Mandi particularly—belongs as much to us as it does to the Muslims. Nobody can dislodge us from our city.' And he would pause a little before adding: 'If, God forbid, that comes to pass, I shall be with you, although we are not married, till death do us part.'

Munni Bai was not one to let it go at that. 'What will you do with your rich wife? You can't commit bigamy, much less murder!'

Raj Kamal would leave her room at that point, saying, 'We'll cross the bridge when we come to it.'

Munni Bai's other lover was Jafar Khan, who claimed to be a thoroughbred Pathan. 'Today you are not exclusively mine because rich kafirs are as attracted to you as I am and they can outbid me. But when Pakistan is formed and after we have driven out all the kafirs you, Munni Bai, will belong only to Jafar Khan.' This was his most frequent boast.

Munni Bai would set him the same poser she did to Raj Kamal, and his reaction would be the same as that of his unknown rival. 'I have been making love to you, Munni Bai, because you are a fairy, a hourie, from behisht and a hourie can only be a Muslim. I am sure of that,' he would say.

Both Raj Kamal and Jafar Khan showed conviction without either of them revealing its source. Munni Bai would tell the latter: 'Suppose your dream of a nation of and for the Muslims is fulfilled and then you discover that I am not a Muslim, what will you do?'

Jafar Khan would stare banefully at Munni Bai for a second or so and then say, 'If, Allah forbid, it is discovered that you are a Hindu, I shall convert you to Islam and marry you.'

Munni Bai treated this bravado with just as much contempt as she did Raj Kamal's boastings. If Raj Kamal was totally dependent on his rich wife, even for his meals, not to speak of his extravagances, Jafar Khan and his wife were both more or less equally poor. Munni Bai had it on good authority that every time Jafar Khan spent a night with her, smothering her with currency notes, he was afraid of being arrested the next morning for theft or burglary. Therefore, there was more fear than passion in his love-making.

Munni Bai would persist: 'Tell me, honestly, Jafar Kahn. Would you find me less desirable if you discovered just now that I wasn't a Muslim? I really don't know whether I am a Muslim or a Hindu. I was found on a road halfway between a temple and a mosque. Maybe that is symbolic of the fact that I am part Hindu and part Muslim.'

'How can anyone be part Hindu and part Muslim? I feel it in my bones that you cannot but be a Muslim,' he would say decisively and also a bit testily.

Munni Bai had known too many men even in so short a life not to be able to read Jafar Khan's thoughts. She knew that what he really felt in his bones was not that she was a Muslim, but that he who was finding it difficult to maintain one wife would not be able to assume the responsibility of taking care of another being.

Then began those memorable months of disgrace by the end of which the Hindus had won, the Muslims had won, but humanity had lost. As an area frequented by members of all communities Hira Mandi, it had initially been presumed, alone would be immune to destruction. But the hope proved false.

Professional jealousy which had festered for years found an outlet in communal frenzy. The rioters and arsonists were made to believe by frustrated denizens that Ma, like every other inmate of her establishment, was a Hindu. Consequently, the establishment had to be wound up before it could be burned down.

With her wards in tow, Ma fled Lahore before it was too late. Only Munni Bai seemed to wish to tarry a little. She kept looking even in the frenzied crowds with flaming torches for Raj Kamal and Jafar Khan, but there was no trace of either. Maybe Raj Kamal had managed to cross the border and was waiting for her on the other side, but whatever could have happened to Jafar Khan? And to think that both had promised to abide by her through thick and thin!

Finally, Ma and her wards reached the refugee camp in Delhi, tired but all in one piece. True, here they lacked the comforts to which they had got accustomed in Hira Mandi, but at least there was no danger to their lives.

They were grieved to see countless refugees mourning the loss of their kinsmen. But Ma and her group had no kinsmen, only clients. Therefore there was no sense of loss. They could not have cared less if all their clients had been done to death. They had rendered services for what they had been paid for, and so they were quits. Human bonds are not forged in commercial transactions.

With the passage of time popular frenzy abated; murderers and arsonists had either tired of what they had been doing or had run out of objects of hate. It was not yet back to business; but the business of destruction was nearly over.

The authorities announced one day that such of the refugees as wanted to leave the camp and start life anew would be given all assistance. Munni Bai kept hoping that some day, somewhere, she would run into Raj Kamal and remind him of his promise to take care of her. Why, she would even remind him of his promise to marry her!

Munni Bai had seen brides and envied them. She had herself had bridals without ever being a bride. She wished to be one.

One day Ma returned from a round of the city of Delhi and announced to her flock that she had fixed up a house for them to live in. It sent a wave of jubilation through her companions. With their meagre belongings held close to their chests they trooped out of the camp, engaged a tonga and got into it.

Ma gave an address to the tongawalla and after what looked like eternity the vehicle stopped in front of a partly damaged house.

The tongawalla addressed Ma: 'Bibiji, this is the house where Salma used to stay with … er … companions. What a beauty she was! Nawabs and rajas used to visit her frequently. She has now gone with her group to Hira Mandi in Lahore.'

In no time at all, women giggling and joking appeared on the balconies of the surrounding houses. One look at them and it was clear to Ma and her group that they were kindred spirits. Meanwhile the tongawalla said, 'Bibiji, this is known as G.B. Road.'

It was then that the ugly reality of the situation dawned on Munni Bai. She turned to Ma and asked in a voice without emotion, 'Ma, the Muslims asked for a Pakistan and they have got it. The Hindus wanted to see the back of Muslims and they now have a Hindustan and are happy. We asked for nothing. Why, then, have we got all this suffering?'

Ma did not answer the question, instead, led her party into the room.

Within days the newcomers were accepted as part of the 'community.' Despite all her harrowing experiences, Munni Bai had managed to retain her charm. Word soon spread that an exceptional beauty had landed from Hira Mandi where her name had been on everybody's lips. But Ma, who knew all the tricks of the trade, also knew how to handle the publicity. She quickly spread the word that the beauty from Hira Mandi would be accessible only to the very rich.

Munni Bai's neighbour told her: 'I am afraid Ma is going about it in the wrong way. Where are the very rich now? So many Hindus and Muslims have perished in the holocaust and so much property has been destroyed that I doubt if there is any rich man around, either a Hindu or a Muslim. Even the poor belonging to both communities have perished.'

The same night two limousines stopped in front of the house one hour after another. The first disgorged a raja, who sent in his compliments ballasted with currency notes and expressed the desire to spend time with the fabled beauty from Hira Mandi. He was obliged. But no sooner had he left than another limousine arrived, disgorging a nawab who desired the same satisfaction, paid generously for the service rendered and departed.

Before retiring for the night Munni Bai asked Ma: 'Ma, Pakistan has been formed but the nawabs are as rich in India as they ever were. The Hindu rajas have been shouting from housetops that such of them as have not been butchered have been pauperised. Yet they have so much money for one night's enjoyment. Then who lost and who died in the Partition?'

—Translated from the original in Urdu by Md. Vazeeruddin

Nuha Samara

(1944–1992)

NUHA SAMARA WAS BORN in Tulkarem, Palestine. In 1948, her family fled to Beirut. In 1962, she began to write for Beiruti newspapers; many of her newspaper publications have been short stories. Her works include *In the Swamp City* (1973) and *The Tables Lived Longer Than Amin* (1981), which she wrote during the Lebanese Civil War. At the end of 1975, she left Beirut for Doha, Qatar, and a year later, she moved to London, where she stayed for two years. Exile then took her to Paris. In 1982, she returned to the Middle East and worked in Limassol, Cyprus, as the editor of the women's section of the Al-Shahid magazine.

In a letter she once wrote, she said: "My primary concern is the Arab woman and her means of expression." Samara is one of the Beirut Decentrists, a school of women writers whose literary production emerges out of the civil war, especially during the 1975 to 1982 period. The leitmotiv of the Decentrists' writings is the role of women in ending the violence.

In this story, a woman's husband leaves her in the war zone to enjoy the safety of another country. In response, the woman cuts her hair, changes her whole physical being, and builds an inner core of hardness. While learning to live alone within war, she reassesses the roles she and her husband have played in prewar times.

Two Faces, One Woman

Calmly she went to bathe. She had learnt how to hold on to time, how to touch things calmly. She undressed slowly. As she washed her long, blond hair she remembered him and how he had loved and admired her hair: "The hair of a palomino"; "It fills me with desire for you"; "The day it's short I'll leave you for another woman."

Ever since the beginning of the war, she had accustomed herself to bathe quickly, fearing that a shell might hit and kill her when she was naked. Her death would become a funny story for the neighbors to repeat!

She felt afraid … and decided to finish quickly. Why shouldn't she admit that he had chosen to abandon her with her helpless father! She dried her hair thoroughly. And then, sitting in front of the mirror, she set up another one behind her and began to cut her hair. She saw the locks fall, but felt no sadness. It's a lie that women make themselves beautiful for men. … Now that the man had gone she could stop lying. In the mirror her features hardened. Then she had an idea. She took some hair dye and, mixing it into a paste, she brushed it on to her hair. Then she washed her hair and contemplated it in the mirror. Her features had become more sharply defined; this bleached hair made her look like a Nazi officer. She wanted him to see her now, to rid him of those sweet images. What did he mean by abandoning her in the filthy war, where survival depended on chance alone! He knew perfectly well how the daily chores of war-time existence exhausted her. And her father … what an enormous responsibility! How could she carry him down to the shelter in his wheelchair when the shelling got heavy? And what of the neighbors' questioning, infuriating glances: "He left her the responsibility of this helpless old man!"

Earlier her father had lived with her sister and her four children. It was he who had suggested that they should bring him here to lighten her sister's accumulated responsibilities. He had driven there under the bombs and had quickly brought him back, like a conqueror. Exactly a month later his director had given the choice between staying and transferring to Paris … and he had chosen the latter.

He stuttered a lot as he announced his decision. She remained silent, neither encouraging, nor dissuading him. He knew her well. She didn't interfere in anyone's decisions. She muttered under her breath: "It's your right to choose to stay alive."

She wondered if he would have chosen to travel had she not aborted the baby a few months ago. Would she have retained her passivity? Two days after this decision, he told her that he was leaving the next day. Throughout those three days he noticed that she couldn't look him in the eye. She had even lost interest in following the news of the war. … And when the dining room window shattered after a shell exploded nearby, he had held her tight and said: "Be strong in my absence!"

And that's how she was now. … Her features were those of a man, her demeanor that of a Nazi in Hitler's army. She went to the wardrobe, and put on a pair of jeans and a khaki shirt. She looked ready to go into battle, all she lacked were weapons. And then she remembered. She opened an old cupboard and took out his pistol. Why hadn't she agreed to his friend Manah's suggestion to train near the house? She could do that in the early hours of dawn while her father was asleep, when the sounds of shells and death had receded.

She contacts Manah immediately. He responds quickly and tells her that she's made an excellent decision. She tells him of Abdallah's departure. He's surprised, and then he understands, and is quiet. Then she hears him reassure her: "You've made a great decision. Tomorrow morning at six, we'll see you over there."

In the morning ... Manah was not there. But he had given her name to the drill master. All those present were men. Not one of them looked at her curiously, nor admiringly nor even lustfully as he had. ... Was it the war? Or was it her new face that made her look like a Nazi officer? The training exercises were not difficult. The sound of the first bullets exploding out of her pistol didn't frighten or disturb her ... She was amazed by her lust to kill. When the bullets exploded in quick succession, she wished that the dummies that were falling had been people. When it was over, the drill master congratulated her on her courage, and she answered: "I want to complete the training. I want to know all fighting techniques."

At night the shelling increased, but she was no longer afraid as she had been before. She heard the neighbors scream as they rushed down to the shelter. She decided to carry her father in his wheelchair down to the shelter, not forgetting to take some bread and cheese. Probably the toughest thing that day was the neighbors' looks. Ohh! ... How she hated to be pitied. The only pity she had been able to stand had been his when he returned home and saw her cooking and cleaning. After returning from a day's teaching, he would mutter something she could not understand: "Ah, the beautiful proletariat!" She never asked him what that meant, but when she dusted his office, she noticed many titles about revolution and change and books stuffed with the word "proletariat." She wasn't at all curious to read any of these books. Maybe she didn't have the time. But then, she'd never seen him read any of them. He preferred to chat with friends, to inhale her food and to smoke an ivory narghile, of which his friends made fun. At one point Manah had said to him:

"Words! This revolution about which you keep talking doesn't go with this narghile of yours!"

Down in the shelter she felt ravenously hungry. She gave her father some bread and cheese. In time with the pounding shells he started to gnaw. She loathed the sound of chewing. All that was left of the people in the war was greedy mouths that did nothing but chew. The shelter was like the Day of Resurrection with all those kids screaming. She touched her stomach where the embryo had been on that day that she had rejoiced to have aborted it. Had she known at the time that her relationship with him could not stand this?

A neighbor asked her presumptuously:

"Where's Abdallah?"

"He's gone."

"Where?"

"Paris."

"Why?"

"They transferred him."

She didn't tell her that his company had given him the choice between staying and leaving, lest the woman pity her even more!

"Has he seen what you've done to your hair?"

"Yes."

She had to lie. Why should everyone know what she'd gone through. The neighbor went on:

"I'm not surprised that Abdallah's gone. I overheard him talking to my husband a while back here in the shelter, and he said that he couldn't stand it. Don't forget, it's been a year and a half! But why didn't he take you with him?"

"How could I leave my father? My sister's already left with her husband and children."

The neighbor shook her head, not quite convinced. Then she said pointing to her father: "May God help you with this responsibility." She turned to her responsibility. He was gnawing at the bread and cheese as anxiously as someone eating his last meal. All his appetites in life had turned to eating. Every day he'd ask her what there was to eat, and whether they had enough money for it.

He had given her his whole salary before he left, and as usual had left the money on the table. He knew that she hated to take the money out of his hand. He noticed that she hadn't hidden the money and he chided her: "Be careful! Everyone's become a thief!"

And when it was time for him to go, he stood there in embarrassment wanting to kiss her, and he said: "Take good care of yourself. If you need anything, go to my brother or uncle. I'll get in touch through my uncle."

Words ... words!!

Most of the people in the shelter were sleeping, completely exhausted. They had spread out their bedding and had fallen asleep. Even her father was asleep in his rocking chair. She covered him with a blanket, and then went up to the apartment calmly. The shells persisted outside, lighting up the skies and then going out, shining and then disappearing. Like red and green traffic lights. She remembered peace time, when these traffic lights used to work.

She felt very calm when she found herself alone. From birth, she had never been quite alone. Her family and siblings had always been there. After marriage, either he or his absence had been there. But now she was completely alone with the night. She sat in front of the hall mirror in her apartment hallway, where there were the safest corners. Suddenly she felt like taking off her clothes. She contemplated her body in the mirror, it was still radiant. She started to touch it as though bewitched, as though noticing it for the first time. She felt a desire to possess it, and she touched herself until she climaxed. The she thought: "I have to have a lover!"

She thought about the men she knew, most of whom she knew through Abdallah. She had not once thought of any of them as men. They had different voices. She could remember their voices clearly, but she could not remember their features, their heights or sizes. She saw them through him. Whomever he had liked, she had liked. And he had really liked Manah and praised her in front of him! Manah ... Maybe he was the one to pursue? He had been his best friend, and his was the only face she could clearly recollect. This was the man. He was almost primitive with his bulging muscles, the hair emerging from the open shirt and his black, piercing, captivating eyes ...

Manah. Why not? She decided to talk to him the next morning. She was a bit embarrassed when she saw him at the training ground. He approached and shyly asked her how she was. Did she need anything in Abdallah's absence. She didn't hesitate to ask him if he could find a hospital for her father where she could be sure that he would be well cared for. He promised to arrange something as soon as possible. She went on to tell him about her anxiety for her father during bombardments. Sometimes she couldn't find him a doctor when he had a relapse. He praised her for her rational decision. Then he said before leaving: "I'll be in touch as soon as I've found something suitable." Manah wasn't long in contacting her. One morning he told her of a suitable, safe place and he promised to get an ambulance to transport him. And then he asked: "How is he?"

She noticed that he avoided mentioning her husband's name. She answered briefly that he had asked his uncle about her and had tentatively asked if there was anything she needed.

When he left, she hurried to her father to tell him of her plan. She assured him somewhat harshly and peremptorily that this was ideal during the war, and that his safety and food would be surer there than with her. He looked distracted and sad, and shook his head a lot because he had difficulty in speaking. In the end she assured him that this was just for the duration of the war, and that when it was over he would return to her.

She rushed out so as not to burst into tears. In her room she began to undress. Manah's face leapt out in front of her. Why was her body beginning to awaken to desires of which she had been unaware when she had been with him? Was it his absence? Or the repeated reports of death? He had accused her of frigidity, and she had never responded because she hadn't had the right keys to her body.

And when he had insistently made love to her during the war, she had questioned him and he had answered confidently:

"When you keep hearing of death your desires increase. This is particularly true during wars. Europe went through its moral decline after its two wars." And he went on: "In the face of death all values go by the board. All that remains alive are the limits of the body and the pulse of feeling and instinct."

Another time he had said something that was hard to forget: "The most important consequence of this war is that our pursuit of work, social relationships and petty misguided ambitions has slowed down. It has reduced us to life size. ... But if it goes on we may lose ourselves once again, but in another way ... "

How often had she looked back on her life with him before the war. Her marriage had been a rush between her work as a teacher and a wife. He had been very concerned about his clothes, his food and the cleanliness of the house. He had often exploded in anger, swearing and slamming the door when he hadn't found things exactly right. She was quite used to this, because her father had been like this, and also Manah sometimes when he was with her husband. And her response to these explosions had been the same as her mother's ... silence! She had only felt a refusal grow in her after he had left. The only difference between her and her mother was that she worked outside the home. The only difference between him and her father was that he didn't object to her sitting with his friends when they came over, and he wasn't ashamed to express his feelings for her openly. Whereas she had never heard her father praise her mother in front of others. Her father was a man: not once had he left his family, and he had shouldered his responsibilities until he was paralysed two years after her mother's demise. How embarrassed she had been by his openness in front of his friends. He had exaggerated, as though wanting them to feel dissatisfied with their wives. But when they had left, he would pick up any old newspaper as though he had not said all those passionate things a few seconds ago. At first she couldn't understand the change, couldn't explain it. She had attributed it to moodiness, because he had often said that he was moody, his temper mercurial.

—&   —&   —&

Manah had been on her mind when she opened the door after a wild night of shelling spent in the shelter with her father. He looked a little disturbed:

"Have you prepared all your father's things? The war might last."

"Will it?"

"Probably. Your drill master has given you an 'A.' He says that you shoot with an amazing ability that he doesn't find in men. I wonder if you can hit all your targets?"

"Yes. And particularly now that he's gone!"

He interrupted her: "Where's your father?"

"In the bedroom ... Here."

Her father's face was tense, as though he were on his way to the gallows. She loved the way that Manah stroked his tired face and held her father's hand, saying:

"Listen, Uncle. We're doing all this for your good. These inhuman conditions have compelled us to put you in hospital where everyone will take care of you. In the hospital they will protect you against this damned war. You'll get food, drink, shelter, electricity and medicine. I'll always make sure you're O.K. ... and so will your daughter. If ever you need anything, just let me know. ... "

"And now?"

He carried her father from the bed to the wheel chair. He indicated that she should bring the case and follow him. Fortunately, the lift was working that day. She rushed after them, and they got into the ambulance.

When they arrived at the hospital after a silent trip, her father's face reflected all the harshness of the war. She followed them into the hospital. She tried not to look through the partially open doors of rooms housing the injured and the maimed of the war. Manah murmured reassuringly:

"He'll be in the geriatrics ward, not here."

She relaxed when she saw how clean the place was and when she realized that he was going to be put into a sunny, private room. She kissed him. Not a single tear. This war was tough. Manah took her hand. She trembled and he must have felt it.

She heard him say: "I left my car at the hospital entrance so we can return together." She followed him as though bewitched. When she sat next to him she was as calm and relaxed as though she were his wife. He said:

"You had no other choice. Imagine what would have happened if your house had been hit, or if you had needed a doctor during a bombardment. What would you have done?"

Silence. Then she heard him say: "He's in the proper place now."

When they arrived at the house she asked him if he wanted some morning coffee, and he answered, his black eyes laughing: "I'd love to have some of your famous coffee!"

In the elevator, he stared silently at the lights that indicated the first floor, the second ... the fifth then the seventh ... She felt very embarrassed when they were alone together without his shadow or the shadow of her father. She rushed to the kitchen to prepare the coffee. All this silence excited her. On purpose she started to make lots of noise with the dishes. When she went in to the sitting room, he had closed his eyes and he looked washed out. He noticed her moving around, and said quickly:

"Imagine! I almost fell asleep. The last three nights I've hardly slept."
He sat up and asked her gently: "Are you depressed to be alone now?"
"No. I need to be alone."
"You're strange. ... Most women living alone complain a great deal."
"Not me."
"That's why he was happy with you."
"Who said he was happy?"
"That's what he had us understand."
She handed him the coffee and he began to talk about the war, and
analyzed the reasons for the resumption and intensification of the fight-
ing. Then he got up and said: "I'll drop around often. I need to talk to
you."
"So do I."
When he had closed the door behind him, the air was filled with his
smell and her father's sad face, and she decided to call and find out how
he was.

↤   ↤   ↤

After taking her father to hospital she hadn't even considered going
down into the shelter. Most of the people kept insisting that she go
down. But she didn't.

There, on her own, she could dream a lot about Manah, and a little
about the future.

What would she do if the war were to end and life returned to its regular place and he came back? And the school, and his friends' and family's
stupid faces and eternal visits, and his anger and whims for what he
wanted and didn't want. She felt incapable of touching him after today.
In the past she had been content with him and submitted to his moods.
But today the balance had been upset. He'd just escaped to Paris. What
did he feel when he saw those beautiful, elegant Parisian women who
were enjoying themselves while she was a prisoner to her responsibility,
her loneliness and to death? Wouldn't he be confused by the compari-
son? At night whom would he hold? She well knew that he couldn't live
without a woman, without touching, especially after the second drink.
When his revolutionary friends had left he would sniff and lick her. Once
she had fallen asleep with him kissing her body, content as a child, and
she had heard him say frantically: "You're mine ... mine ... a thousand
times mine."

It was that day that she realized that however much she submitted to
him, he was never fully satisfied that she was his. He had said to her
once that she wouldn't let him feel that she belonged to him, that she
was like happiness: only felt after it was gone.

The sounds of the shells and the explosions returned, the daily blanket of this city which enfolded the inhabitants like a peasant woman's

clothes enfolded her. She began to feel the warm pulse of her new life. The white space of time ahead was hers to contemplate. Again she took off her clothes in front of the mirror in the hallway. She saw Manah's face, and she felt embarrassed as she touched herself, as though he were actually watching. She felt a terrible longing for him. She knew his phone number. Why shouldn't she contact him, and use all her feminine tricks and wiles? Tell him that she was afraid and he would come over and hold her through the night. And she would drown in love in his body. But if that were to happen, how difficult it would be to return to the distant traveller. She knew that she couldn't maintain relationships with two men at the same time. She remembered that his uncle had brought her a letter from him two days ago and she hadn't yet looked at it. His writing was like his body: sensitive, supple and full of curves ... reading handwriting is like making love to the writer.

"My darling. Here, far away it's hard to forget, and it's hard to remember. ... I'm living like someone who is postponing his life. Beirut had not given us the space for expectation and hope. And yet, I am living it. My time and my space are defined by it, even though I'm far away in Paris. ...

"Peacetime Beirut is not as beautiful and passionate as war-torn Beirut. Because of her we become vicious in love with vice, and mystics in love with mysticism. I am filled with loneliness, longing and waiting. I recollect the city's face and yours, and feel that I am still intimately connected to it and to you. I feel that my amputation has been a kind of treachery. My darling, I am suspended between life and death. Every morning I am amazed that I can keep going. Every morning as I awake out of the confusion of my dreams I forget where I am, but am filled with the old joy, probably part of my childhood. This joy drives me to get up and wash my face, shave and dress. And as I go through the streets to work I discover the delusion of this joy, and I wonder why and I find it in Beirut and in your face. Both possess me to the point of suffocation. I walk through the streets like a lost child not knowing where the path is leading.

"The women of Paris are beautiful and they remind me of a phrase from Byron: 'If all the women of the world had but one mouth I would have kissed it and been happy.' How I miss your mouth, your long hair, my corner in front of the TV, my records, my bed, the smell of your cooking when I come home from work. How I long for the warmth of old! I'll be back when the war's over, that's what my director promised when he knew how I was suffering. Today he said to me laughing: 'You Beirutis, you're like fish out of water. I don't want you to die like a fish!'

"Pray for peace, so that I can return to you ...

"Love always,

"Abdallah"

His last words revived all her anger at his departure. Was he only with her during times of peace, love, cooking, and warm beds? She hurried to the telephone and dialed Manah's number. He wasn't there.

She'd try tomorrow and the day after and even when the war was over … And even if he returned from Paris …

—Translated from the Arabic by Miriam Cooke

Mahasweta Devi

(1926–   )

MAHASWETA DEVI IS ONE of India's most important writers. Her stories about the struggles and courage of women have often been included in anthologies of twentieth-century literature. She has an M.A. in English from Shantiniketan and in 1979 was awarded the prestigious Sahitya Akademi Award for her works.

"Draupadi" first appeared in 1978 in *Agnigarbha* (translated as Womb of fire or Fires underground), a collection of short political narratives. In the introduction to that volume, Devi states that "life is not mathematics and the human being is not made for the sake of politics. I want a change in the present social system and do not believe in mere party politics."

The protagonist of this twentieth-century short story, a tribal woman who lives in poverty, bears the name of one of the most important female protagonists of *Mahabharata*, Queen Draupadi. Draupadi is the wife of the five Pandava princes from the Sanskrit epic. When one of her husbands loses his kingdom to another prince in a dice game, Draupadi challenges the victorious prince's right to her. She prays to the god Vishnu/Krishna to save her honor when the evil prince and his companions try to dishonor her by attempting to pull off her sari. Her prayers are answered, and every time one sari is pulled off, another appears miraculously to cover her. Draupadi endures many hardships and adventures as she lives with her husbands in exile. Using her skill with words as her primary weapon, she struggles courageously against injustice. She also uses her clothes and her physical appearance to remind her husbands and the world about the injustices she and her husbands have suffered. As long as she is a dispossessed queen, she refuses to dress herself in the ornamented clothes of a married woman and leaves her hair in an unadorned braid. The symbolism of women's clothes, as mentioned in the introduction, appears often in the literature of war. (See for example works such as Chitra Divakaruni's "Indigo" and Daisy al-Amir's "The Future" in this anthology.)

Mahasweta Devi's twentieth-century story, "Draupadi," is set in the context of the sociopolitical, militant Naxalite movement, which began as a peasant rebellion in the Naxalbari area of West Bengal in 1967. Draupadi, also called Dopdi in this Bengali story, is not a queen exiled to a forest. She is a poor peasant woman, familiar with the forest, who is actively participating in the war against injustice. No divine being intervenes for this woman when she is tortured, but she, like the legendary queen, uses her physical presence to make her statement to the world. Instead of cleansing her body of the wounds inflicted upon her and removing her tattered clothes, she presents herself as she is to Senanayak, the army officer, as the explicit manifestation of his and his men's cruelty and injustice to her as a woman.

The translator, Gayatri Chakravorty Spivak, italicized words that were in English in the original story.

Draupadi

Name Dopdi Mejhen, age twenty-seven, husband Dulna Majhi (deceased), domicile Cherakhan, Bankrahjarh, information whether dead or alive and/or assistance in arrest, one hundred rupees ...

An exchange between two liveried *uniforms.*

FIRST LIVERY: What's this, a tribal called Dopdi? The list of names I brought has nothing like it! How can anyone have an unlisted name?

SECOND: Draupadi Mejhen. Born the year her mother threshed rice for Surja Sahu (killed)'s at Bakuli. Surja Sahu's wife gave her the name.

FIRST: These officers like nothing better than to write as much as they can in English. What's all this stuff about her?

SECOND: *Most notorious* female. *Long wanted in many ...*

Dossier: Dulna and Dopdi worked at harvests, *rotating* between Birbhum, Burdwan, Murshidabad, and Bankura. In 1971, in the famous *Operation* Bakuli, when three villages were *cordonned* off and *machine gunned,* they too lay on the ground, faking dead. In fact, they were the main culprits. Murdering Surja Sahu and his son, occupying upper-caste wells and tubewells during the drought, not surrendering those three young men to the police. In all this they were the chief instigators. In the morning, at the time of the body count, the couple could not be found. The blood sugar level of Captain Arjan Singh, the *architect* of Bakuli, rose at once and proved yet again that diabetes can be a result of anxiety and depression. Diabetes has twelve husbands—among them anxiety.

Dulna and Dopdi went underground for a long time in a *Neanderthal* darkness. The Special Forces, attempting to pierce that dark by an armed search, compelled quite a few Santals in the various districts of West Bengal to meet their Maker against their will. By the Indian Constitution, all human beings, regardless of caste or creed, are sacred. Still, accidents like this do happen. Two sorts of reasons: (1) the underground couple's skill in self-concealment; (2) not merely the Santals but all tribals of the Austro-Asiatic Munda tribes appear the same to the Special Forces.

In fact, all around the ill-famed forest off Jharkhani, which is under the jurisdiction of the police station at Bankrahjarh (in this India of ours, even a worm is under a certain police station), even in the southeast and southwest corners, one comes across hair-raising details in the eyewitness records put together on the people who are suspected of attacking police stations, stealing guns (since the snatchers are not invariably well educated, they sometimes say "give up your *chambers*" rather than give up your gun), killing grain brokers, landlords, moneylenders, law officers, and bureaucrats. A black-skinned couple ululated like police *sirens* before the episode. They sang jubilantly in a savage tongue, incomprehensible even to the Santals. Such as:

Samaray hijulenako mar goekope

and,

Hende rambra keche keche
Pundi rambra keche keche

This proves conclusively that they are the cause of Captain Arjan Singh's diabetes.

Government procedure being as incomprehensible as the Male Principle in Sankhya philosophy or Antonioni's early films, it was Arjan Singh who was sent once again on *Operation Forest* Jharkhani. Learning from Intelligence that the above-mentioned ululating and dancing couple was the escaped corpses, Arjan Singh fell for a bit into a *zombie*like state and finally acquired so irrational a dread of black-skinned people that whenever he saw a black person in a ballbag, he swooned, saying "they're killing me," and drank and passed a lot of water. Neither uniform nor Scriptures could relieve that depression. At long last, under the shadow of a *premature and forced retirement,* it was possible to present him at the desk of Mr. Senanayak, the elderly Bengali specialist in combat and extreme-Left politics.

Senanayak knows the activities and capacities of the opposition better than they themselves do. First, therefore, he presents an encomium on the military genius of the Sikhs. Then he explains further: Is it only the opposition that should find power at the end of the barrel gun? Arjan Singh's power also explodes out of the *male organ* of a gun. Without a gun even the "five K's" come to nothing in this day and age. These speeches he delivers to all and sundry. As a result, the fighting forces regain their confidence in the *Army Handbook.* It is not a book for everyone. It says that the most despicable and repulsive style of fighting is guerrilla warfare with primitive weapons. Annihilation at sight of any and all practitioners of such warfare is the sacred duty of every soldier.

Dopdi and Dulna belong to the *category* of such fighters, for they too kill by means of hatchet and scythe, bow and arrow, etc. In fact, their fighting power is greater than the gentlemen's. Not all gentlemen become experts in the explosion of "chambers"; they think the power will come out on its own if the gun is held. But since Dulna and Dopdi are illiterate, their kind have practiced the use of weapons generation after generation.

I should mention here that, although the other side make little of him, Senanayak is not to be trifled with. Whatever his *practice*, in *theory* he respects the opposition. Respects them because they could be neither understood nor demolished if they were treated with the attitude, "It's nothing but a bit of impertinent game-playing with guns." *In order to destroy the enemy, become one.* Thus he understood them by (*theoretically*) becoming one of them. He hopes to write on all this in the future. He has also decided that in his written work he will demolish the gentlemen and *highlight* the message of the harvest workers. These mental processes might seem complicated, but actually he is a simple man and is as pleased as his third great-uncle after a meal of turtle meat. In fact, he knows that, as in the old popular song, turn by turn the world will change. And in every world he must have the credentials to survive with honor. If necessary he will show the future to what extent he alone understands the matter in its proper perspective. He knows very well that what he is doing today the future will forget, but he also knows that if he can change color from world to world, he can represent the particular world in question. Today he is getting rid of the young by means of "*apprehension and elimination*," but he knows people will soon forget the memory and lesson of blood. And at the same time, he, like Shakespeare, believes in delivering the world's *legacy* into youth's hands. He is Prospero as well.

At any rate, information is received that many young men and women, *batch by batch* and on jeeps, have attacked police station after police station, terrified and elated the region, and disappeared into the forest of Jharkhani. Since after escaping from Bakuli, Dopdi and Dulna have worked at the house of virtually every landowner, they can efficiently inform the killers about their targets and announce proudly that they too are soldiers, *rank and file.* Finally the impenetrable forest of Jharkhani is surrounded by real soldiers, the *army* enters and splits the battlefield. Soldiers in hiding guard the falls and springs that are the only source of drinking water; they are still guarding, still looking. On one such search, army informant Dukhiram Gharari saw a young Santal man lying on his stomach on a flat stone, dipping his face to drink water. The soldiers shot him as he lay. As the .303 threw him off spread-eagled and brought a bloody foam to his mouth, he roared "Ma-ho" and then went limp. They realized later that it was the redoubtable Dulna Majhi.

What does "Ma-ho" mean? Is this a violent slogan in the tribal language? Even after much thought, the Department of Defense could not be sure. Two tribal-specialist types are flown in from Calcutta, and they sweat over the dictionaries put together by worthies such as Hoffmann-Jeffer and Golden-Palmer. Finally the omniscient Senanayak summons Chamru, the water carrier of the *camp*. He giggles when he sees the two specialists, scratches his ear with his "bidi," and says, The Santals of Maldah did say that when they began fighting at the time of King Gandhi! It's a battle cry. Who said "Ma-ho" here? Did someone come from Maldah?

The problem is thus solved. Then, leaving Dulna's body on the stone, the soldiers climb the trees in green camouflage. They embrace the leafy boughs like so many great god Pans and wait as the large red ants bite their private parts. To see if anyone comes to take away the body. This is the hunter's way, not the soldier's. But Senanayak knows that these brutes cannot be dispatched by the approved method. So he asks his men to draw the prey with a corpse as bait. All will come clear, he says. I have almost deciphered Dopdi's song.

The soldiers get going at his command. But no one comes to claim Dulna's corpse. At night the soldiers shoot at a scuffle and, descending, discover that they have killed two hedgehogs copulating on dry leaves. Improvidently enough, the soldiers' jungle scout Dukhiram gets a knife in the neck before he can claim the reward for Dulna's capture. Bearing Dulna's corpse, the soldiers suffer shooting pains as the ants, interrupted in their feast, begin to bite them. When Senanayak hears that no one has come to take the corpse, he slaps his *anti-Fascist paperback* copy of The Deputy and shouts, "*What?*" Immediately one of the tribal specialists runs in with joy as naked and transparent as Archimedes' and says, "Get up, *sir!* I have discovered the meaning of that 'hende rambra' stuff. It's Mundari *language*."

Thus the search for Dopdi continues. In the forest *belt* of Jharkhani, the *Operation* continues—will continue. It is a carbuncle on the government's backside. Not to be cured by the tested ointment, not to burst with the appropriate herb. In the first phase, the fugitives, ignorant of the forest's topography, are caught easily, and by law of confrontation they are shot at the taxpayer's expense. By the law of confrontation, their eyeballs, intestines, stomachs, hearts, genitals, and so on become the food of fox, vulture, hyena, wildcat, ant, and worm, and the untouchables go off happily to sell their bare skeletons.

They do not allow themselves to be captured in open combat in the next phase. Now it seems that they have found a trustworthy courier. Ten to one it's Dopdi. Dopdi loved Dulna more than her blood. No doubt it is she who is saving the fugitives now.

"They" is also a *hypothesis*.

Why?

How many went *originally?*

The answer is silence. About that there are many tales, many books in press. Best not to believe everything.

How many killed in six years' confrontation?

The answer is silence.

Why after confrontations are the skeletons discovered with arms broken or severed? Could armless men have fought? Why do the collarbones shake, why are legs and ribs crushed?

Two kinds of answers. Silence. Hurt rebuke in the eyes. Shame on you! Why bring this up? What will be will be ...

How many left in the forest? The answer is silence.

A *legion?* Is it *justifiable* to maintain a large battalion in that wild area at the taxpayer's expense?

Answer: *Objection.* "Wild area" is incorrect. The battalion is provided with supervised nutrition, arrangements to worship according to religion, opportunity to listen to "Bibidha Bharati" and to see Sanjeev Kumar and the Lord Krishna face-to-face in the movie *This Is Life.* No. The area is not wild.

How many are left?

The answer is silence.

How many are left? Is there anyone *at all?*

The answer is long.

Item: *Well, action* still goes on. Moneylenders, landlords, grain brokers, anonymous brothel keepers, ex-informants are still terrified. The hungry and naked are still defiant and irresponsible. In some *pockets* the harvest workers are getting *a better wage.* Villages sympathetic to the fugitives are still silent and hostile. These events cause one to think ...

Where in this picture does Dopdi Mejhen fit?

She must have connections with the fugitives. The cause for fear is elsewhere. The ones who remain have lived a long time in the primitive world of the forest. They keep company with the poor harvest workers and the tribals. They must have forgotten book learning. Perhaps they are *orienting* their book learning and sincere intrinsic enthusiasm. Those who are working practically will not be exterminated so easily.

Therefore *Operation* Jharkhani *Forest* cannot stop. Reason: the words of warning in the *Army Handbook.*

2.

Catch Dopdi Mejhen. She will lead us to the others.

Dopdi was proceeding slowly, with some rice knotted into her belt. Mashai Tudu's wife had cooked her some. She does so occasionally. When the rice is cold, Dopdi knots it into her waistcloth and walks slowly. As she walked, she picked out and killed the lice in her hair. If she had some *kerosene*, she'd rub it into her scalp and get rid of the lice. Then she could wash her hair with baking *soda*. But the bastards put traps at every bend of the falls. If they smell *kerosene* in the water, they will follow the scent.

"Dopdi!"

She doesn't respond. She never responds when she hears her own name. She has seen in the Panchayat office just today the notice for the reward in her name. Mushai Tudu's wife had said, "What are you looking at? Who is Dopdi Mejhen! Money if you give her up!"

"How much?"

"Two–hundred!"

Oh God!

Mushai's wife said outside the office: "A lot of preparation this time. A–ll new policemen."

Hm.

Don't come again.

Why?

Mushai's wife looked down. Tudu says that Sahib has come again. If they catch you, the village, our huts …

They'll burn again.

Yes. And about Dukhiram …

The Sahib knows?

Shomai and Budhna betrayed us.

Where are they?

Ran away by train.

Dopdi thought of something. Then said, Go home. I don't know what will happen, if they catch me don't know me.

Can't you run away?

No. Tell me, how many times can I run away? What will they do if they catch me? They will *counter* me. Let them.

Mushai's wife said, We have nowhere else to go.

Dopdi said softly, I won't tell anyone's name.

Dopdi knows, has learned by hearing so often and so long, how one can come to terms with torture. If mind and body give way under torture, Dopdi will bite off her tongue. That boy did it. They countered him. When they counter you, your hands are tied behind you. All your bones are crushed, your sex is a terrible wound. *Killed by police in an encounter … unknown male … age twenty-two …*

As she walked thinking these thoughts, Dopdi heard someone calling, Dopdi!

She didn't respond. She doesn't respond if called by her own name. Here her name is Upi Mejhen. But who calls?

Spines of suspicion are always furled in her mind. Hearing "Dopdi" they stiffen like a hedgehog's. Walking, she *unrolls the film* of known faces in her mind. Who? No Shomra, Shomra is on the run. Shomai and Budhna are also on the run, for other reasons. Not Golok, he is in Bakuli. Is it someone from Bakuli? After Bakuli, her and Dulna's names were Upi Mejhen, Matang Majhi. Here no one but Mashai and his wife knows their real names. Among the young gentlemen, not all of the previous *batches* knew.

That was a troubled time. Dopdi is confused when she thinks about it. *Operation* Bakuli in Bakuli. Surja Sahu arranged with Biddibabu to dig two tubewells and three wells within the compound of his two houses. No water anywhere, drought in Birbhum. Unlimited water at Surja Sahu's house, as clear as a crow's eye.

Get your water with a canal tax, everything is burning.

What's my profit in increasing cultivation with tax money?

Everything is on fire.

Get out of here. I don't accept your Panchayat nonsense. Increase cultivation with water. You want half the paddy for sharecropping. Everyone is happy with free paddy. Then give me paddy at home, give me money, I've learned my lesson trying to do you good.

What good did you do?

Have I not given water to the village?

You've given it to your kin Bhagunal.

Don't you get water?

No. The untouchables don't get water.

The quarrel began there. In the drought, human patience catches easily. Satish and Jugal from the village and that young gentleman, was Rana his name? said a landowning moneylender won't give a thing, put him down.

Surja Sahu's house was surrounded at night. Surja Sahu had brought out his gun. Surja was tied up with a cow rope. His whitish eyeballs turned and turned, he was incontinent again and again. Dulna had said, I'll have the first blow, brothers. My greatgrandfather took a bit of paddy from him, and still gives him free labor to repay that debt.

Dopdi had said, His mouth watered when he looked at me. I'll put out his eyes.

Surja Sahu. Then a *telegraphic message* from Shiuri. *Special train. Army.* The *jeep* didn't come up to Bakuli. *March-march-march.* The *crunch-crunch-crunch* of gravel under hobnailed boots. *Cordon up. Commands* on the *mike.* Jugal Mandal, Satish Mandal, Rana *alias* Prabir *alias* Dipak, Dulna Majhi-Dopdi Mejhen *surrender surrender surrender. No surrender surrender. Mow-mow-mow down the village.* Putt-putt-putt-putt—*cordite* in the air—putt-putt—*round the clock*—putt-putt. *Flame thrower.* Bakuli is burning. *More men and women, children …*

fire—fire. Close canal approach. Over-over-over by nightfall. Dopdi and Dulna had crawled on their stomachs to safety.

They could not have reached Paltakuri after Bakuli. Bhupati and Tapa took them. Then it was decided that Dopdi and Dulna would work around the Jharkhani *belt.* Dulna had explained to Dopdi, Dear, this is best! We won't get family and children this way. But who knows? Landowner and moneylender and policemen might one day be wiped out!

Who called her from the back today? ⌐

Dopdi kept walking. Villages and fields, bush and rock—*Public Works Department* markers—sound of running steps in back. Only one person running. Jharkhani *Forest* still about two miles away. Now she thinks of nothing but entering the forest. She must let them know that the *police* have set up *notices* for her again. Must tell them that the bastard Sahib has appeared again. Must change *hideouts.* Also, the *plan* to do to Lakkhi Bera and Naran Bera what they did to Surja Sahu on account of the trouble over paying field hands in Sandara must be cancelled. Shomai and Budhna knew everything. There was the *urgency* of great danger under Dopdi's ribs. Now she thought there was no shame as a Santal in Shomai and Budhna's treachery. Dopdi's blood was the pure unadulterated black blood of Champabhumi. From Champa to Bakuli the rise and set of a million moons. Their blood could have been contaminated; Dopdi felt proud of her forefathers. They stood guard over their women's blood in black armor. Shomai and Budhna are half-breeds. The fruits of war. Contributions to Radhabhumi by the American soldiers stationed at Shiandanga. Otherwise, crow would eat crow's flesh before Santal would betray Santal.

Footsteps at her back. The steps keep a distance. Rice in her belt, tobacco leaves tucked at her waist. Arijit, Malini, Shamu, Mantu—none of them smokes or even drinks tea. Tobacco leaves and limestone powder. Best medicine for scorpion bite. Nothing must be given away.

Dopdi turned left. This way is the *camp.* Two miles. This is not the way to the forest. But Dopdi will not enter the forest with a cop at her back.

I swear by my life. By my life, Dulna, by my life. Nothing must be told.

The footsteps turn left. Dopdi touches her waist. In her palm the comfort of a half-moon. A baby scythe. The smiths at Jharkhani are fine artisans. Such an edge we'll put on it, Upi, a hundred Dukhirams—Thank God Dopdi is not a gentleman. Actually, perhaps they have understood scythe, hatchet, and knife best. They do their work in silence. The lights of the *camp* at a distance. Why is Dopdi going this way? Stop a bit, it turns again. Huh! I can tell where I am if I wander all night with my eyes shut. I won't go into the forest, I won't lose him that way. I won't outrun him. You fucking jackal of a cop, deadly afraid of death, you can't run around in the forest. I'd run you out of breath, throw you in a ditch, and finish you off.

Not a word must be said. Dopdi has seen the new *camp,* she has sat in the *bus station,* passed the time of day, smoked a "bidi" and found out how many *police convoys* had arrived, how many *radio vans.* Squash four, onions seven, peppers fifty, a straightforward account. This information cannot now be passed on. They will understand Dopdi Mejhen has been countered. Then they'll run. Arijit's voice. If anyone is caught, the others must catch the *timing* and *change* their *hideout.* If *Comrade* Dopdi arrives late, we will not remain. There will be a sign of where we've gone. No *comrade* will let the others be destroyed for her own sake.

Arijit's voice. The gurgle of water. The direction of the next *hideout* will be indicated by the tip of the wooden arrowhead under the stone.

Dopdi likes and understands this. Dulna died, but, let me tell you, he didn't lose anyone else's life. Because this was not in our heads to begin with, one was countered for the other's trouble. Now a much harsher rule, easy and clear. Dopdi returns—good; doesn't return—bad. *Change hideout.* The clue will be such that the opposition won't see it, won't understand it if they do.

Footsteps at her back. Dopdi turns again. These three and a half miles of land and rocky ground are the best way to enter the forest. Dopdi has left that way behind. A little level ground ahead. Then rocks again. The *army* could not have struck *camp* on such rocky terrain. This area is quiet enough. It's like a maze, every hump looks like every other. That's fine. Dopdi will lead the cop to the burning "ghat." Patitpaban of Saranda had been sacrificed in the name of Kali of the Burning Ghats.

Apprehend!

A lump of rock stands up. Another. Yet another. The elderly Senanayak was at once triumphant and despondent. *If you want to destroy the enemy, become one.* He had done so. As long as six years ago he could anticipate their every move. He still can. Therefore he is elated. Since he has kept up with the literature, he has read *First Blood,* and seen approval of his thought and work.

Dopdi couldn't trick him. He is unhappy about that. Two sorts of reasons. Six years ago he published an article about information storage in brain cells. He demonstrated in that piece that he supported this struggle from the point of view of the field hands. Dopdi is a field hand. *Veteran fighter. Search and destroy.* Dopdi Mejhen is about to be *apprehended.* Will be *destroyed.* Regret.

Halt!

Dopdi stops short. The steps behind come around to the front. Under Dopdi's ribs the *canal* dam breaks. No hope. Surja Sahu's brother Rotoni Sahu. The two lumps of rock come forward. Shomai and Budhna. They had not escaped by train.

Arijit's voice. Just as you must know when you've won, you must also acknowledge defeat and start the activities of the next *stage.*

Now Dopdi spreads her arms, raises her face to the sky, turns toward the forest, and ululates with the force of her entire being. Once, twice, three times. At the third burst the birds in the trees at the outskirts of the forest awake and flap their wings. The echo of the call travels far.

3.

Draupadi Mejhen was apprehended at 6:53 P.M. It took an hour to get her to *camp.* Questioning took another hour exactly. No one touched her, and she was allowed to sit on a canvas camp stool. At 8:57 Senanayak's dinner hour approached, and saying, "Make her. *Do the needful,*" he disappeared.

Then a billion moons pass. A billion lunar years. Opening her eyes after a million light years, Draupadi, strangely enough, sees sky and moon. Slowly the bloodied nailheads shift from her brain. Trying to move, she feels her arms and legs still tied to four posts. Something sticky under her ass and waist. Her own blood. Only the gag has been removed. Incredible thirst. In case she says "water" she catches her lower lip in her teeth. She senses that her vagina is bleeding. How many came to make her?

Shaming her, a tear trickles out of the corner of her eye. In the muddy moonlight she lowers her lightless eye, sees her breasts, and understands that, indeed, she's been made up right. Her breasts are bitten raw, the nipples torn. How many? Four-five-six-seven—then Draupadi has passed out.

She turns her eyes and sees something white. Her own cloth. Nothing else. Suddenly she hopes against hope. Perhaps they have abandoned her. For the foxes to devour. But she hears the scrape of feet. She turns her head, the guard leans on his bayonet and leers at her. Draupadi closes her eyes. She doesn't have to wait long. Again the process of making her begins. Goes on. The moon vomits a bit of light and goes to sleep. Only the dark remains. A compelled spread-eagled still body. Active *pistons* of flesh rise and fall, rise and fall over it.

Then morning comes.

Then Draupadi Mejhen is brought to the tent and thrown on the straw. Her piece of cloth is thrown over her body.

Then, after *breakfast,* after reading the newspaper and sending the radio message "Draupadi Mejhen is apprehended," etc., Draupadi Mejhen is ordered brought in.

Suddenly there is trouble.

Draupadi sits up as soon as she hears "Move!" and asks, Where do you want me to go?

To the Burra Sahib's tent.

Where is the tent?

Over there.

Draupadi fixes her red eyes on the tent. Says, Come, I'll go.

The guard pushes the water pot forward.

Draupadi stands up. She pours the water down on the ground. Tears her piece of cloth with her teeth. Seeing such strange behavior, the guard says, She's gone crazy, and runs for orders. He can lead the prisoner out but doesn't know what to do if the prisoner behaves incomprehensibly. So he goes to ask his superior.

The commotion is as if the alarm had sounded in a prison. Senanayak walks out surprised and sees Draupadi, naked, walking toward him in the bright sunlight with her head high. The nervous guards trail behind.

What is this? He is about to cry, but stops.

Draupadi stands before him, naked. Thigh and pubic hair matted with dry blood. Two breasts, two wounds.

What is this? He is about to bark.

Draupadi comes closer. Stands with her hand on her hip, laughs and says, The object of your search, Dopdi Mejhen. You asked them to make me up, don't you want to see how they made me?

Where are her clothes?

Won't put them on, *sir.* Tearing them.

Draupadi's black body comes even closer. Draupadi shakes with an indomitable laughter that Senanayak simply cannot understand. Her ravaged lips bleed as she begins laughing. Draupadi wipes the blood on her palm and says in a voice that is as terrifying, sky splitting, and sharp as her ululation, What's the use of clothes? You can strip me, but how can you clothe me again? Are you a man?

She looks around and chooses the front of Senanayak's white bush shirt to spit a bloody gob at and says, There isn't a man here that I should be ashamed. I will not let you put my cloth on me. What more can you do? Come on, *counter* me—come on, *counter* me—?

Draupadi pushes Senanayak with her two mangled breasts, and for the first time Senanayak is afraid to stand before an unarmed *target,* terribly afraid.

—*Translated from the Bengali by Gayatri Chakravorty Spivak*

A. Rahmani

(1948–   )

A. Rahmani was born in 1948 in northern Iran. She has an M.A. in sociology from Sussex University in England, where she now lives. "A Short Hike" was published in 1984. It celebrates women's courage as displayed even under the most oppressive conditions of the religious patriarchy that marked postrevolutionary Iran. Clothes and children are the focus of this story. A woman removes her veil and asserts her own freedom in a land that has just fought for its liberty. A young boy demands that she put on her head-cover and threatens to inform on her. In much war literature, we read of children as victims of physical brutality and violence. In "A Short Hike," written during the first year of the war with Iraq and three years after the Iranian Revolution, we see children as victims of ideological violence. A child's mind, not his body, is maimed; and instead of protecting the child, a woman finds herself confronting him.

A Short Hike

The orange sun perfected the art of spreading its wings on the snow. The first snow had continued for several days non-stop. The city gradually turned white. In the white of the pavement, people looked like poisoned mice, moving from one line to another. There was something prevalent, heavy, and permanent in the air, something that made breathing, forgetting and escape difficult. It was as if each moment was ever-present, and it was. We lived the past three years experiencing this illusion. When we woke in the morning, its presence imposed itself upon our minds, transforming it into a cold, dark space, and it stayed. And we, the poisoned swarm, living the moments between childhood and old age simultaneously—unaware of the customary sense of Time—swung back and forth. At times, we childishly turned the event into an imaginary one, a journey into fantasy, into the depths of Hell, or to the gathering of Devils. Oftentimes, we were patient and resigned, as seasoned as old people.
...

Every one of us had devised a stratagem fitting his or her circumstances. Some planted trees and flowers, some jogged, some wrote, and others knitted, sewed, fed the dogs, the cats, the chickens, the pigeons. And still that heavy, poisonous air prevailed, continuously contaminating people's lungs, minds, and the atmosphere. To become political beings, however, was a necessity emanating from the circumstances. In a sense, we had all become political beings. We read newspapers, we listened to the news on all the other radio stations that broadcasted in Persian, we gave each other shelter, we hid each other's banned books, and thus we lived in this network of daily necessity.

I said that we were all political beings; whether optimists or pessimists, believers of this or that theory to change the prevalent poisonous atmosphere, or members of this or that organization, this was a prerequisite to our survival. Before, under the previous regime, you could do as little as withdrawing to your safe corner, closing off your eyes and ears, or choosing a solitary life in a secluded area, to survive. But now things were different; everything was closed out there, as if you were faced with an iron door: the university, the bookstores, the movie houses, the theaters, the bars, the streets. ... To survive under these circumstances, you could no longer stay on the sidelines. There was nothing there to hang on to. This was why, except for the few agents of corruption and darkness, all of us, despite our varying viewpoints, were political.

Last night, a couple, who were my friends, stayed over at my house. We extinguished the candles—as our neighbor was a member of the 'Party of God'—the Hezbollah—and sat and talked into the wee hours. The sight of the first rays of the sun on the mountains tempted us, so we left the house, taking along my mother, too.

There was a line of cars from Mahmoodieh to Valenjak, and the flock of pedestrians climbing the slopes of the hills extended as far as the eye could see. Everyone seemed to be in the same mood: eager to see the expanses of snow and the open solitariness of the rocks lying under its humble surface and the clear, kind sky—a sky unaffected either by the distant, sluggish Heaven or the tangible, convenient Hell. Lately staying home had become as unbearable as going out. Both had turned into traps, driving us to such insane acts as pounding our heads against the walls, hoping to end our miseries that way. A futile act.

We passed the gate opening to the slopes designated for public use, surprised to find it open. On a Friday? Permission to pass through the gate would be granted to those who abide by the Islamic code of conduct! The guards, armed or unarmed, were driving on the road leading to the chair-lift, imposing their unpleasant presence on people, and "fraternally" splashing the soft dirty snow all over them. There were many guards inside the ticket office with pointed guns, inspecting the size of our head-covers, and permitting those who passed the test to go on to enjoy the "fresh" air. The area around the office and the mini-bus station was covered by slogans: advice, warnings, declarations of Enjoining the Good and Forbidding the Evil, and finally threats—all crooked and nonsensical statements by this or that agent of punishment by Hell-fire. There were pictures, too: some showing men wearing turbans and some of the children who had unquestioningly offered their necks as projectiles for the canons of their government's establishment. "Waves of Martyrs," "Caravans of Martyrs," "Lineage of Martyrs," ... As if mothers of the Martyrs had tolerated nine months of pregnancy, the labor pains, and all the subsequent anxieties to be endowed with the honor of having their sons' pictures decorate ridiculous posters hanging from trees whose fruits perish as quickly and easily as this, before tasting the sun that is needed for their maturity. Then the government announcements came. Announcements of organizations rooted in the spiritual world but established in this earthly world! The "Forbidding" section was prohibiting the unveiled women from entering the area. The Ministry of Guidance was recounting the various kinds of adultery ... adultery involving the eye, the throat, the nose ... and so on.

There were people, too, either passing by or waiting in the bus line. Someone, possibly in his sixties, carrying a walking cane used by professional mountain climbers and wearing a carefully trimmed beard, had come with his dog. Later I heard a young woman ask him, "Are you an architect?" Was there supposed to be a connection between her question and the man's appearance? Then I saw a woman wearing a long veil halfway soaked in the mud, trying to climb the rocks. I could see a pair of military boots sticking out of her veil. I could also see her pants, her Islamic gown, and even her sweater; she reminded me of the inside layers of an onion. She was annoyed by the impurity of the architect's dog. Someone passed us hurriedly and bade us a "Take it easy!" in the manner of professional mountain climbers. He must have been one of those people who draw their daily dosage of satisfaction from greeting people who had fallen behind. Then I saw a few women, probably colleagues in some office, in their overcoats, high-heel shoes and fancy purses. They strolled ahead without any concern that they might be blocking other people's passage. The path was not wide enough to accommodate all the people. When there was no car, people used the road. Coming towards us was a group of school children accompanied by their coach, who was a member of the Revolutionary guard and to whom I would not entrust my child, if I had one, under any circumstances. They ran along the gravel side of the road and shouted, "God is Great!" "Death to Anti-Revolutionaries!" ... thus passing their leisure time.

We rented a chair-lift at the second station. When we got off, my mother and my friend's wife joined the people waiting for tea, and my friend and I moved on for a short walk. My friend's brother had left the country illegally a few days ago. He had yet to notify anyone of his whereabouts. He was one of the many people with no choice but to escape across dangerous borders. The revolutionary guards besieged his parents' house periodically and forced their way into the house. They arrested him once before his escape. He confused them by acting as if he were someone else and they let him go. A few days later, after realizing they had been tricked, they tried to confiscate his father's house. He stayed at our house for a few days, too. A few days after he left our house, they came after him again. My friend told me that once he had gone with his brother and friends to the mountains and stayed for a few days. He pointed to the area where they had set up their tents and prepared for the climb to the summit. The conversation absorbed both of us. I knew he was troubled and needed to talk.

After we were finished talking, we jumped down a steep rock, both feeling much lighter.

I saw the line of the school children coming down the opposite slope. I was watching them as they ran, rolled around, and played with each other. I thought to myself, "How could anyone confiscate their merriment and liveliness and institute such cruel concepts as sin, misery, elegy, and miracles in their place? No matter how hard the preacher tried, acting like a clown in ridiculous children's shows on T.V., trying to turn the saints Muhammad and Ali into familiar heroes who kill the Indians in massive numbers, he would never succeed in getting close to their minds. Not a chance! Even their epics turned out clumsy and sickening."

The wind had blown off my head-cover. It must have happened while my mind was wandering beyond the present surroundings. A voice, a male voice, shouted something from the end of the line. The children were closer now and I was carried away, enjoying every moment of the scene they created. The voice brought me down from the clouds:

"Put your head-cover back on!"

It was a young boy's treble voice. It prompted me to laugh.

"Even a sky as wide as this, mountains as white as these, and the vast expanse of trees underneath your very feet, aren't enough to distract your attention from a meager, uncovered head?"

"One must note the Bad and the Good!"

"When you were learning the Bad and the Good, didn't they teach you to mind your own business?"

"I'm not acting beyond my scope. It's respect for the principle of Enjoining the Good and Forbidding the Evil."

"Who said a bare head is Evil? The wind has removed my head-cover. You don't have to look!"

"I'm not just defending my rights; it's for everyone's sake."

"Who asked you to speak on Everyone's behalf? Other people can express their opinion themselves. Besides, who said Everyone minds a bare head?"

The children were slowly gathering around us. The voice of my young assailant had grown weak and hesitant. He said, "Our coach has instructed us to speak up." I thought he probably didn't understand the significance of his action. I started to respond, "Your coach isn't Everyone ... ," when a rough, nervous voice stopped me.

"What is it? What's the matter?"

He threw an angry gaze at the boy. A gaze that could frighten any young boy his age out of his wits.

"Didn't I tell you not to argue with people? What's the matter?"

I volunteered, "It's nothing. Just a minor disagreement between him and me."

I had intended to end the fuss, but I made him more agitated. How could there be something just between him and me, not involving them? He didn't even look at me. Instead, he repeatedly shook the boy's body violently, waiting for a response. The boy was flabbergasted. I imagined him thinking, "Now, what do I do? I don't believe my good intentions have created such a big mess!" And I imagined myself responding to him, "That serves you right," when a voice coming from the group of children said:

"Sir! He only told her to put her head-cover back on!"

I wondered if the word "sir" was intended for the man standing in front of me: a mercenary revolutionary guard who worked as a coach but acted as a pathetic preacher in his spare time; a man reduced to considerations of sins and inhibitions who, unable to harness his own, was desperately determined to control others so that he might have peace; or maybe a deprived soul whose contact with the earthly world was primarily through the television programs of the past regime, leading him to believe that the world was full of debauchery just as Jamilah's belly dance and vulgar songs?

The "sir," who was wearing a dark green jacket and a pair of army boots, who was skinny and pale, whose eyes looked ill and frightened, and who did not look at the person he was talking to, said:

"I don't see what the argument could be, then. You must put your head-cover back on. What made you think you could argue against that?"

How arrogant! Who did he think he was to order people around like that? If he had a gun, I would at least understand where he was coming from. Has it really become this easy? I thought perhaps his students' "dutifulness" has boosted his courage. If I don't confront him now, his Hezbollah party, they become both the law and the law enforcement agent at the same time: condemn another citizen, arrest her, and execute the punishment? This was a bad joke history had played on those who believed in breaking the traditional boundaries of the present order of the division of labor!

A few revolutionary guards had shown up and circled around me, aiming their guns towards the crowd. They did not ask me anything. They didn't even look at me. The so-called coach told them the story of my insolence and asked them to take me "there." The guard then looked at me. I imagined him saying to me, "You are a conspirator!"

My throat was dry out of anger. I saw a canteen in someone's hand. He looked queer, although there was nothing in particular wrong with his appearance. Had I noticed it earlier, I wouldn't have asked, but it was too late and I started:

"Will you give me a glass of water?"

He looked startled. To make sure I was talking to him, he looked around. Then he became nervous and stepped back, pathetically calling, "Why me?" And then he was lost in the crowd.

Meanwhile two of the guards left. I imagined that they hadn't found the event as exciting as they expected. Or perhaps they were up to something else, since they hurriedly ran all the way down the slope. One of them stopped suddenly, as if he remembered something, and shouted, "When you're finished, come down to see. ... " I didn't hear the rest because of the wind, but the guard who stayed behind waved to him in agreement.

Then he made a gesture I interpreted as an attempt to compose himself. He was very young. He turned to face the crowd and yelled, "Gentlemen, please don't gather here! Come on, go mind your own business!" Then he addressed me, "You come with me!" We started to walk: the guard, me, and the so-called coach who didn't forget to remind his students of their duties. The children started shouting the slogan, "Death to Unveiled women!" They had formed their lines behind us and started following us right away. They threw a few small rocks randomly at me, but as they managed to build up their courage, the number of rocks that bounced off my body increased, indicating a systematic and conscientious attempt at stoning me.

I was not intimidated. You must be a woman to understand how much of the efforts of this massive body of turpitude is directed toward the creation of devices to make women believe that they are contemptible. And if you, as the object of these attempts, fall into their trap, then you have accepted their values and will naturally fall apart. You have to interpret each rock and each shout of "Death to Unveiled Women!" as the sign of their desperate reaction to your resistance. As insignificant as it may seem to you, your struggle to hold up your chin and your endeavor to convince yourself that you exist, is an expression of our freedom—despite those vultures' attempts to reduce our existence to those of slaves whose only recognized right is to breathe. They want me to believe that I do not exist, or make me accept the distorted, unidentifiable images of their Islamic holy saints as my role models.

What is so special about "outside" after all? It's a purgatory, at best. And we, the people, are kept in suspense on a bridge as narrow as a strand of hair waiting to err and be shoved; and "there" was the Hell awaiting us.

We walked down the hill to the station. The coach had calmed down considerably, and exchanged a few words with the guards. It was clear that they didn't work for the same Komiteh and didn't know each other. The children had fallen behind and added a little spice to their shouting activities, chanting, "Death to Anti-Revolutionaries!"

The guard was much younger than the coach. A young man of about sixteen, with a strong, healthy bone structure and a beard, fluffy but tight, that betrayed the boundless effort he invested in its growth. He was also more talkative than the coach. It was evident from the way he talked that he wasn't impressed by the coach. He talked about the heavy volume of responsibilities he was given by his district's Komiteh; about the problems created by both his enemies and friends on the weekends; about the two missing schoolboys they had to search for the previous week; and about himself and how, because of the recent state of alert, he hadn't slept in twenty-four hours. It was evident that he had little tolerance for leisure time activities. The coach was slowly getting the message: acting more Catholic than the Pope, in someone else's District? He looked confused. The guard was looking for a justifiable offense or a way to rid himself of the intruder. Whichever it may have been it was apparent that he didn't have much in the way of authority to arrest anyone. In his own district's Komiteh, maybe ... Things could have looked different there. ... The least he could do was to reprimand me. But here? Even the other guards had abandoned him. Where then was this cooperation between revolutionary organizations they so boasted about? Even I, the convicted party, had sensed this guard's restlessness, his uneasiness over being there and his anxiousness to get rid of these intruders.

On the way back I saw my mother and friends standing some distance from the restaurant and the tea house. My mother was holding two glasses of tea, one waiting for me. It was probably cold by now. I didn't feel like drinking tea anymore. I felt nauseous again. For the last two years nausea had seized me occasionally, both at home and in public. I thought to myself, "This is not as bad as the attacks of asthma, headache, and nettle-rash other people are suffering from. ... " The thought consoled me. I stopped under the pretext of tying my shoelace. Before I knew it, my mother, using her motherly wisdom, had struck up a conversation with them. In my ear hummed all the world's bees. I was exhausted; I wished to hand down the load I was carrying to my mother. I wished to stay beside her and be protected against all the worries, fears, and nightmares of the past few years. I didn't want to stay out there any-more. I had completely lost my desire to get fresh air. I was only thinking about my mother's hands. I wanted to touch them; to feel their consol-ing, real weight, to make sure that compared to my mother's real hands, all that had happened, the tumult, the shouts of "Death to Unveiled Women!" the rocks, the coach's sick look and the guard's gun, had been imaginary.

The guard seemed pleased to have finally found a conciliator. I heard him report that this woman (he meant me) had refused to put her head-cover back on, that the children had been about to beat me up, that he had gotten there in time to save me, and that he was now trying to get me out of there. I was too tired to argue with him. Besides, it wasn't wise. I was supposed to be lucky to have gotten away with that much already. If the coach and the guard had cooperated with each other ... If the guard had known someone in that district's Komiteh ... If a few people had spoken up on my behalf ... Who knows? One could lose her life as easily as that. These days, the distance between life and death was not bridged by a first degree or second degree offense, a four-year or ten-year or a life-time sentence, but by a mere event ... Such as a hike.

The conversation went on and the coach who realized his words were less effective than he had imagined, stood there silent, listening to my mother and the guard. My mother was benevolently advising them to stop the acts that discredit the revolution and Islam, acts that give the wrong people an excuse to take it upon themselves to become agents of the government, to frighten everybody by threatening to take them "there" and to spread among people exaggerated lies and stories. I was wondering how anyone could possibly exaggerate the existing savagery and barbarism ... I should ask my mother later if she meant what she said. The guard went even as far as claiming that no one had intended to take me away and that I had insisted on it myself. And my mother suc-ceeded in mediating between us, and things got cooler. They left and the children followed them.

We were in no mood to stay around to enjoy the mountains and our little exercise. Silently we sipped our tea and walked downhill toward the exit. My stomach was intensely upset, as if a hand was pulling the mus-cles violently. My ears were filled with noise. I could occasionally hear the people's voices in the tumult created by the noon hour call to prayer and other humming noises: "What's this expiation we are condemned to pay ... If only more women dared to ... Such a pity ... This is one of those cases of serving a prison sentence before you're proven guilty ... Actually I'm against speaking up in protest; it makes them bolder ... " I thought to myself, "This must be the wife of the man I requested a glass of water from." "How many times we asked them not to ... A heroine ... War-time ... Fight against imperialism ... " Why don't I throw up? "We should have confronted them from the start ... A few days ago I saw the same thing on the street ...

I cannot bear it any longer. We take a short-cut. We leave the road and the crowd behind. A stream of water is flowing in a gap between two rocks. Sometimes it disappears under the snow, but it soon surfaces again a few yards away. Cheerful, care-free, and mischievous, it is capable of amusing us all the way to the end of the valley. We lose it some distance below. We carefully look for it. The snow has covered the rocks. We walk cautiously lest we slip on the snow-covered rocks.

—Translated from the Farsee by Soraya Sullivan

Daisy al-Amir

(1935–   )

DAISY AL-AMIR WAS BORN in Basra, Iraq. She earned her B.A. from the Teachers' Training College of Baghdad. In 1963, she went to Cambridge, England, to do research on Arabic literature under the guidance of orientalist A. J. Arberry. However, to her dismay her father refused to pay the tuition. On her return to Iraq, she stopped in Lebanon, where she got a job in the Iraqi Embassy in Beirut as a secretary and later as assistant press attaché. When war broke out in Lebanon in 1975, she was appointed director of the Iraqi Cultural Center. She returned to Iraq after the Israeli invasion of Lebanon in 1982. In 1990, she came to the United States and stayed for a year. She is currently in Beirut.

Her first collection of short stories, *The Distant Country That You Love*, appeared in 1964. In 1969, she wrote *Then the Wave Returns*, a collection of short stories that she dedicated to Samira Azzam, a Palestinian woman writer. Daisy al-Amir has written two short story collections on the Lebanese Civil War: *In the Vortex of Love and Hate* (1979) and *Promises for Sale* (1981), in which "The Future" appeared.

As many of the works in this anthology show, women seldom remain inactive or passive in a war. They record war experiences so that others will know their sufferings. They call upon helpers, poets, divine beings, and other women to alleviate their grief. They look to nature, their children, even their enemies in hopes of finding peace. In "The Future" a woman asserts her belief in a future without war by defying the course of safety and rationality. She buys a dress and refuses to take shelter from exploding bombs, and her actions stop and frustrate a soldier, at least briefly.

The Future

She paid for the dress, quickly, though she was not at all certain that it was the right size. But she was certain that it was made of a heavy cloth that would be good for spring or fall. Now it was the middle of summer, maybe there would be another fall and another spring. And yet, would they come? Would spring and fall come? Last spring and fall had not happened. Time had stood still, as it had stood still in all the four seasons of the year. But it had not stood still for the fighting which never stopped, and which assassinated every moment and every whisper and every emotion and everything ... everything ... She quickly hid the dress in the bag. She didn't want to admit to herself that she had committed a crime in buying this dress. The murderous war dominated everything. Two years, weeks, and months? No ... no ... she could no longer concentrate. She could no longer count the number of weeks in these many months, nor the number of days and the number of minutes and seconds, and she ... she ... she waited, as everyone else waited, minute by minute, for news ... news that was not horrifying. News that did not tell of vast destruction and of absolute darkness. ...

She had bought the dress from the house next door to the one in which she lived. She had not crossed the street nor gone downstairs. The woman in the next-door house sold clothes.

The shops were still operating. When she thought about buying the dress she felt as though tar was being thrown on her and her house, that burning, flaming tar which is thrown onto the houses of those who have been disgraced, so that all passersby should know that the woman in this house had been vilified and that her hair had been cut off and her house set aflame and ... she touched her hair with one hand and grabbed hold of the bag which hid the dress with the other.

The dress was for fall, and now it was summer. Whoever was still alive was either a prisoner of his own house, or else he was lucky not to have been caught by a sniper's bullet (either aimed or shot at random), or else he was a coward, or had not been kidnapped by the guards at the barricades, or his religious faith had not made him a martyr. Who could tell how many ways there had been, throughout history, of killing a person?

She had bought the dress at a moment when she could not even afford bread for the next few days. If those days should come, would she be able to afford fuel for heat and cooking? ... Would there ever be a night without hunger cramps? She had bought the dress at a moment when hundreds of thousands could not find a roof over their heads. And hundreds were longing for a crust of bread, and hundreds more were lying dead.

Lebanon was dying; the fighting made headlines in the world press and broadcasts. All were trying to describe graphically this horror, this sickness for which there was no cure.

If only she had saved a little of her money. Would it not have been better not to buy the dress? If only she had kept this money in her purse? Or in her closet? If she were to put the dress in her closet with her other clothes, how could she make certain that she would not lose any of them? The whole house was exposed to burglary—possessions, money, owners—what was the difference between buying a dress and hoarding the money for its purchase? Everything might be looted. This dress she had bought, where had its seller acquired it? How had all those dresses displayed there come into her hands? Had people brought them in? How had they been paid for? And did those who sold the dresses buy them? Did they import them? Did they make them themselves? Rumors of thefts from commercial establishments, banks, offices, and private homes were rife.

Some armed groups kill for a national cause and die gladly as martyrs; other armed groups just fight to loot. Where are the former groups? And where are the latter? And who has robbed whom? And who has held on to possessions of those who are not armed? The fighters permit themselves to steal, to loot goods and souls. Where is the armed element which defends the national cause when it sees the other gang looting and plundering?

Is the national cause the looting of the nation? Is the national cause the plundering of the individual's property and his soul?

That dress was bought with dirhams earned by the sweat of her brow. And so was the dress she was wearing now. *That* purchase had not been a disgrace.

Someone else ... someone else should be doused with hot, burning, flaming tar, and his house, too, so that all passing by should know it. The real shame must be burnt and proclaimed abroad. She rummaged through the bag to touch her dress. It was still there, all rolled up. She wanted to show it to someone and explain that she had bought it from a shop that did not deal in stolen dresses, it was not stolen. She wanted to shout out loud: I haven't stolen ... I haven't stolen ... I have not and shall not steal ... I shall wear this dress next spring or fall. Next? She was not expecting anything. She did not know what season this was, nor why thinking about the seasons following each other and waiting for the moment might be the end ... the end ... death.

Had she only one second left it would be enough to enjoy having bought a dress, not stolen it, and it would help diminish her rage. What matter if she never got to wear the dress? The important thing was the pleasure she derived from the act of buying it. What should she save her money for? The future? Was there a future? Would she witness tomorrow's sunrise?

She wanted to feel that life continued, she wanted to feel the desire for possessions, she wanted to anticipate the coming days. And suddenly she realized that she wanted to go on living, to look forward to the future, to fall and to spring. She had a new dress to wear, she wanted to feel that she might not die at any moment. Was she trying to justify herself, to rid herself of a feeling of shame? Buying a new dress ... while people were starving to death and rockets and grenades were exploding all around her? Death was waiting at every corner, and she held on tightly to the dress, as if by clinging to it she were clinging onto life itself.

Lebanon was dying, calling for help. And the whole world injected more deadly poison and plunged in more daggers.

The world was covering its ears, closing its eyes; it stretched out a furtive finger to steal, then sent provisions in a ship that never arrived, sent delegations to sell the truth ... or falsehoods ... hope, accomplishments, faith, lies. ...

All this is happening in Lebanon, and she ... she was buying a dress for a fall she knew would not come?

The saleswoman said she had been forced to sell dresses from her home since her husband and children had lost their jobs, and this was the way she could earn their keep. The woman was forever trying to justify her business as a means of keeping the family alive. And here she was buying a dress, for an autumn that would not come. Would it save her from starving? Would it save her from the sniper and the rockets and grenades exploding all around her? Would it light up the darkness she was so afraid of? Or could it make her wait less anxiously for the fall and the summer preceding it? She folded the bag so it should not look so large. She folded it, shrinking its size, so that she might forget that she was carrying her very own dress in that bag.

An armored car passed ... some shots were fired to frighten her and she was not afraid.

She was used to the bullets and the cannons and the explosions and the rockets ... and the darkness ... and she was used to none of it.

She had not died yet with all the many dead and wounded and disfigured whom she saw and of whom she heard and did not hear, but ... was it right that she buy a dress with the excuse that she had not yet died? Would she be able to hang on to it? Would her house not be looted? Would she be able to get a doctor? Would a doctor get to her if she became sick? If she were wounded? If she were hit? Would the guard at the barricades allow her to explain to him that she would die if she didn't got to the hospital? And the fighters? What did they care about the word Death, experiencing it at every second and hour and day and week and month throughout these two years? What did this individual matter? Or whether the number of the dead was increased tenfold or a hundredfold or a thousandfold or if he remained alive? Since when has a living individual been important in the eyes of fighters who are exposed to death all the time?

Fighters are exposed to death here,but they are protected by a barricade, there are some weapons with which they protect themselves. ...

Weapons and fighters and leaders and presidents and parties and followers and organizers who approach and move away from each other, who support and oppose each other, who curse and praise each other, and she ... she was this individual like so many others who do not belong to any of those; how could she get rid of fear of the moment, of the hour and of the day? Of the memories of the days gone past?

Would tomorrow come? Would there be a new day with a new sun after the long, dark night, lit only by rockets? And she? She had bought a dress suitable for fall! The saleswoman had said that it would do for spring as well as for fall. Which season was the nearest? And when would the days come when she could truly feel and see? when the whole world did not close in on her, neither the sky nor the buildings?

A grenade fell at the entrance to the building. She was not afraid, nor did she jump and run away. She stood stock still contemplating the shattered glass and listening to the screams of the terrified. Where had she got this bravery from? Was she holding on to the future in a bag that she was hiding under her arm? The inhabitants of the building rushed to the shelter. She stood at the top of the stairs and watched them running and screaming, carrying their little ones; she could not tell who was more frightened, the young or the old. Who among them would live another second and for whom was death waiting? And she ... she felt the dress. Her soul was grieved to death, unable to find a justification for the purchase of a new dress.

The grenades increased, shattering the walls and windows. She went down the dark stairwell, holding on to the bannister. She reached the door of the shelter. She did not know what had compelled her to stop and prevented her from running into the depths with the others.

She felt the dress and calmed down. Who could tell her at this instant why it was that she had bought the new fall dress? And if anyone saw her, how could she convey her contentment at carrying her new spring dress?

More grenades and rockets fell close by. The screaming and wailing increased and she tightened her hold on the bag. Uniformed fighters entered the building. All wore beards and carried all sorts of arms on their shoulders. One of them came rushing towards her, shouting and yelling, "Get into the shelter, can't you hear? Can't you see? Why are you standing there? The shelter is the only place that will save you from getting killed." And he lifted his Kalashnikov, shooting into the air. The panic increased and shouts rose to where she stood. She stood there as though paralyzed, and the fighter's fury increased. He came closer, screaming at her, "Go down! I told you to go down to the shelter. What are you doing here? Move! What is it that you are holding on to so tightly? Are you worried about it? Give it to me and go down." And her grip on the bag with the fall/spring dress tightened. She did not answer. The shouting started again, and he screamed at her again, his bullets reverberating. He stared at her furiously and she screamed at him, "This is my future, this is for fall and for spring." She clasped it to her breast, and now his greatest fear was that she would pounce on him.

—Translated from the Arabic by Miriam Cooke

Anonymous Afghan Woman

IN THIS SELECTION, an anonymous Afghan woman—a woman who has dared to love, has dared to learn to read and write—speaks to us, records for us her suffering and her decision to fly to freedom if the names of her beloved husband and son appear among the executed freedom fighters.

In one brief passage we read of the unending grief of women who live daily with war and their determination to struggle for freedom. As discussed in the Introduction, the use of language, not tears, to communicate their experiences becomes important to women such as this poet-recorder of Afghanistan's struggle against the Communists.

Testimony

Our faces thrust between the bars of the prison gate, we wait, clinging to the cold iron, a silent crowd of women, wondering if we will see our husbands, sons, brothers, again. My son is inside the stone walls with his father for whom he carried his gun. Suddenly the names of the political prisoners are posted. The women's eyes strain in the cold, their sockets as frozen as the ground under the prayer rugs the old men bring to the gates to pray for sons, nephews, grandchildren who are tortured or executed inside the walls, among the many men who chose the freedom of their god or death. I've told no one such blasphemy, but my husband is my only god, my son, my only prince of heaven.

Outside the walls, we wait and wail and hope and a woman screams from behind her veil, seeing that her son's name, and her husband's, too, are there among the executed. We know there are no more men left in her family or she would not be here alone. Only the women who have no men left in their families come to the prison gate alone. I am not so lucky as to know my fate. I am no heroine like Naheed. I carry no flag like Malalai. I'm no poet like Rabia Balkhi. I simply wait. I will return again in the morning to wait and wait … my mind hanging from a thread like the rag the old woman makes tearing at her veil as she weeps—exposing her withered face in the madness of grief. We envy her tears as she knows her fate. While we wait, holding our vigil at the cold iron gate.

To find my way through the street, I must pass the old palace again, where the guards are displaying the blood-soaked rugs. They dragged us in the street to show us where women and children were massacred yesterday by the soldiers. They show us to warn us to behave. I make my way back to the camp where my daughters with mangled frostbitten fingers wait by the gate. These words are useless. I will be dead when you read them … I, a woman who dared to dream of love, of poetry, of a life of reading. I taught myself to read, to write, hour after hour before the firelight … I've decided that when I see my husband's beloved name, my son's among the executed of the prison, I will tear my veil from my face and take my daughters with me into the frozen mountains. We will run and the bullets will fly after us and set us free from this wait to be free.

—Adapted to English by Daniela Gioseffi with Emira Omar

Mridula Garg

(1938–   )

MRIDULA GARG has an M.A. in economics from Delhi University and taught there from 1960 to 1963. She has written collections of short stories, a number of novels, and a play.

"The Morning After" (originally published in Hindi as "Agli Subah") is from her 1980 collection of short stories titled *From the Glacier.* The story is set in the context of the assassination of India's prime minister, Indira Gandhi, by her Sikh bodyguards on October 31, 1984. The assassination set off violent clashes between Sikhs and Hindus in which many people were attacked, wounded, and killed, regardless of their political beliefs. Women trying to protect the sons of other women, even of women considered to be "the enemy," in an effort to stop the insanity of war may be one of the most important elements of women's mythology of war. In this story, a Hindu mother tries to save her son's friend, a young Sikh man, but is in the end betrayed by her own son.

The Morning After

Bansal Babu and Manku—'the people downstairs'—were calling "Bhabiji! Satto Auntie! Oh Bhabiji! Auntie, Satto Auntie!"

"How loud these people shout!" That's what she thought at first, as usual, and then she stopped. Some hours ago they had made just such an uproar and she had disliked it, but the news they told her was so terrible and chilling that the uproar had died its own death—Indira Gandhi was treacherously gunned down by sixteen bullets.

What next! She came out of her room chanting "Shubh—shubh" and leaned from the balcony.

"Don't let the children out, Bhabiji, there is a riot in the city."

"I saw with my own eyes four Sikhs being killed, Satto Auntie. They killed them and threw them on that side of the bridge," Bansal Babu's son Manku told her with wild gestures. She shivered while watching him talk, but did not follow what he said.

"Sikhs? Why did they kill Sikhs?"

"Didn't you hear? Indira Gandhi was murdered by Sikhs."

"But the radio said that her own guards shot her down."

"Yes, yes, they were Sikhs ... " said Manku with a voice shaking with excitement.

"So what? Those two killed her, that doesn't mean the whole community murdered her," Ashok threw in as he was stepping out.

She saw that Sarbjeet was about to step out of the room with Ashok and Ajay. Swiftly she turned inwards and pushed Sarbjeet against the back wall of the room. Then she called in an angry voice, "Ashok, come back here!"

As a surprised Ashok turned back, she pulled him in and bolted the door from inside and then stood facing them, panting. "What happened?" All three boys were staring at her in surprise. She beckoned them towards her and caught Sarbjeet's wrist tight and whispered, "Don't step outside and don't let anyone know that he is here!"

All three boys laughed out loud.

She shut Sarbjeet's mouth with both her hands, "Shush, no noise!"

"What's the matter with you, mother?" Ashok forgot to laugh and snapped at her angrily.

"Haven't you heard? There is a riot in the city, and people are killing Sikhs."

"Nonsense! You believe any old rumour from anybody. Don't you know 'the people downstairs,' how good they are at making a fuss?"

"Maybe there was a killing or two, Auntiji," said Sarbjeet, turning aside her hand, "What's that got to do with us?"

"I'll go to see what's happening outside," said young Ajay and he leaped to unbolt the door.

"No!" She caught his wrist and squeezed it, "Don't you dare do anything without asking me."

She bolted it again and stood in front of the door as if she were another door!

"You boys don't know this, but the same thing happened in 1947. Sarbjeet is in danger. We'll have to hide him here."

"What danger can there be for me, Auntie?" said Sarbjeet, "Everyone knows me here!"

"That *is* the danger," was her instant reply. "Everyone on the block knew Babuji as well. He was the ticket collector at the railways, so everyone knew him. That is why ... No! Don't waste time, come with me." She took Sarbjeet by the hand and pulled him to the store-room nearby.

"Sit here. No lights on! I'm locking the door from outside. If you hear three knocks, then you know it's me."

"Auntiji, you must have seen a good spy film lately. All right, as you please! Here I sit. But is there any provision for breathing here?"

She didn't laugh. "There's the window." She showed him a hole in the wall and started to lock the door.

"Wait Auntiji, at least give me something to eat, you know in the afternoon ... "

She had turned before he could finish, filled a dish with some food and a bottle with water, and returned to him. When she locked him in and came back, Ashok and Ajay were upset with her.

"You haven't seen it, so you don't understand. I have seen it. I was just ten in 1947. My own Babuji ... " she choked.

"That's the limit, Mother. Then the whole country was being torn apart. Why would anyone kill anyone without reason now? Are people mad?"

"They're not, but they become so."

"Do they all become mad?"

"Not all, some."

"Buy why?"

"Even if the instigators are a handful, that's plenty. All you need is a match to set fire to a heap of straw. As soon as people become a mob, something happens, either a festival or a war. The man in a mob is no longer a man ... "

Ashok laughed. "Whose speech are you repeating?" he asked.

Before she could answer, Ajay asked, "But where do these people come from?"

He was only being curious, but instead of answering him, she was stumped by his query. Really, where do they come from, these rioters, these murderers? Until yesterday, everyone was busy with his own job. Nobody had any business with the rest of the world. Then how did they find each other out today, how did they form a gang today, and how did they start killing others by ganging up on them? Who are these people, where do they come from and then again, where do they go to hide?

"Tell me, Mom, where do they come from?" Ajay repeated the question.

"From nowhere. Mother is imagining things," snapped Ashok.

Just then there was another noise from downstairs. This time with just one call of "Bhabiji" she opened the door and leaned from the balcony.

"What is it, Brother?" she asked in a voice made deliberately sweeter.

"Is Ashok at home?"

"Yes sir, yes, he is."

"Is there any friend of his there?"

"No, sir. He went a long time ago. He came in the morning, then when you went to the Medical, he said, let me go see, and he went."

"If he returns, don't let him in the house."

"No, sir, who can trust them now!"

"Why not?" screamed Ashok, "Aren't you ashamed, Mom?"

"Shut up!" she snapped at him.

"Well, these people were selling sweets, they were taking revenge. What could they do but kill them. Is Hindu blood water?"

"Did you see them dancing Bhangda, selling sweets?"

"What then? Are we telling lies!"

"Did you really see them?" There was a great deal of mistrust in Ashok's voice.

"These people were not going to learn a lesson without a beating. They killed so many Hindus in Punjab, and we kept quiet ... "

"Why did you?" Ashok interrupted. "It would have been brave of you if you had killed them there. What do you get by killing people over here?"

"Great! My child! How can you make excuses for the enemy? If we don't kill them, they will surely erase every trace of Hindus, don't you know that? Why, Bhabiji, am I not saying the right thing?"

"Yes, sir, it is very true, quite right," she said.

"You believe him, do you really believe him? I ... no ... I won't believe him." Ashok was getting upset, not with her but with himself as it were.

"How will you find that out by sitting in your mother's lap, little prince? Come out and see for yourself," Bansal Babu dared him.

"Yes, yes, I'm going out," cried Ashok in a choked voice. He roughly pushed aside his mother who had confronted him and shot out of the house just as he was.

"Ashok, Ashok!" she went on shouting. "Brave Bajrang, guard him, guard him," she chanted for a long time after he had gone.

Inside the store-room Sarbjeet's hand stopped in motion. He had broken off a bite of the roti and was about to put it in his mouth as he heard what Satto Auntie was saying. "I am sitting here chewing roti and these people ... " The bit of roti fell back in the dish. He got up and started towards the door. From underneath the door, the light of the room outside was coming in. By now he was used to seeing in that feeble light. The door was locked from outside. He felt all the way up to search for the bolt from inside. There was no bolt inside! When they opened the door from outside, he would be without a weapon, helpless, utterly dependent on their mercy! He searched every inch of that cage-like room with his hands. The only thing he laid his hands on was a large piece of wood. Clutching it with both hands, he sat up, watchful.

Everything was dark and quiet, just the way it is in the first quarter of the night. The radio was going on in the middle of that silence and darkness, but monotonously, as if it were tired, beaten, its voice was being absorbed in that silence. Some notes of sitar, some melody on veena, sometimes words of a bhajan. "Om Shantih Shantih Shantih." Offerings of prayer for the departed soul, silence, painful prayers. How can a person go on to kill someone when he is drowned in misery? She, too, was suffering such a shock at his passing away that in her heart she could hear the voice saying, "Don't let anyone suffer what I went through." It was almost seven years now. Do wounds like this ever heal? Even now, her heart ached and hurt like a blister. How he wanted to live in his own house! After so much trouble, he had been able to build a house, a couple of rooms, but he couldn't enjoy it even for a day. We had to rent it out to others. Well, that's what helps us out now. Otherwise, how were we to live on the meagre salary of an embroidery teacher in the government school? Anyway, we have a roof over our heads. Bansal Babu is not a bad man. At least he doesn't demand a rent increase every day. He didn't bother me in my difficult times. It is ten years now I've lived in this room. I'm better off than millions. When we came as refugees, aunt and uncle sheltered us. However it was, at least it was shelter. Mother used to say, "Satto child, we've been robbed, yes, but now pray that no one should set fire anymore, no blood be shed, no head be cut off, may no one ever lose his honour. Yes, may no father ever be sacrificed anywhere in front of his daughter, no child in front of his mother … !"

In the middle of the darkness the dogs started barking. She was startled. Ashok hadn't come back yet. Who knew where he was wandering. "Oh Brave Bajrang, please guard him."

The dogs were silent now. The fear enveloped in the silence was melting. The Mira bhajan on the radio was "I have only my Mountain-bearing Cowherd! No one else for me, no one else … I have … " The words soothed and lulled her.

What a fool I am, she thought. How quickly I panic. Ashok was saying the right thing. What happened thirty-seven years ago had a different cause. The whole nation was being divided then. The English brought about our partition. Otherwise, Hindustan was like a giant tree, anyone could come and seek shelter here. But even a Banyan is a big tree, under which nothing grows, nothing can grow. Dhur, may my thought perish, who knows why I think such crazy thoughts. Let me get up, go and open the door of the store-room. The poor child sitting in the dark must be cursing me. A little smile began to play on her lips. Dhur! May my intellect burn! I didn't even ask him if he wanted more roti. I am really confused, just as Ashok says.

"Mom, won't you give us any food today?" Ajay asked just then and her smile became more natural.

"Come son, let me give you food. Silly me … " She left the four-poster bed and just then a loud shriek tore apart the silence. Then everything was silent again.

"Hear that?" she whispered with her hands holding her heart.

Ajay nodded.

She grabbed his hand, and with a finger on her lips, admonished him, "Not a sound!"

She turned up the volume of the radio and to its peaceful music started doing what she had to do very slowly. In a corner of the room was a tallish cupboard. That was the only thing that would cover the store-room door. Directing Ajay with gestures, she removed the cupboard with his help and placed it in front of the store-room. Now no one could see the lock hanging from the store-room door. Now the attention would be on the cupboard instead of on the door. Then she removed the four-poster bed and put it in another corner. She made him move the two chairs and the wooden box. Now whoever saw it would think that the furniture in the room had always been like that. All the time she made sure there were no scratch marks from the furniture on the floor and prayed that the people downstairs would not hear the sounds of the furniture being moved about. Oh yes, she almost forgot: wherever the furniture had been, there were big patches of dust and dirt; she must wipe them out with a wet cloth. No broom should be used, because they would hear it downstairs, and wonder, why is she sweeping after sunset? It is after all inauspicious to sweep after the sun has set.

Suddenly it was completely dark inside the store-room. Even the light trickling from the room was no longer there. Sarbjeet tried to bend down and look under the door and felt as if the wall of the room had moved and covered up the door. What had these people done? Why did they turn of the lights? They had imprisoned him in total darkness. "Wahe Guru, how did I get stuck here! No weapon in my hand, no window to jump out and run, no key to open the door; is there no way to escape this choking darkness?" "No lights on." He remembered Satto Auntie's words. "Oh, that means there is a light in here. I will turn it on, at least once." With arms extended, he searched the wall from one end to the other. No switch was found. "So I can't turn the light on from inside. Satto Auntie lied. Oh God!"

He had not expected this from the mother of Ashok and Ajay. For five years he had come to her house; he is like one of her own sons. He was Ashok's schoolmate and now is in the last year of college with him. They're getting ready to open a scooter shop in partnership and today, this ...

Is it his fault that Indira Gandhi was murdered by her Sikh guards? Why did the bastards kill her? Why did they become traitors? They had taken an oath to save her life, they had eaten her salt to guard her, and they murdered her with their own hands! And an unarmed woman at that! Not just one shot! Sixteen bullets! This is no bravery of a Khalsa. We don't even strike an animal twice. If it is killed in one strike, fine; else we leave it. Who knows, maybe they were the shaven ones who disguised themselves as Sikhs and shot her. They did the bad deed, and the Sikhs get the bad name. Yes, that's what must have happened. Our people may be hot-tempered, but they are not traitors. Then why am I sitting here like a coward? So if I have no weapon, I have hands and feet! I'll break the door down and I'll make Ashok's mother see it as it is. I'll tell her, "Spit out your anger, Auntiji, it's all a lie. Don't fight with your own, just because the others influence you. Tell me the truth, am I not like a son to you?"

Just then a red glow of fire rose up from inside and outside the storeroom. He was blinded. He didn't understand anything for a moment. Such a fire comes from a funeral pyre, had he not seen it at the funeral of Bhaiyaji? How come the funeral fire is breaking out here? Is this a burning place in a cemetery? Wahe Guru, this is fire, real fire! Through the little holes of this room I can see flames shooting up high. The fire is in this very block! Right behind this house! And who knows, maybe even in front of this house. Or ... Wahe Guru, maybe this whole house is on fire. They threw me alive in the fire and ran away, all of them, the traitors! What do you think, murderers, I won't be burnt alive in this fire. I am a Khalsa! I will die only after killing as many as I can kill. *Jo bole so nihal, Sat shree Akal.*

He made up his mind and pounded on the door with all his might.

"Oh my God, what is this boy doing! Does he want the whole world at the door? Be patient, son, be patient. What happened? Should I open the door and go in to see ... ?" She was still not able to decide when there were thudding feet climbing the stairs.

"Bhabiji, Satto Auntie, Oh Bhabiji, did you hear? The gang of Sardars is attacking! They're firing from the Gurudwara!" Bansal Babu and Manku couldn't stay downstairs, they marched right up. She leapt out and collided with them at the gate of the stairs.

"Did Ashok come back?" asked Manku.

"No, where is he?"

"Why did you let him go? What if something happens ... ?"

"Oh, Brave Bajrang, please guard my child!" With hands on her head she leaned against the wall.

"Didn't I tell you, you can't trust these Sardars? Did you watch the fire outside?"

"Ashok ... " was all she could say in a broken voice.

"Did the Sardars set this fire?" asked Ajay coming out.

"Who else?"

"But it looks as if the fire is in the Gurudwara itself."

"So? If they start shooting, will we not set fire? Or should we give them a drink of water, you think? We won't claim to have a name if we don't burn them alive."

"Ashok ... " Satto repeated in a broken voice. "Where did Ashok go ... ?"

"Let me see," said Manku, "Come with me." He pulled Ajay and took him out.

"Brother ... oh ... " she started crying.

"Don't worry, Bhabiji. Why should you worry when we are with you? Ashok will be back. Manku will find him and bring him back. Is he gone?"

"Who?" her voice shook up.

"That one ... Ashok's friend?"

After that one time, Sarbjeet had not pounded on the door anymore. The loud shrieks and calls from downstairs were clear in his ears. He was clinging to the door. His grasp on the wooden board was tighter. He was holding his breath and waiting to hear the woman's reply. But even straining his ears he could not understand what she had said. Why is this woman speaking in such a whisper? The people downstairs are making such an uproar! Who knows what plot is being cooked. This is not the time to break down the door and get out. This house is not on fire, at least that much is clear. The mistress of the house is still inside. Everyone seems alert. It will be better to strike at the right moment.

"Is he gone or not?" Bansal Babu repeated.

"A long time back ... " Satto answered still crying. Even the ears of Bansal Babu caught it only with difficulty. "By now he must have been slaughtered."

Bansal Babu went back. She came in the room and lay down on the four-poster bed and started to chant the names of the god Hanuman.

Standing beside the door, Sarbjeet was alert. Only this door stood between him and Death. His hands tight on the board were ready. If he had to die, he would, but with bravery.

Although torn by flames, night is still night. A moment came when Sarbjeet standing beside the door, and Ashok's mother resting on the four-poster bed, both fell asleep.

Each night turns to morning. That night did too. But some mornings are darker than night. The morning of the first of November was just such a frightful morning.

He came back silently to his own house, and knocked softly, as if afraid that a louder knock would collapse the rafters. At first knock, Satto sprang from the bed and was at the door. As soon as her "Who is it" was answered in a whisper, she opened the door just enough to let him in.

With a glance at him her mind and heart went berserk. How could Ashok's father have returned now after seven years! His youthful body had burnt on the funeral pyre right before her own eyes. There had been no room for doubt. His young face, made old by Death, had not parted for a moment from her.

With a leap, the man bolted the door and pulled her into the room. "We can't keep him in the house, Mom," he said. She was startled to hear "Mom" from him. Oh yes, this is only Ajay, her own little son. But what has happened to his face? How did he age, from fourteen to forty, in one night?

"What … ?"

"I made a stupid mistake; I went to the police station."

"So?"

"I asked them to help him. They said, 'What kind of Hindu are you? If you had killed him, and then come here, we would have helped you.'"

Satto grabbed his hands. "What happens now?"

"Only one thing to do. He has to shave his hair off."

"He'll never agree."

"He'll have to," said Ajay in a rough, harsh voice. "I'll tell him everything I saw."

Startled, she looked at her son. Was this the same boy who asked last night, "Where do they come from?"

"Hurry up, we have no time, we must get him out of here," he said.

"Why? What's the danger here?"

Satto asked but before he could answer, she knew. Shouts shot up from both sides of the street at once and surrounded her. "Kill, Kill, Kill! Don't let him get out alive!"

Ajay pulled her behind the cupboard. She opened the store-room door and tore in. Startled by all the noise, Sarbjeet had just woken up, but the board had slipped from his hands. Before he could grasp the board, the woman was inside. With both his fists tight, he raised his hands above his head to hit her on the head when she took him in her arms.

"Son! My gem, be quick. The danger's here. Cut your hair and run away with Ajay. You have no other chance."

By then Ajay, too, had come inside. Ashok's razor blade and scissors were in his hands. Stunned Sarbjeet was still standing with his hands raised. Outside there were shrieks of pain ringing in the air as well as the shouts.

A truck and some scooters came roaring up to their house and stopped and flames rose from a house across the street. And the shrieks! Oh, those blood-curdling shrieks! Still their hands went on working like machines. As soon as Sarbjeet's face was clean-shaven, she gave him Ashok's clothes to wear. The same clothes in which the people of the block had seen him many times. The second set of clothes was on him when he had stepped out of the house last night. He had not returned … Where did you go, Ashok? There was a cry in her heart. But this was not the time to think and weep.

"Auntiji … " Sarbjeet wanted to say something with choking voice while he dressed, but this was not the time for goodbyes.

"Hurry up," said Ajay. "The mob's busy with the other house. You ride the bike; I'll be on the backseat." That was right, this way the mob would see more of Ajay and less of Sarbjeet.

Both mounted Ashok's bike and started off at the edge of the mob.

No one from Bansal Babu's house was paying any attention, all were busy watching the spectacle from the roof top. She gathered up the cut hair. She locked the store-room door again. She was unable to decide what to do with the hair when she was pulled out against her will by the unrestrained shouts of the mob. Leaning over the balcony, she looked down.

What kind of mob is this! Are these young boys in a religious war or in a parade? No one's face has any pain of sorrow, no remorse, nothing except the madness of elephants in heat. Then too, in 1948, there was a murder! Then too, people gathered; they observed the wake. There was no fire even in the kitchen stoves then, in anyone's house that night and the morning after. And now ... the houses are being burnt down. Is this a funeral or a festival?

Leaning from the railing she watched. Ajay and he, Sarbjeet, were not yet out of range of the unholy intentions of the mob. "Brave Bajrang, Brave Bajrang!" She tried to keep up her chant but noticed that right in front of her house, four young boys were dragging a man down onto the road. "Leave him alone, you monsters, leave him alone!" She wanted to follow her scream down but stood there petrified. A white car came and stopped at the curb. From inside the car a man looked out and screamed. With a jolt in her heart, she recognized him; this was the one she had voted for last time. Even the Sikhs of the neighborhood had given him their votes. Before she could calm down, he was shouting, "Stop them, stop them, the shaven Sardar is on that bike!"

"NO!" she screamed with all her might. "Look at this hair!" She held Sarbjeet's shorn hair in both her hands and raised them high. The flames of the fire made the hair shine. "The boy is locked up in my room. Come and get him. Leave *him* alone; he's my own son. Come up quick. Don't let him escape!" She was acting as if possessed.

Was it the heat of the fire or was it her own encouragement? The mob, their wolf-like tongues lolling, leapt towards her.

"There he is ... " she said pointing towards the cupboard. Their strong bare hands split the sides in two shoves. It was full of things. They turned towards her, mad with anger. "Behind the cupboard, in the store-room!" she said. Before the words were out, the mob pulled the cupboard away and attacked the wall behind. There was no need to bring the key; the youthful hands broke the lock along with the latch. Ready with their sticks and knives, they crowded the door, and peered inside. The empty room mocked them.

"Lies! A pack of lies! Where have you hidden him? Tell the truth!" Who knows how many men shouted all at once and attacked her.

"Have shame, demons, have some shame." She shouted at them, "Is this really your religion? Is this what makes you Hindus? What if your child were in his place? Should someone burn your Manku alive? Should they beat your Harish to death? Have pity, my brothers, have pity! You have children, too, you, too, have old mothers and fathers! Come join me, let us save that Sardar in the house across the street!" Leaning on the railing of the balcony, she pointed towards the house across the street and became silent. She was getting ready to jump off the balcony like a madwoman, when someone hit her on the head with a steel rod. Sarbjeet's hair was drenched in Satto's blood.

"Ashok ... " was her last word before she became unconscious. She had spotted her own son on the edge of the mob.

—Translated from the Hindi by Vidyut Aklujkar

Jane Singh

JANE SINGH WAS BORN in Yuba City, California, to Punjabi immigrant parents who were farmers and were very active in the Gadar Party, which had been organized to fight for India's independence. She has a Ph.D. in South Asian studies from the University of California, Berkeley, and was an outreach coordinator at the University Center for South Asian Studies. She teaches in the Ethnic Studies Department at the University of California, Berkeley. She was the organizer and curator of a national exhibition, "Peoples of South Asia in America," and the coordinating editor of *South Asians in North America: A Selected and Annotated Bibliography* (1988).

As the following nonfiction selection shows, the Indian struggle for independence from Great Britain was waged by Indians not only in India but also in places such as North America, where Indians had immigrated. Many years after independence was won, an immigrant mother remembers, and her daughter records, the struggle for freedom. The events as well as the poems and songs composed by Indians far from India remind them of their struggles on behalf of their motherland.

Interview with Nand Kaur Singh: Gadar Indian Nationalist Poetry in America

> *The time is right for Hindustanis to join together,*
> > *rid the country of wretched discord.*
> *The tyrant drinks the blood of Hindustan mercilessly,*
> > *humiliate this worthless government.*
> *Hindus, Muslims, Christians and Sikhs,*
> > *do not align yourselves with this cruel regime.*
> *Let us join forces for the sake of Hindustan,*
> > *let us set aside our religious differences.*
> *Listen to the pleas of the nationalists,*
> > *bring freedom to your country.*
> *Enlist with Gadar forces,*
> > *quickly take over Hindustan and make it Prosper.*
> *The time to declare your freedom is near,*
> > *people of Hindustan, destroy the oppressors.*

Let the blight of misery and hunger go to England,
raise the cry of victory for Gadar.

THE GADAR PARTY was a nationalist organization which was founded in 1913 on the West Coast of the United States and Canada by Indian immigrants, political activists and students. The word "gadar" means revolt or revolution. The Gadar Party headquarters were established in San Francisco, California; the building was called the Yugantar Ashram. It remained a political center and a meeting place for the community until after Indian independence in 1947. A Gadar memorial building stands on the same site today.

I had heard a lot about the Gadar Party from my husband who had returned to Punjab in 1922; we were married that year and left for the United States in 1923. The first Gadar Party meeting I attended was in Stockton, California, in 1924. I did not know any of the speakers, but I was impressed by the number of people who attended; there were about 300 Indians at this gathering. The next Gadar Party meeting I went to was in Marysville in January, 1925. There were several speakers who talked about India's freedom. One person said there was no reason why 32 *crores* of Indians could not drive a handful of British out of their country. I really liked to hear what the speakers had to say. People also recited poetry during the Gadar meetings; some would repeat Gadar poems and others would recite their own compositions expressing their feelings about the independence struggle.

We went to the Gadar meetings every year. There were three or four gatherings each year and we went to as many as we could. I really looked forward to these meetings which were held regularly into the 1930s. We also received the Gadar newspaper at our home. It came about once a month and usually included poetry along with articles written on various subjects. The poetry was later collected into a pamphlet called *Gadar di Gunj.*

I remember many of the poems and still have one or two copies of the *Gadar di Gunj.* We used to sing the Gadar songs everyday. After supper, we would sit down and start to sing. The songs were very touching. My husband would read the songs or poems in Punjabi. Later I had the urge to read the poetry myself when I was at home alone with the children. I would read them everyday. To me the poetry was powerful. I liked the message that we could drive the British out of our country, that they had no right to be there, that it was our country.

We worked very hard for Indian independence. People made so many sacrifices. Most of the immigrants from India in those days were Sikhs. Many Sikhs, along with some Muslims and a few Hindus, returned to India in 1914 to lead a revolt against the British. There were many who died in this attempt.

How the Gadar Forces Were Enlisted in 1913
by The Gadar Founders

Recognizing that it was time to make the ultimate sacrifice
    for the nation,
    you drew a line on the battlefield Baba.
Crossing the line yourself, you challenged,
    let the brave ones come forward and lay down their
        lives Baba.
Along with Nidhan Singh, Kartar and Usham Singh,
    young Santokh Singh also leapt across Baba.
Comrades like Jawala Singh came forward and said,
    we are prepared to sacrifice our lives wherever you
        say, Baba.

The Sacrifices and Braveries of 1914

All the brave ones returned to their country,
    they went to India and planted the root of Gadar.
They swung from the gallows for the sake of the nation,
    they spent years incarcerated in jails.
They did not hesitate, nor did they retreat,
    they did what they swore they would do.
Well done! Bravo to you and your comrades,
    who devoted yourselves to preserving the nation.

They went to India to fight for freedom. When India gained its independence in 1947, we thought we had succeeded; but now in the Punjab it is again like that. We feel cheated, as though our work went to waste. We thought we had helped India, our India, gain freedom. And now the government is oppressing the public again; they are making trouble all over the country.

There was much talk of unity in the Gadar meetings. I remember one speaker saying we could do anything in India if we were united. This was at a meeting in 1925 or 1926. It was very moving; the whole hall thundered with applause. Over the years, several nationalists from India toured the U.S. and met with the Indian community. There were special meetings to welcome these individuals in San Francisco, Marysville, Sacramento or at the *gurdwara* in Stockton. I particularly remember the time that Sarojini Naidu came to California in 1929. We heard her speak at a meeting in Sacramento and we were so impressed with what she had to say that we went to Stockton the next day to hear her speak at the *gurdwara*. She explained that Mahatma Gandhi had asked her to go on an international tour to tell the world about India's desire for freedom from colonial rule. She told him that she could not go because her daughter was ill, to which Gandhi replied, "My dear, my whole country is ill, you must go." After the talk in Sacramento, she came over to me and asked if she could hold my baby. She said she was amazed that the child had not cried once during the three-hour meeting. I think she must have been missing her daughter.

Sarojini Naidu was famous for her poetry, but she did not recite any during the meetings I attended. I had read her poems, however, in Punjabi magazines like *Istri Jivan* and *Phulwari* to which we subscribed. At first my husband would bring home Punjabi newspapers or magazines from the local Indian store or from a friend's house. Later we subscribed directly to monthlies such as *Istri Jivan* and *Phulwari* because we did not want to miss any of the issues.

I liked poetry and I thought that Gadar poetry was unique. When I read the poems I felt happy. I thought one day our country would be free, and like America it would have all the amenities, making people's lives easier. The Gadar Press sent free literature in Punjabi, Urdu and English to all who wanted to read. I enjoyed the collections of poetry, the *Gadar di Gunj*. I learned many of the verses and taught them to my children. My sons would sing the songs at the Gadar meetings and at the *gurdwara*. The *Gadar di Gunj* became a part of our household. There is a nice poem from the last page of an issue of *Gadar di Gunj* printed in 1931. It's called "The Last Message of the Gunj" and it is written in the voice of the *Gunj*. The first verse reads:

> The path to the heart is through the heart,
>> I come from the heart to you.
> The Gadar workers have strung together choice flowers,
>> I am a beautiful, fragrant garland.
> From the collected breath of the compassionate ones,
>> I have made a river of nationalism flow.
> Selecting pearls from the seven seas,
>> I have created a precious necklace [of verse].

Jahanara Imam

(1923–)

Born in Mushidabad, India, in 1923, Jahanara Imam has an M.A. in Bengali literature and language and a B.A. in education from Dhaka University. She was a Fulbright scholar in the United States in 1964–1965 and a participant in the International Visitors Program (United States) in 1977. Her autobiography, *Another Life*, portrays a Muslim family in rural Bengal during the first half of this century. *The Days of '71* is her account of life in East Pakistan (now Bangladesh) under occupation by the West Pakistani military.

Of Blood and Fire: The Untold Story of Bangladesh's War of Independence, in which the following selections appeared, is Jahanara Imam's personal journal of the events of 1971, when many of her friends and family, including her beloved son, joined the freedom fighters. Her anguish as she describes the events, her frustrations and fears as she waits to hear news about the friends and relatives who have disappeared, and her grief as she discovers the loss of people who are integral parts of her life are depicted in the journal entries. By keeping a record of the events and her emotions, Imam reveals the importance of remembering and documenting her experiences as a woman caught in a war. By presenting everyday matters, including family illnesses, preparation of food, and visits to friends, in the context of a brutal military oppression and the valiant resistance of people she knows very well, Imam describes the effects of war on the very fabric of a woman's life as a householder. As discussed in the Introduction, women documenting their memories of war is a crucial element of the waging of peace and the creation of a women's mythology of war and peace. Re-membering is a crucial strategy for survival.

Of Blood and Fire

Thursday, 25th March, 1971

I was fast asleep. Suddenly I woke up at a very loud sound. Rumi and Jami came rushing to our room. "What's the matter?" Deafening sounds of heavy guns, the intermittent sounds of machine guns, the whistling sound of bullets filled the air. The tracer balloons brightened the sky. We all ran up to the roof. South of our house, across the playground, are the University Students' dormitories—Iqbal Hall, Mohsin Hall and a few other buildings of the University quarters. All the noise came from that direction. There were screams of anguish and heartrending cries of the victims along with the sound of weapons. We could not stay there for long because of the sparks. Rumi quickly lowered the black flag and that of independent Bangladesh.

Suddenly I remembered that Barek and Kasem were in the outhouse on the ground floor. We all rushed down. As soon as we opened the wooden door to the courtyard our alsatian dog Mickey rushed in and started moaning pathetically and rolling on the ground. I called Barek and Kasem. They came in quickly. I told them to bring their beds and sleep in the drawing room.

Mickey refused to move out of the room. It seemed that all the noise of the guns and the light of the tracer balloons had badly shaken him. Rumi lovingly patted his head and said: "Don't be afraid, Mickey. You will stay with us upstairs." But he refused to go upstairs either. He was looking for a corner. Finally he crept into a dark corner under the staircase and curled up quietly there.

I lifted the receiver. The phone was dead. Hearing Baba's voice, Rumi was holding his hands and telling him something in a whisper.

There was no sleep for the rest of the night. I went upstairs again. There was fire visible at a distance. We could still hear the sound of different types of guns, big and small. The tracer balloons continued to inflame the sky. There were sounds of people crying for help all around. The pillars of fire were getting bigger and higher in the North, South, East and West.

Nobody uttered a word. Rumi and Jami opened up the polythene packets and unloaded the contents into the commode, a little at a time lest it get blocked, and then pulled the flush. Jami washed the mortars and pestles very carefully with dish-washing powder to remove the smell of chemicals.

After that, Rumi packed all his books on Marx, Engels as well as Mao Tse Tung's military writings into a polythene bag. We did not know where to keep them. We didn't want to bury them underground because it would spoil the books. Then I remembered a gap between Barek's room and the boundary wall. We threw the packet of books in there as soon as the faint light of dawn appeared on the horizon. Rumi covered the packet with a few dried fronds of palm.

Friday, 26th March 1971

At six o'clock in the morning I heard a faint voice calling me. I ran to the window and looked out nervously. I saw Kamal Ataur Rahman, curled up under a tree in the garden. Kamal is an Honours student at the Dhaka University and stays in the Mohsin Hall. I rushed down and opened the door. Rumi and Jami helped me to bring the semi-conscious Kamal indoors. He had spent the night with a few other students in a bathroom in the Hall. Due to the bright tracer balloons he did not dare to come out at night. As soon as the morning light appeared they all left the bathroom and fled in different directions.

After some nursing and breakfast, Kamal felt a little better. We switched on the radio. After recitation of the Holy Quran only one piece of music was being played over and over again—the instrumental rendering of a popular patriotic song. At 7 o'clock in the morning I went to our neighbour, Dr. A.K. Khan's place to use their telephone but it was also dead. Gradually some more faces appeared at the windows of our neighbourhood. There was terror on every face. Everybody had spent the night awake and nobody knew what was really happening. All the telephones were dead.

I returned and kept sitting in front of the radio. I told Jami, "Go wake your grandfather up. Wash him and feed him with the help of Barek."

Kasem left the breakfast tray on the table like an automaton. Nobody touched any food.

At 9 o'clock, the instrumental music suddenly stopped and a harsh voice was heard on the radio. Curfew was announced all over the city until further orders. People were also reminded of the punishment for violating curfew. Martial law was announced and all the articles of the martial law were read out. The announcements were made in Urdu first and then in English. The pronunciation, style and accent betrayed the Army background of the announcer. Probably the military government could not find any more suitable person at this time.

Curfew for an indefinite period! Even without curfew nobody would dare to go out amidst the shootings and firings. There was no end to the sound of the gun shots. The pillars of fire were getting bigger and bigger and now we could see them from our windows. The dark smoke covered a large part of the bright blue sky over the city.

Mickey continued his moaning all morning. His alsatian nature had been changed by the sound of non-stop gun shots. We all in turn tried to cheer him up and feed him but to no avail.

Baba was another problem. We had a hard time explaining to him why the Pakistani troops were killing the innocent people. I was afraid that his blood pressure might go up again.

The telephone was dead. The radio station was crippled. There was curfew outside and the unending sound of all types of guns made our lives miserable. There was no way of knowing what was really happening. Under the circumstances the only first hand information could be obtained from Kamal Ataur Rahman. From the morning he had been repeating his story to satisfy my curiosity.

"What were you doing at 12 o'clock last night, Kamal?"

"I was writing an essay on Patriotism in Bengalee literature. I was going to read it on the radio on the 27th."

"When did you first hear the gun shots?"

"At around midnight. A friend of mine came and told me: 'You are still here! Don't you know what's happening all around? The soldiers are coming to attack our campus. I am leaving. You better do the same.' But we never had a chance to leave. The firings started almost immediately thereafter. As soon as the sky was brightened with the tracer balloons the firings increased. From my room on the 5th floor I quickly came down to the ground floor. On the south of Mohsin Hall is the Iqbal Hall and the Muslim Hall is next to it. It appeared as if the heavy guns were pounding the Iqbal Hall. Some of the bullets were entering our Hall too."

"Didn't they attack your Hall?"

"No, though we were expecting an attack any moment."

"Where else did they attack?"

"I don't really know. But it appears that the Iqbal Hall, the Muslim Hall, the Jagannath Hall and the Shaheed Minar were the main targets. Most of the sound came from that direction."

"Do you think that they have razed the Iqbal Hall and Muslim Hall to the ground? What about the students, are they all killed?"

"There is no way of knowing. We were hiding in the bathroom in the ground floor. We could hear the noise of window panes shattering all around us the whole night."

When I left Kamal, Rumi told me: "Don't ask him any more, Mother. Can't you see it hurts him to repeat his nightmarish experience?"

"I can see that. But I want to know what is happening."

"There is nothing to know Mother, whatever was to happen has happened."

I looked deep into Rumi's eyes. He lowered his gaze. He has become somewhat quiet and withdrawn since last night. I remembered Rumi's prediction—it had finally come true.

Rumi must have been thinking, "Didn't I tell you? Have you at last been thrown out of fool's paradise?"

How long could one stay indoors under such conditions? I opened the door and went to the porch. The road in front of our house is a cul-desac. Branching out from the Elephant Road it ends just beyond our house. There is an advantage to a blind alley, because there is very little traffic. Sometimes we neighbours talk to each other on the road. It is like a common courtyard. Since the house was built in 1959, we would spend time chatting on our road every time there was a curfew. But today I did not dare to step out of the porch. I could still hear the whistle of the bullets. I could hear dogs barking and people screaming—a very faint sound from a distance. Or was it my imagination? Could people still be alive and cry for help after such a shower of lead? Surprisingly, all the birds have disappeared. I could not even hear a crow.

I peeped over the boundary wall and looked at the main road. There was no sign of any life there. Had I continued to stare I could probably have seen truck loads of troops passing by. But I had no interest in them. The house opposite ours belongs to Mr. Hussein. I could see him moving restlessly from his chair in the drawing room to the door and then to the verandah and then to the chair again. On the left is Dr. Rashid's house. He was also moving between the front room and the verandah nervously. As I turned back, I caught sight of that sticker on the rear window of the car—'Each letter of the Bengali alphabet represents one of us'. I asked Rumi to take of the sticker immediately.

Just before evening the electricity went off. Our cup of misery was full to the brim. There was some respite in the sound of gun shots. Mickey also appeared somewhat more composed. He went out and sat on his favourite wooden box on the left of the courtyard. He also ate some food.

I took out some candles and lit them. I placed them at different places on the ground floor and the top floor. Barek and Kasem have stayed indoors the whole of today. In the evening I told them to bring their beds into the guest room and asked them not to go out into the courtyard at night. Gratefully, they brought their beds inside. I felt as if we were all sitting in Noah's Ark.

There is not one radio in good condition in the house. On 20th February when we were all out there was a theft in the house and our expensive radio was stolen. After that we were using Kitty's radio. But since she left for Gulshan we have been managing with Rumi and Jami's little portable two-in-one. It is hard to get the BBC on it. All India Radio has so far only said that there are troops on the streets in Dhaka and nothing more. Dhaka TV station is closed. There was nothing to do and so we had early dinner. As we were leaving the dining room, Rumi suddenly remarked: "Mickey is rather quiet. Looks like he has finally overcome the shock."

Jami said: "We should bring him inside."

We opened the door and went to the courtyard. In the flickering candlelight we saw Mickey lying in the courtyard. He was dead.

Wednesday, 21st April, 1971

I have been having a debate with Rumi for the last few days. Had he quietly sneaked out at night like his friends to join the war of liberation, I would have been spared the agony of taking a painful decision. But right from his childhood I have taught him not to hide anything from me. So I am caught in my own trap. Rumi insists on joining the war with my consent.

But how could I allow him to go? This is the age for studies, not warfare. He has just completed his 12th grade and has got admission in the Illinois Institute of Technology in the United States. On 2nd September, the classes will start and he has to be there by the end of August. It will take him four years to complete is graduation in Engineering. How could he go to war now?

We were discussing this matter at Nasir's house. Dr. Nasirul Huq is a paediatrician in the Holy Family Hospital. He is also trying to go to the United States. He might leave within a week. Till recently, Nasir agreed with me, but today he spoke in a different tone. Angrily I said, "Now I know why Rumi comes here so often. He must have won you over to his side during the last few days."

Rumi was playing with Nasir's little girl. He said, "You are wrong, Mother, I come here only to play with this little poppet. I didn't discuss this subject with Uncle at all. But Mother, had I used a fraction of the arguments that I used in my discussions with you, Uncle would have been convinced long ago. It is an age-old truth that the main responsibility of a student is to study and build up his career. But haven't the events of March 1971 turned it into an untruth? Do you find normal conditions anywhere around you? The whole country has been turned into a firing range for the Pakistani Army's target practice. Our condition is worse than the Roman gladiators. The gladiators had at least a slim chance of escaping from the clutches of the lions but we don't even have that. We are made to stand blindfolded with hands tied behind our backs and within seconds we fall like ninepins before the Pakistani bullets. Is it the proper environment for studies? Is this the time to pore over books in preparation for the future?"

"But you are going away to the United States in September. We might even send you earlier. You are not going to study here."

"Mother, if in the present conditions you insist on my going, I might go. But all my life I would live with a guilty conscience. I might come back from the United States with an impressive degree and become a renowned engineer but I would never be able to hold my head high again. Do you want that Mother?"

Rumi has won prizes for debates in schools and colleges, so he is not to be defeated easily.

I shut my eyes and said slowly, "No, I don't want that. All right, I give in. I sacrifice you to the cause of the nation. You may join the war."

Thursday, 22nd April, 1971

It seems that time has stopped since yesterday. Yesterday at this time Rumi and I were at Nasir's place. What did I say? Nasir, Leena, Rumi—everybody were stupefied. Rumi, too, had not expected such a dramatic turn. He beamed in joy and hugged me as if he was a little boy who had just got ice-cream money from his mother. Nasir tried a faint smile. Leena left the room carrying the child in her bosom.

I could not sleep last night. I could not discuss it with anyone. At the breakfast table Kasem said that he wanted to go home. Earlier, I had refused him leave twice. Someone had got permission to go to war, so why couldn't Kasem go home for four days only? I said, "Okay, you may go."

After that I became busy. I told Sharif, "Please send the car back after you reach the office. I have to go to Thatari Bazar."

Sharif said, "You come along with me now. I'll get down at the office and then you may go wherever you want."

These days the soldiers commandeer private cars. It has become a routine affair. But they spare the cars which have lady passengers.

The situation in Thatari Bazar was no better than other places. It was burnt down on the night of 25th March. Some repair work was going on now. I got down from the car and asked the chauffeur to accompany me.

The atmosphere was tense and abnormal. The shopkeepers looked disinterested and wore a faraway look. The floors were wet. Why did they have to wash the floors? Did anything happen here? I had an eerie feeling. I bought some minced meat and quickly came out. I felt that I would rather go to New Market for the rest of my shopping.

Lulu came when we were having lunch. I asked him to join us. While eating, Lulu said: "Do you know Aunty, yesterday the Biharis slaughtered some Bengalee meat-sellers in Thatari Bazar?"

"You can't be serious. I was there this morning. I didn't notice any panic or nervousness among the shopkeepers there. Had it been true could the shopkeepers have been so relaxed? It must be a rumour."

Though I feigned disbelief, a chill ran down my spine.

After lunch I asked Kasem to get some chicken and fish from New Market.

Sunday, 1st August, 1971

Three American astronauts landed on the moon today and took a stroll. If I could get a ramshackle spaceship I could take a quick trip to Melaghar, only a few hundred miles away, and see Rumi.

Rumi left 48 days ago but I feel as if it has been 48 months. Sometimes I wonder, "Is there really someone named Rumi or is it an illusion?"

I had a thorough medical check-up today including blood test and X-rays and Dr. Nurul Islam prescribed some medicines. But I know my cure lies not in the medicine prescribed by Dr. Nurul Islam but on a special medicine that is in Melaghar. Who will bring me that medicine?

Kaleem came in the afternoon. He looked rather sad. His wife's brother Latif who had come from Nilphamari informed him that the Pakistanis have killed his elder sister's husband. Kaleem's wife Salina was extremely shocked and wept disconsolately. Salina's sister's husband, Makbul Hussein, used to live in Chilahati. He was a very simple and decent person. In March when the Army action took place, Salina's parents with their three sons were staying in Nilphamari. At that time, the Bengalee soldiers of East Pakistan Rifles, East Bengal Regiment, the Ansars and the local youths built up a resistance force. Salina's elder brother Abu was a commander in this force. On 7th April, the Pakistani troops captured Nilphamari and the resistance forces were dispersed with their arms and ammunition. Some went over to India and the others to the neighbouring districts. Salina's father also went to India with his family but came back after three months. There is free movement between Nilphamari and India. Abu is now working for Swadhin Bangla Betar. Dr. A.K. Khan returned today from Rajshahi on a month's leave.

Wednesday, 4th August, 1971

The days and nights are now crowded with events. There is an unending stream of visitors and we are getting used to frequent sounds of explosions. We don't sleep well unless we hear one or two loud bangs. Dada Bhai, Murtaza, Banka, and Fakir all feel the same way. Some of my friends jokingly say that the sale of Valium has gone down because the sound of explosions work as an excellent sleeping medicine. Some nights if I don't hear the sounds I feel alarmed. Have the Pakistanis caught the boys?

No, that is not true. Even if there is no explosion in the early part of the night there is invariably a blast later on to soothe our nerves.

The boys are getting more and more daring every day. The people have nicknamed them 'The Scorpions'. Yesterday, just before sunset, some of the Scorpions threw a grenade at the Army checkpost near the State Bank. The soldiers could not get any of them. The Swadhin Bangla Betar reports that those of the Scorpions facing the Pakistanis in a frontal warfare at the borders are also showing tremendous courage and valour, disregarding all hazards to their lives. They are fighting for a cause and they believe that death for the motherland is a death of honour. They would rather embrace martyrdom than dishonour.

Someone was singing in the Swadhin Bangla Betar—
>We the young sailors must cross this turbulent ocean;
>We the young soldiers fight for our freedom,
>We the young ones have no anchor and no sense of time.
>We only know to hold the rudder firm and row forward.

As I listened, tears rolled down my cheeks.

Sunday, 29th August, 1971

Today Hafeez returned from his country home. He had gone there in the middle of March with his mother. Only his elder brother Wahid, stayed back. Wahid also left in the first week of April with Chinku to join the Liberation War.

In the afternoon Hafeez came to see Rumi but Rumi was not in. He had left after breakfast and said that he had to attend a meeting and meet Chullu.

I told Hafeez, "I don't know where he has gone. He doesn't tell me anything these days. God knows what has happened to all the young people these days. They have become so irresponsible."

Hafeez tried to defend Rumi and said, "Aunty, Rumi is not like that."

Rumi came back in the evening and was happy to see Hafeez. The two of them went upstairs to the privacy of Rumi's room.

At 9 o'clock, I called them for dinner. Rumi said, "Mother, Hafeez will stay overnight. We are not yet through with our exchange of information."

A spare bed was placed in the room by Rumi and Jami for Hafeez. Rumi said, "Mother, I have a headache. Could you please give me a massage?"

I sat on his bed and ran my fingers through his hair. Jami and Hafeez were talking in a low voice. Masum came from his room and sat on Jami's bed. He shut the connecting door so that Baba was not disturbed.

The radio on the bedside table was tuned to the Calcutta Station, and the famous song which immortalised Khudiram was being played—"Don't hold me back, Mother, I would smilingly go the gallows for the cause of the nation."

Rumi said, "What a strange coincidence, Mother. Only this afternoon I heard this song on the radio and again at night the same song. Rarely do they play the same song twice the same day."

I was fast asleep. Suddenly I woke up at a loud knock on the door and heard voices of people. I looked out of the window on the eastern side. Oh my God! The whole road was full of soldiers. I could see everything in the bright street lights. I ran up to Rumi's room and found the four of them standing petrified in the centre of the room. I looked through the western window and saw soldiers on the road in front of Mr. Bazlur Rahman's house. Through the southern window I could see the empty space in front of Dr. A.K. Khan's house filled with green-helmeted soldiers. In the north there were soldiers in our garden. The house was surrounded on all sides by the troops. Rumi said in a shaky voice, "It seems there is no way to slip out. They have brought a few hundred soldiers. The street-lights are so bright that not even a cat can pass unnoticed."

In panic I was looking all around and thinking of a way to get Rumi out. But there was no way. All the windows of the house and the verandah are covered with iron grills. There is no way to get out by the back door as the road is full of soldiers. Meanwhile, the knocking on the door was getting louder and there were angry voices. At that very moment I felt as if I was acting like a puppet. As if I was simply responding to the pull of the strings of a puppeteer. I looked at Sharif and said, "Let's go and ask them what they want." The two of us came out on the eastern verandah. Sharif yelled, "Who's there? What do you want?"

Someone in a harsh voice replied in Urdu, "Open the door. Don't keep us waiting."

Sharif replied: "What do you want at this time of the night?"

This time the other voice was somewhat mellow, "Please open the door, we will tell you what we want."

Sharif and I went down. I looked at the wall clock. It was ten minutes after twelve. The main door opens on the porch. There are collapsible shutters on two sides of the porch. When the shutters are drawn the porch becomes a garage. Sharif unlocked the collapsible door. A rather young Army Officer accompanied by some soldiers entered. In a shaky voice I asked, "What can we do for you?"

The officer introduced himself, "I am Captain Quayyum. I'd like to search your house."

I said, "Why?"

"Just a routine search. How many people live in this house?"

I said, "My husband, father-in-law, two sons, my nephew and myself."

"What are the names of your sons?"

"Rumi and Jami."

The officer and soldiers moved forward. I moved aside and said, "Look, my father-in-law is old, blind and a patient of hypertension. If you want to search the house please do so but please don't wake him up."

Captain Quayyum looked like a young college student, fair, slim with a soft voice. The Subedar following him was middle-aged. His Urdu accent indicated that he was a Bihari. Captain Quayyum, the Subedar and a few other soldiers spread all over the house in a minute. They opened every cupboard, every drawer, searched every nook and corner of the house. They tiptoed into Baba's room and did not wake him up. They talked to

Rumi, Jami, Hafeez and Masum and asked them to go downstairs. Nervously I asked Captain Quayyum, "Why? Why do you want them to go down?"

Capt. Quayyum replied, "We would like to do a little bit of routine interrogation" and then he looked at Sharif and said, "Would you come down also?" I accompanied them. Downstairs Captain Quayyum asked Sharif, "Is that your car?"

Sharif replied, "Yes."

"Would you please follow us?"

I got scared and asked, "Where are you taking them?"

Quayyum replied, "We will just go down to the Ramna Police Station for a routine interrogation. They will be back in less than an hour."

I said, "I will also come with you."

Until now Sharif was absolutely quiet. Now he said, "No, you stay back. Baba is alone."

I replied, "No, I will go."

The Subedar told me in broken Bengali, "Madam don't worry. They will be back in no time."

Sharif looked at me. I thought he wanted to tell me something. I tried to compose myself. I saw Rumi, Jami and Masum moving towards the police van. Captain Quayyum sat beside Sharif. Sharif reversed the car and drove away.

I don't know how long I kept standing in the porch. I had lost all sense of time. I went inside and switched on all the lights. The main door remained open. I went up to Baba's room. He was fast asleep. Then I went to the roof top and switched on the lights there. I climbed down and once again stood on the porch. Then I moved on to the road and came back to the porch. For a while I stood on the verandah and then walked restlessly between the porch and the road. Half an hour passed, one hour passed and then one and a half hours; but they did not return. Impatiently, I moved back and forth. The night watchman of our neighbourhood told me, "Madam, you better go inside." I didn't listen to him. The main door remained open. Again I went upstairs on the roof and then came down. The night guard said, "Madam, you better not go inside leaving the main door open. It is not safe." I didn't listen to him. I walked down to the main road again and then came back. There was some trace of annoyance in the nightguard's voice when he said, "Madam, aren't you going to sleep tonight?"

Sleep? He must be joking. How could I sleep until they came back?

Wednesday, 29th September, 1971

Thirty days ago from today Rumi was taken away. During these thirty days I have not heard anything about him. There are many others who are also without any trace. Though *Pagla Pir* insists that they are all alive, he could not get any information about Rumi, Altaf Mehmood, Bodi, Jewel, Bakar, Bashar, Hafeez, Mamun, Majid, Shamsul Haq or Jahangir.

I went to visit Begum Sufia Kamal today. Jhinu had told me that she wanted to see me. Begum Kamal hugged me and said with tearful eyes, "Only last year Rumi went with me on flood-relief operations in Barisal. He came to me and said 'Aunty, could you please persuade Mother to let me go with you?' When I asked you, you said, 'Of course, what objection could I have if he goes with you? I know you will look after him as your own son'. There was a tie of deep affection between the two of us. Whenever he came he hugged me and kissed me. After returning from Melaghar, I was one of the first ones he visited. And this Altaf poor fellow—I was instrumental in his marriage with Jhinu. He also disappeared. And look what they did to Alvi—they beat him up mercilessly. They have killed and tortured all the ones I loved so much." Her voice was choked with tears.

I held her and said, "Please, please calm down."

She said "I am calm, my heart has become numb like a stone. See how I continue to live and carry on with my daily routine."

"When did Alvi visit you?" I asked.

"The day he was released. Rana brought him here. Do you know Rana, son of Lutfur Rahman and grandson of Poet Golam Mostafa?"

"Yes, I do. He is the one who picked up Nuhail, Alvi and the others from the road in front of the M.P.A. Hostel." Sufia Kamal gave me an enquiring look. I said, "When Nuhail, his three brothers and Alvi were released, they walked from the M.P.A. Hostel to the main road and sat down there. They could not walk any further as they were extremely weak. Lutfur Rahman was driving by and he picked them up. Nuhail told me about him. I see them almost every day at *Pagla Pir's* place. How's Alvi now? Where is he? Do you see him?"

"Yes, I saw him twice more. I think he has gone back to Melaghar. At first he could not walk but after medical treatment he is better now. Alvi probably has taken Dr. Rashiduddin along with him. You know his elder brother was Gyasuddin who was killed by the Army in the University on 25th March."

Saturday, 2nd October, 1971

Our old cook Bura Miah has come back. I needed him badly as I could not cope with all the cooking and other household work. He has come at an appropriate time. Bura Miah has been with us for the last sixteen years. He had left us in January as he was suffering from ulcer. The white-haired, white-bearded Bura Miah looks distinguished and has an imposing personality. Besides cooking, he is also a sort of guardian to all of us. It was a relief for me when he took over charge of the kitchen.

Tuesday, 5th October, 1971

It is Shab-e-Bharat tonight—the night when Almighty God allots the destiny to each of us. Last night Sharif, Mother and Jami prayed the whole night. I could not keep awake long because of my weakness. Mother insisted that I should go to bed.

As is customary on Shab-e-Bharat chapatis, sweets, and meat dishes were prepared. Some of it was distributed among the relatives and the rest among the poor.

Everybody fasted today except me. Fasting is recommended at Shab-e-Bharat. In the evening as they were all getting ready to break the fast, there was a loud bang. The sound came from a distance but it was a familiar sound.

I hadn't heard it for at least a month.

There was a trace of a smile on Sharif's face "Did you hear that?" he asked.

"Yes, I think it came from somewhere far away."

"From now on you will hear it nearby also!"

"What do you mean?"

"A new group has arrived."

Sharif shut his mouth as soon as Mother and Laloo entered the dining-room.

For the next two hours I didn't have a chance to talk to Sharif in private. There were rotis and halwa coming from our neighbours. There was a queue of beggars who were waiting for food at the gate. Meanwhile, Dada Bhai and Murtaza came along with packets of roti and halwa. Sharif and the two of them went upstairs to our room and switched on to Swadhin Bangla Betar.

At bedtime, when we were alone, Sharif told me that a new group of guerillas have come from Melaghar and have set up their camp in the outskirts of Dhaka at Savar. Their Deputy Leader is Bachchu, Manzur's nephew and Banka's brother-in-law.

The guerillas have rented two houses—one in Farm Gate and the other in Fakirapool. Banka and Manzur are paying for all the expenses. They are looking for more houses. The boys are scheduled to resume their operations tonight. The bang that I heard was probably the beginning of the renewed operations. I look forward to hearing more of them.

—Translated from the Bengali by Mustafizur Rahman

Aliya Talib

IN "GREENING," THE SECOND selection by this author included in this anthology, the heroine is not waiting passively for her warrior-husband's return while turning her son into his image, as was the case in "A New Wait." This mother and wife is making sure that she will not be complicit in the perpetuation of war by giving birth to and socializing a new generation of killers.

Greening

The continuous volleys make his tank vibrate. They accelerate. Each labor spasm produces a great joy mixed with conflicting feelings that crowd his imagination, burning with the borders of the country whose beautiful hem the enemy wanted to kiss.

A loud, strident sound against the heavy iron body which held them all together.

"I think it's a mortar shell."

"Never mind. It's not made much of an impact."

More hits against the burning body with the green eyes.

"I'll show them what will happen if they dare to scratch her."

A strong attack, a battle and then under him various objects collide into each other. Ammunition. Smashed bodies. The sound of shells falling close by.

"Don't go any further! Stop!"

But he's not hearing. The roar in his burning ears prevents him from taking in what was being said. Another hit stopped the tank. His furious looks will it to go on. It's got to go on; this is not the time to return. We've got lots to do. Useless. They opened the tower and got out like tigers. They roll on the ground which is fragrant with the smell of gunpowder. Death was creeping on to the necks of the attackers. A red land that refuses to allow foreign feet to step on it.

The skirmish went on for a long time. A gushing wound in his left hand which he did not notice until it became numb. He began to feel a weakness holding him back.

"You've lost a lot of blood. You should go back."

"No. It's stopping."

"Please. Go back. Otherwise we'll all bring you."

"No. No. I'll return alone."

His return was not peaceful; he was returning undaunted. He didn't know how to return he was so weak. A thick fog blurred vision. His wounded hand. He was struggling against his hemorrhaging body's collapse. Fog. Fog. Fog.

"You promised me, Darling, that you would not give birth before I return, didn't you? Is your womb still pure awaiting my return? Has our child remained where he is, true to the promise that you made me? He has not smiled yet. I am confident that he will wait for me. I must be the first to see him. My kiss will be the first thing to be placed on his cheek. Where are you? Can you hear? I can almost feel your hot breath on my face. I can feel my fingers plunge into your beautiful hair."

A pungent smell of medicine filled his nostrils, a brilliant white flashed before his eyes, which were fighting to stay alert. In the hospital he would have to resist sleep. He must struggle against weakness. Two loved ones were awaiting him, they were expecting from him a vision of life. He had to return to the battle. He had to hasten the time of the meeting. She might give birth while he was not around. No. Impossible.

A sharp upward motion threw off the cover. The nurse approached anxiously and tried compassionately to return him to bed.

"You've got to sleep. Please!"

"Sleep? When there's someone expecting life from me?"

She failed to convince him. The doctors were unable to convince him to stay.

They gave him medications and bandages and the last bottle of blood that had been sent for him. He closed the last opening of his military shirt.

He was overwhelmed with joy as he tried to catch up with the last of the army that was returning to the front.

"We'll meet soon. Wait for me."

"In how many days will I give birth?"

"Very few," the woman doctor replied and she smiled reassuringly. Her thoughts wandered far, far away.

"I'll wait for you. Be sure of that."

She had become accustomed to sitting next to the radio and breathing in the news of victory written by the loved ones who included among their numbers the dark beloved.

-ə   -ə   -ə

"Why did you come back so quickly?"

"Should I have waited longer?"

The commander smiled in admiration at the knight standing in front of him with the readiness of a hero.

"Good. Go. God give you success."

"Ready, Sir."

The delicious vibrations to which he had become addicted from the old tank returned as he stroked it and spoke to it. He was a new warrior who was going to fight.

"I'll never let them hit you."

Their hits increased. The combatants were singing inside the deaf lump that held them.

"We'll annihilate them. All of them. I'll see my baby soon."

The firing increased and the fighting became fierce. He moved closer. Mortars rained down upon him. He didn't look at all worried, and his joy and enthusiasm did not leave him. The tank sustained many hits. Neither he nor his companions paid any attention to them.

"It is we who must make them retreat."

"We must ... we must ... "

He became more enthusiastic. Both of them were wide awake. Hot drops covered her face. Salty drops surrounded his eyelids. The veins in her face were distended. His hands gripped the trigger. The meeting was close, their hands stretched out. The smile grew. A sharp pain below the waist. The beating of the cudgel in her back increases. His bladder burst. Strong labor pains overcome her.

The hits increase. An insistent, violent anxiety fills him. His hand grabs hold of his weapon with difficulty. Swift labor pains invade her body.

She didn't say a thing. Not a groan of pain. She must not give birth before he returns. He must be the first to see him. It was not yet time for the meeting. You must not come out, baby, before his face can embrace your little cheeks. You will learn the meaning of the word embrace from his strong arms.

His beautiful hair fell over his dimming eyes with a simple splendor as he fired the last shot in his gun barrel. His hands grab his lower body. Pain that overcame the last of any future resistance.

"We've got to go to hospital."

"No. I'll last another day."

"But, you're in great pain and you could give birth at any instant."

"No. Not before he returns."

A beautiful, majestic flag in front of their house embraces a brown coffin. Two green, lovely eyes. His mother screams in agony. His father collapses in front of the door. His brother rushes forward to embrace him. His sister slaps her face. The children's apprehension increases as they hold on to their little planes with their small insistent hands. Big as far as he is concerned. The people collect in front of the house. They lower him with humility and respect and love and gratitude. She stands among them. She is struggling against impossible pains. Her body shakes, the labor pains increase. The baby wants to get out. No, not now. Not before the beloved knight dismounts ... and sees you, and your small hands touch him. Not now. Her pains are infinite. Don't go near his pure tomb. Don't touch him. Not before he embraces his son who is about to come.

They drag her indoors. The women surround her. Their screaming drowns out the screaming of the agonized woman, the beloved out of whom life was pouring. Life which promised her survival.

The newborn is brown with green eyes. He does not cry. His eyes do not move. At peace.

"Don't take him. Don't look at him. It is he who must see him first." They lower the little one into the beautiful coffin draped with heroism. He kisses with his little lips the face of the hero lying there submissively.

In the eyes of the beloved shine looks of pleasure that roll down with the grief-stricken tears.

"I gave you my word ... you would be the first to embrace him."

—Translated from the Arabic by Miriam Cooke and Rkia Cornell.

Huda Naamani

(1930–   )

HUDA NAAMANI WAS BORN in Damascus, Syria. After her father's death in 1938, she was raised in her maternal grandfather's Damascus mansion. She is descended from the Ghazzis, who were landowners and politicians, and the Nabulsis, scholars and mystics who trace their lineage to the Prophet Muhammad. She attended the Lycée-Français and the Franciscan School and in 1946 received her Baccalaureate. In 1947, following family tradition, Naamani joined the law school at the Syrian University. Upon graduation she joined, as a court attorney, the firm of her uncle, Said al-Ghazzi, who was prime minister during the regime of Shukri al-Quwatli. In 1952, she was awarded a graduate scholarship in political science to Stanford University. Her mother objected, and Naamani declined the grant. She then married her cousin A. K. Naamani, twenty-three years her senior. She flew with him to Cairo, where he became dean at the American University. During a two-year stay in England, she studied history, Sufism, philosophy, classical literature, and the Islamic arts at the School of African and Oriental Studies. She and her husband moved to Beirut in 1968.

Her publications include *To You* (1970); *My Fingers ... No* (1971); and *I Remember I Was a Point, I Was a Circle* (1980), her major cluster poem of nationalistic songs calling for universal peace. The latter was published in 1993 in the United States in a bi-lingual Arabic-English edition; the translation that follows is from that edition. A member of the Arab Writers Union, she contributes regularly to *Al-Nahar*, the Beirut daily newspaper. Her two plays on the Lebanese Civil War are to be published shortly.

In the dreamlike sequence of poems/verses included here, Huda Naamani uses imagery from religion, memories of love, and descriptions of nature to weave a heavenly vision of peace, an end to the Lebanese Civil War.

I Remember I Was a Point, I Was a Circle

You carry your torch,
Your roots bloom like a revivified corpse.
Is the ant without its red bricked roof?
Has the garden, with the lawn, with the swings and with
the flute grown distant?

Is the ant without its golden mirror?
Did the anklets, the lips, the pastries, and the drop of water lose their way?

Has hope been in vain?

You may possess the sea.
The ebb and flow have many wings,
and kisses only the sky beholds.

The gold that is you,
The meadow that is you,
The heritage you tread on.
Divinity and heroism but
Chariots for your eyes.

What if you were to drown?

Is is possible you may catch the wave?
There is no need for your disappearance.
The pulse spawns a pleasant froth, and
Hope pursues its dance,
Rain drips over children's hands.

There is no reason for your pallor,
A white fragrance hugs the pains of prison,
Winter steps awaken the returning dream, a sweet music
are
The creaks of oarlocks: they dispel delusion's many deaths.

Your departure is of no consequence,
Your face is white-washed in a harvest of tears,

Your specters are not your beseigers, instead
Your orchard is the ornament of the world,
Your purpose is in the cadence of wisdom,
The compassion of nations.

You may find the bottom of the abyss, but
Nothing in bewilderment is to be called defeat.
There is no doubt except your fear,
No scream except on a bed of stone, for
Happiness has garments of glass, shimmering
for you to see nakedness, one's own, ours, surviving ...

Were you to stumble? What then?

You might attain the depths
To the Phantom of your patience, you could reach out, for
A fuel of a lamp, intense and meek,
Apropos of your compassion, for
A choice of honor of pearly praise.
The strength that is in you, for
The controversy that is you
Earthquakes of light,
Embracing horizons.

With the veil of beauty, you will fly.
Soar!
You are destined for the heavens, nor
Ships rest except on your cloak, salt badges, woven.
Your steps tread in the air, on high
You inspire a saint,
You heal a saint,
You reveal a saint,
None may follow save your shadow,
None but the forest ablaze below you.
As a prophet, you shed tears,
As a prophet, you start the fire,
AS a prophet, you can put out the flame.
You may be rewarded ...
    You may be rewarded by God.

We seek escape,
You tighten your grip,
You create me a child anew,
Water remains enchanted,
I stretch out my hand to you,
Your meadows come into view,
Your voice echoes in mine,
As the summer float of a tree's fragrance,
I toss my house keys on your breast,
You fall to your knees.

I follow you,
We impress our bodies on the snow,
The spirit abides on the horizon,
We tell each wave, it is not delirious,
We will heal the wounds of every stone,
We will prune every branch with our lashes,
Every infant will be guarded by a star in the heart.

You follow me,
Glass takes the place of wakefulness,
The dawn remains a butterfly,
We traverse horizons,
We carry goblets of light,
We bend and stoop to the mountains,
We burn, and continue to rise on our self-made thermals,
We shine as the light of God,
Glare at every door, set afire every shadow.

You embrace me,
I pray on your chest,
You whisper to me,
They did not tarnish the bloom in you,
I whisper back,
They did not break your spine,
Our steps are upwards, our bones still work,
Our six pillars stand firm, the ages carry no threats!

I embrace you,
We are ablaze,

One copper piece melts into another,
We calm the tempests of blood,
We restore the gush of fountains,
We forgive the unjust village,
The unjust Village? Not to be specified?

Apologies, then, O Beirut,
To you, resounding thunder,
You promise, a city atop a city,
Your dowry, that of ageless Zanoubia,
Your beauty, that of a magnolia tree.
With doves warbling at your waist,
With bouquets of flowers at your knees,
With a twenty-one sun salute,
And your dream that remains unexplained.

You were killed ...
    you killed ...

Your death, Your Joseph, Your death!
They tossed him to the bottom of the pit,
They came repentant to you with their father,
They claim the wolf devoured him,
They spattered his tunic with bogus blood,
Careful, wife of Aziz,
Patience, passionate woman.
Where are your wine pressers,
Your bread vendors,
The seven ears of grain,
The green Cow,
Where are the guided tours
    to the watering places,
Who will meet the announcer of the Gospel?
The bargain hunter,
with a full birdfeeder resting on his head.

Where are the ladies,
You gathered on the stages, having
Slashed their hands with knives, and
Asked God's forgiveness?

Have mercy, O Queen,
Your tenderness, Beirut.
You teach that death on your breast,
Is a life past resurrection,
Love is a tulip in the blood, a balloon in the blocked artery.
Your heart a cave all astir, our
Homeland a lake that nurses the night, waiting for the
    light.

You teach us to linger at your breast
   for drop after drop after drop.

Sorrow, our altar of sponge, our mirror in the sea.
The moon, a surprise that says loneliness, image in water,
    to sky-disk
The heavens, an expanse that frightens the children.

In vain, we say:
   Gypsy of the night,
   River of emerald,
   Braids of a doll.

In vain, we say:
   Rock of perplexity,
   Dizziness of the hungry,
   Sting of words.

In Vain, we say:
   You are a virgin,
   A Magdelene.

You rain down pearls,
You rain down honey,
You rain down suns.
Hope is to be tireless in search …

You rise to a meadow of dew,
You shine forth purity,
You stream forth nectar.
   Peace, Peace.

God almighty is the true King,
He traverses the heavens.

Has God come down?
Has God come down?

The self forswears self satisfaction,
Destroys understanding,
Destroys the tilling.

You rain down kindness,
You rain down gentleness,
You rain down flames.

Light and wetness have taken on flesh,
Space filling
Incantations, the throat sings, tears
Fill our eyes, fill our silence, till the heart fills!

   Peace, Peace.

The voice hisses like a whisper, a message ...
The voice winks like a star, the eye of crystal dome ... says

"Sorrow not for what you have lost"

We shall not lose hope, My God, we Shall not lose hope.

"Rejoice not in what you have," it says ...

We will not rejoice, My God, we will not rejoice.

"We will assign two companions to each of you,
   and we will nurture light for you."

You give us two companions and you nurture ... we re-
      spond

Blessed be God, the king, the holy,

He is the Mighty, He is the Healer,
He is the Lord, He is the Ever-Here.

His hand is raised like the blade of a sword,
Has the announcer confirmed?

   Peace, Peace.

Is the Heir blessed? Is the all-seeing sworn?

You kneel with waves,
You run with trees,
You weep with valleys,
You genuflect with mountains.
Peace, Peace.

You shout with the waves ...

He is the creator,
Has the all powerful decreed?

He is the just,
   He has gathered.

Has the glorious entrusted?
Has God mandated?

                    —*Translated from the Arabic by Huda Naamani*
                          and Solomon I. Sara

Fadwa Tuqan

(1917–)

FADWA TUQAN WAS BORN in Nablus, Palestine. Her poetry collections include *I Have Found Her* (1958); *Give Us Love* (1960); *The Guerrilla and the Land* (1968); *Night and the Knights* (1969); *Alone on Top of the World* (1973); and *The Nightmare of Night and Day* (1974). Although most of her early poems deal with love, she has also written more directly about Palestine in poems like "Call of the Earth" and "Dream of Remembrance." The latter deals with the death of brothers killed in action. After 1967, she focused more on the West Bank and Gaza.

Dedicated to the spirit of the martyrs—Dalal al-Maghribi and her companions—the following poem uses the image of the bird and nature to speak not of the death and destruction of war but of the sacrifices and heroism of women that will bring peace and an end to suffering. In Tuqan's poem, the poet watches the bird soaring up out of the gloom and sees morning light on the house.

The Gull and the Negation of the Negation

Crossing the horizon, it cut the gloom
On wings of light, it controlled the blue
It wheeled and turned and kept on turning
It knocked at my dark window, and the stunned silence
    trembled:
Is all well, O Bird?
Disclosing the secret, it said not a word
Then disappeared.

⤙ ⤙ ⤙

O Bird of mine, Bird of the sea, I now know
When times are difficult and inert in the vaults of silence
All things move
Seeds grow in the heart of death

Dawn breaks out of darkness
Now I know,
As I hear horses running, the race of death on the shores,
That when the flood comes
This is how the earth washes away its griefs.

O Bird of the sea soaring out of the depths of the gloom
May God grant you goodness
Now I know
Something happened ... The horizon cleared and morning
  light
Greeted the house.

—Translated from the Arabic by Miriam Cooke

Razia Hussain

(1938–   )

RAZIA HUSSAIN WAS BORN in the Dhaka area of Bengal that became East Pakistan in 1947. After a bitter and violent struggle with the West Pakistan troops that were stationed in East Pakistan, the area became Bangladesh in 1971. The poet is a peace activist and an active participant in the struggle for women's rights in Bangladesh.

The war and violence depicted in "The Sound of Leaves" surrounds the narrator. The struggle is not carried out on a far battlefield but on her own land. But the motherland, the earth itself, which is the setting and stage of the war, also offers the poet hope for a new beginning in the sound of the leaves and the sight of the sky. The documentation of the horrors of war in this poem are interwoven with the promise of life and peace. Neither the poet nor the earth, which is being torn apart in the battle to possess her, submit passively to war.

The Sound of Leaves

War, only war, all twelve
months of the year. Our eyes
are cactus plants,
the thorns growing inward
to pierce our
tenderest nerves.

War, only war.
The orchids on the wall,
the ceiling-fan's whirl overhead,
all suffocate me.
Man sheds civilization
like a snakeskin
and bares the horror
of his naked face.

North, south, east, west—
no white-horsed hero
from the legends
will come to rescue us.

Each corner of the sky
is pushed down into darkness,
into the mush of rotting corpses
working their poison
on the air. Breath drowns
in this blind sea named time.

Still, sometimes the sound of leaves
makes me open my eyes to the sky.
Again, the mind begins to build its nest
among quiet wings,
the shadow of the shal tree
falls green
over my house
over the smell
of this warm, wet earth.

—*Translated from the Bengali by Chitra Divakaruni*

Attia Hosain

(1913–)

ATTIA HOSAIN WAS BORN in Lucknow, India. She received a liberal English education at the Isabella Thoburn College and a traditional Muslim education at home. In her twenties, she was influenced by the nationalist movement, and she became a journalist and broadcaster. In 1947, she moved to England, where she has worked for the British Broadcasting Corporation (BBC). She is the author of a collection of short stories, titled *Phoenix Fled and Other Stories* (1953), and a novel titled *Sunlight on a Broken Column* (1961).

Surviving the sufferings experienced during war often involves making a deliberate effort to remember and document the experiences and emotions, but it also often involves trying to forget, maybe even deny, the experiences. In "After the Storm," a little girl tries in vain to suppress her fragmented, tortured memories of violence and the disappearance of her mother and her protectress, through her everyday actions as a servant. Dressed in cast-off clothes, wearing glass bangles that are gifts from her mistress, she remembers her old gold earrings and the gold bangles that her mother had promised her before the war.

After the Storm

The flowers were awkwardly crowded into the small-necked bottle. Its paper label had not been successfully washed away and triumphantly survived in its scratched mutilation.

On and around the bottle there was dust. There was a film of the dust on everything. It crept up with the hot wind that found its way into the room in spite of shut doors and windows. Green paper on glass panes shut out the glare that burned away colour from earth and sky and the sensual delight of vision from the eyes.

The heavy sweet scent of the flowers reached out into the skin-drying air with a cooling touch. The flowers were white and wax-petalled among thick deep green leaves. Their buds were tight, wrapped in slender pale green sepals. They were allies in the battle against the cruel

summer—lying cool on hot pillows—around earthenware water pots—
strung in garlands sold in scented streets by singing men—adorning
women when gold and silver grew heavy with heat and sweat.

This summer the battle was lost before it began. The desolation it
brought was the visible expression of desolate hearts. The tainted wind
blew hot from blazing homes, and carried the dust of devastated fields,
and the dead. ...

She tore me out of the shroud of my thoughts, a child small and thin
with serious anxious eyes and a smile on her face, a garland in her hand.
She looked at the bottle and the flowers.

'Do you like them? I put them there. This is for you too.' I bent my
head and she slipped the garland over with a faint smile and stepped
back.

'I knew you were coming today and I cleaned your room.'

'Who are you?'

'Your servant. I've been put in charge of this part of the house,' she
said with proud responsibility.

'What is your name?'

'Bibi.'

'How long have you been here?'

'A long time. Just before I left home there was the fair at Shahji's tomb.'
She sounded uninterested, then said brightly: 'Do you need anything?
The others are all sleeping. You rest and then I shall bring you some tea. I
have put cold water for your bath in the buckets.'

'Weren't the buckets heavy?'

'Oh no—I always brought water from the well.'

I could not tell her age. Her assured manner made me feel younger
than herself. Her eyes had no memories of a childhood. Her body was of
a child of nine or ten, but its undernourished thinness was deceptive;
she could have been eleven or twelve. There was no telling of how many
years of childhood life had robbed her.

She came every morning with flowers no one else cared to pick and
every evening with garlands no one else cared to thread.

'Aren't they pretty? In my home we had two big bushes near the well. I
made garlands for my mother and aunt.'

The nails of her peasant hands were worn with work. By now I knew
her story, but knew she had to tell it herself how and when she willed.

'Had you any brothers and sisters?'

'After my sister was married she went to live far away; a whole day's
journey by bullock cart. My brother was older than me. He could read
and write. He was clever. You will teach me, won't you?'

She kept her clothes very clean—old discarded clothes which were cut
down for her and hung loosely on her. She wore tight pyjamas that were
easier to clean than loose ones, and she kept her head covered like the

older women, the 'dupatta' that was made from torn cotton sari. She used to dye them herself and was fond of bright colours. Her hair was combed back smoothly from a centre part, oiled and plaited with a rag. The pigtail was short and stood out stiffly. She was not a pretty child, and one would not have noticed her. But she was now a symbol and around her hovered the ghosts of all one feared.

Sometimes she threaded buds into the pierced lobes of her ears.

'I had gold earrings,' she said proudly, but with no reproach. 'My mother said after the next harvest she would buy me gold bangles. When we had feasts I was sorry I had no bangles.'

I had bought her glass ones.

When she brought me tea she said:

'Do you like these English cakes? My mother made such lovely halwa—you would have loved it.'

'Do you remember your father?'

'He died long ago. We lived with my uncle and aunt. He kept labourers to help in the fields.'

⭐   ⭐   ⭐

One day she suddenly put her head on my lap—'I like you. Will you always keep me with you?'

Then I asked her: 'Bibi—how did you come here?'

I wanted to lay to rest my ghosts of imagined horror, and hear her tell me what actually happened.

'The police brought me. I was at the railway station. Then they took me to a place where there were lots of women and children. I ran away from them.'

'Why?'

'I don't know. I got up at night and ran away. Then I came here.'

'Who brought you?'

'The police.'

Her mind refused to fill the gap between the refugee camp and her adoption.

'What happened to your mother?'

Her voice was self-detached—a child telling a fairy story. 'I don't know. I was with Chand Bibi. I had gone to visit her.'

'Who was she?'

'Oh, she was brave. She had a big house where I played. She fought and fought and killed so many of them—then her arm was cut off.'

'Where was your mother?'

'At home. They said the house was full of blood. They said Chand Bibi kept on fighting until her arm was cut off.'

'Who said?'

'Some people—I ran into the fields and a man said "Come this way," and he carried me, we hid in the sugar cane—then he put me on a train, and I came here. See how long this garland is. You can put it twice round your neck.'

In the bottle she had put fresh flowers.

Shukria Raad

(1943–   )

DAUGHTER OF THE LAST emir (or king) of Bukhara, Shukria Raad was born in Kabul, Afghanistan. Her father died when she was one year old, and her mother had to sell her jewelry so as to be able to educate Raad and her sister. She earned her B.A. in journalism in 1964 from the University of Kabul and, fourteen years later, her M.A. in Old Persian linguistics from Delhi University.

During the intervening fourteen years she traveled to Germany, Australia, and the United States to gain firsthand experience in journalism and broadcasting. From 1968 until 1974, she became editor in chief of a children's magazine and then of *Zhwan Doon* (Life), Afghanistan's only weekly political magazine. Throughout that period, she was writing regularly for women's pages in both *Anis* and *Islah* as well as writing series for the *Family Life* program of Radio Afghanistan. While in Delhi, India, she worked for All-India Radio as an announcer and translator. In 1978, she was appointed director general of Television Films in Afghanistan, a post she had to abandon when the Soviets invaded in 1980. After the invasion, she fled to America, where she has worked in the Daree and Urdu programs of the Voice of America (VOA). She has received several awards, including the VOA Excellence in Programming Award in 1985 and 1990.

In "Tears of Joy," a boy who was orphaned during the Soviet occupation of Afghanistan finds his mother.

Tears of Joy

Akram Kahn, the teacher of Jamal Orphanage in Peshawar, was talking to the students:

"Boys. Tomorrow is Friday, and as you all know, once again we are going to send you to see your relatives in town. The bus will leave at exactly eight fifteen from in front of the entrance, exactly eight fifteen. Let me tell you once again that at four P.M., four P.M. sharp, you must be back in front of that bakery. Do not be late!"

Every Friday morning, the boys of this orphanage were taken to the city, to Peshawar, to meet their friends and distant relatives.

Their closest relatives—mothers, fathers, sisters and brothers—all had died in the war.

So their only happiness was to go to the city to see their friends. It had taken them a long time to find these former neighbors and friends from their villages, from back home. At least, a look at a familiar face.

Nazar Mohamad was six years old when they brought him to this orphanage. He was the youngest one. He had nobody. They said that one day when Nazar Mohamad, along with other boys, was playing near the hill, their village was bombed by Soviet planes. They said that Nazar Mohamad's mother and father, his brothers and his little baby sister were all killed. Their mud house collapsed on them—that small mud house, which had been their home for such a long time, became their grave.

Nazar Mohamad never talked much unless he was spoken to. Whenever he was asked something, he looked down to avoid looking into the eyes of the person who asked the question. Then, slowly rubbing the palm of his right hand against his head, he would talk about them.

He talked about his father, about his brothers—especially about his older brother Akbar, the one he thought was the bravest—never afraid of anything. Whenever he mentioned his mother, you could notice a smile on the corner of his lips.

Nazar Mohamad's deep, dark eyes and his smile made him popular among the boys. Everybody knew his story, the story of his life, so short and so sad. He had lost every member of his family at once. Not only that, but he could not find anybody he knew in all the refugee camps of the area.

Nazar Mohamad wanted to go to the city too. It would be a nice change for him. The bus would take him. Akram Kahn was going to accompany the boys. The teacher told him, "You just go with the boys but do not wander off by yourself. Stay with Akram Khan."

The next day, on Friday, two teachers, one of whom was Mr. Akram Khan, as usual accompanied the boys on their trip to the crowded city. The bus dropped them off at the Gulzar bakery. Akram Khan gave all the instructions and told them to be back at four P.M., exactly at four.

Nazar Mohamad never went with the other kids; he always walked with Akram Khan.

Akram Khan would take him shopping and buy him a pen, or candy, or something.

Akram Khan and Nazar Mohamad were the first ones to reach the bus in front of the bakery. They both looked tired.

They got on the bus and sat on the same seats they had sat on in the morning. Akram Khan opened a box of batteries and got busy putting them into his transistor radio.

At four-forty everybody was finally back, and the bus started to move.

The bus could not move fast. The narrow street was far too crowded.

The boys were all tired. Most of them had closed their eyes. Some of them were sleeping, and some pretended to be asleep.

Nazar Mohamad was still looking out of the bus window. He wanted to enjoy every minute of this trip.

Suddenly, he shouted so loud that everybody jumped up, especially Akram Khan, who was sitting next to him.

He was shouting, "Stop the bus! Stop it! Please stop it!"

The bus driver looked in the cracked mirror and asked what to do.

Akram Khan stood up, walked forward, and ordered the driver to stop. Nazar Mohamad kept on shouting incomprehensibly.

He was crying—or was he laughing?—It was not clear what.

He pushed the door of the bus open, jumped out, and started to run.

Akram Khan got out too, He was bewildered, thinking that the only reason for such behavior would be that he dropped the two-color ballpoint pen Akram Khan had bought him that day.

Now all the boys were looking from the windows of the bus. They too were puzzled about why Nazar Mohamad was running so fast, his small body boring through the moving crowd of bearded men and veiled women. Then they saw that also in the crowd a woman was running, crying, pushing everyone aside as she rushed toward Nazar Mohamad.

They met, reached out to each other, and hugged. Their tears ran down their faces, past their smiling lips. The crowd stopped, and men and women stood there watching, forming a circle around them.

And so Nazar Mohamad found his mother. She had just arrived from Torkham on the Afghan border with a new truck-load of refugees.

—Translated from the Pushto by Shukria Raad

Ismat Chugtai

(1915–1991)

ONE OF THE BEST KNOWN and most widely translated women writers of
Urdu fiction, Ismat Chugtai taught in a girls' school in Bareilly and then
went on to train as a teacher at Aligarh Muslim University. Her literary
career began in 1938 with the publication of her short story, "Fasadi"
(sometimes translated as "The Trouble Maker"), in the journal *Saqui.*
When the story was published, some people declared that it was not
Ismat but her brother, Azim Baigh Chugtai, already established as an important writer, who was the real author of "Fasadi." During the 1940s, the
years of the Indian Independence movement, Ismat Chugtai was a
member of the Progressive Writers Association, an organization of writers who used their works to fight for political and social freedom and
justice.

Chugtai's works usually portray women and children who spend their
lives trying to overcome socioeconomic barriers or physical disabilities.
In "Two Hands," a poor soldier returns home without medals or glory
and resumes his former life of servitude. He accepts his wife and her illegitimate child over the remonstrations of his rich employer. It is not war,
the life of a soldier, or even a question of paternity that is important for
this ex-soldier; it is the possibility of having two more hands to help him
earn the family living that matters to him.

Two Hands

Ramavatar was returning home from the war. Mehtarani, the old woman
who cleaned our toilets, came with a letter to father to have it read to
her. Ramavatar was discharged. Finally the war was over and after three
years Ramavatar was coming home. Old Mehtarani's dirty eyes glistened
with tears. She was filled with a sense of gratitude and touched everybody's feet as though they had something to do with Ramavatar's return
back to his home.

She must have been fifty years old but looked seventy. She had delivered ten children, some of them premature, in her youth. Out of all of

them only Ramavatar survived, with great difficulties and prayers. Only a year after his marriage he was drafted. Mehtarani tried her best to save him from going to the front, but all in vain. When Ramavatar came to bid goodbye to her in his uniform, she was greatly impressed by his grand appearance. For her he was no less than a colonel.

The servants were smiling in anticipation of the commotion which would follow Ramavatar's arrival. Everyone was eagerly looking forward to his return. Ramavatar did not go to war to perform active duty. Nonetheless, while he cleaned the soldiers' toilets, some of their pride had rubbed off on him. Perhaps in his khaki uniform he wouldn't be the same old Ramavatar. It would be impossible for him to listen to the scandalous behavior of his wife Gori and contain his feelings of anger and mortification.

How bashful Gori was when she came here as a bride! As long as Ramavatar was here, she would cover herself with a heavy veil, and nobody ever saw her face in the daylight. When Ramavatar had to leave for the war, she had grieved bitterly as if she were becoming a lifelong widow. Granted, for some time, she went about her work carrying her basket of filth, her eyes swollen from weeping. But slowly and gradually her veil began to shrink.

Some said the springtime was to blame entirely, but others said Gori was a woman of loose conduct to begin with. The trouble started soon after Ramavatar's departure. She laughed all the time and moved about with a swinging gait. When she passed by, carrying her basket on her hip and making music with her bracelets, she made people uncomfortable. The bar of soap would slip from Dhobi's palms into the trough. The cook could not keep his eye on the chapati on the griddle. The man who used to fetch water would let his bucket slide all the way down the well. The peon's starched and pinned turban somehow got loose and hung down his neck.

At the servants' quarters, people froze when this femme fatale arrived, darting her arrow-like glances from inside her veil. Then suddenly they would wake up with a start and make fun of each other for acting so foolishly.

Observing their men's attitude, the washerman's wife would smash the pot of starch angrily, the peon's wife would beat on the child clinging to her breast for no fault of his own, and all of a sudden the cook's wife would have a bout of hysteria.

The word 'gori' means fair complexioned, but Ramavatar's wife Gori was fair only in name. In fact, she was dark complexioned, like the backside of the griddle, smooth and glistening. She had wide nostrils and a generous mouth. No one in her family ever cleaned their teeth and even the liberal use of kohl couldn't hide the squint in her right eye. Her waist did not have a particularly attractive swing to it as she walked, and one could see that she was getting plenty of leftovers to eat. She had wide hoof-like toes. The smell of rancid oils hung around her. But despite all this, when she threw an arrow of a glance, it never missed its mark. And yes, her voice was extremely captivating. At festivals she would sing in her sweet, lilting voice, quite different from the rest.

As soon as Ramavatar left for the war, old Mehtarani, her mother-in-law, treated her badly. For no reason at all she would call her names, just to keep her in line. She would follow Gori to keep an eye on her. But now the old woman could not keep up. She had been carrying filth for the last forty years and this had put a permanent arch to her back. It was she who had buried the afterbirth residual sacks when we were born. As soon as Mother would go into labor, she would come and sit at the steps and at times call out to the lady doctor offering some piece of advice. She would bring charms and amulets and tie them to the bed to ward off evil. She had quite a respectable position in our household.

It was strange to understand why suddenly everyone began to detest the daughter-in-law of such a popular old Mehtarani! It was even more amazing that these feelings were not contained within the servants' quarters; even my sisters-in-law did not like to see her around. If my sister-in-law suspected that Gori was sweeping the room where my brother was sitting, she would snatch her breast away from her child's mouth and rush to the spot, lest Gori be casting a spell on her husband when nobody was around. People behaved as if Gori were nothing but a long-horned, dangerous animal at large. They clung to their fragile glassware with both arms to protect it.

When the situation became unbearable, the women of the servicemen's quarters came with their petition to see Mother. Heated discussions ensued concerning the danger of Gori's presence and its consequences. A committee was formed to protect husbands. My sisters-in-law enthusiastically participated in the voting and Mother was elected president.

The women took their position according to their status, some sitting on little stools, some on the edge of the bed and some on the carpet. Pieces of betel leaves were passed around and the old Mehtarani was summoned. Women forced their breasts in their children's mouths to maintain silence in the meeting. The court was in session.

"Why, you wretch, why have you given so much freedom to your beloved Gori? The bitch has made our lives miserable! What do you have in mind? What are you waiting for? Do you want to bring shame to this house?" Mehtarani had a million grievances of her own. These words were the last straw. She burst out, "What am I to do, Begum Saheba? I beat her up and I gave her no food to eat, but really I can't control her."

"Do you think she would starve if you did not give her bread?" the cook's wife said tauntingly. She was from an old established family of

chefs in Saharanpur and was the cook's third wife, and yet she was unhappy. All the wives were unhappy, the peon's wife, the gardener's wife,
the washerman's wife; together these women imbued the courtroom
with gravity. Poor Mehtarani! She just sat there scratching her diseased
calves and listened to their barrage.

At last she said, "Begum Saheba, I shall do exactly as you tell me. But
am I to strangle the wretch?" This vision brought great pleasure to the
women; they could all identify with her feelings and sympathize with
her. Mother suggested, "Send the mischief maker to her mother's
house." "Begum Saheba, how can this be possible?" Mehtarani explained that according to the rules of her community, one has to give a
lot of money to bring the bride home. Mehtarani's family had to sacrifice
their entire life's savings, every penny of it, to bring Gori here. For the
same money they could have bought two healthy cows yielding enough
milk for all; whereas all Gori knew was how to kick up a row. If she were
sent away to her father's he would promptly sell her off to another man.
Furthermore, she was more than just an ornament for her husband's
bed. With her two hands she managed to accomplish the work of four
men. When Ramavatar left, could old Mehtarani manage all that work by
herself? Thanks to Gori's two hands, life was quite comfortable for
Mehtarani in her old age.

The women were no fools. They realized that they were no longer ad-
dressing a moral issue but one pertaining to economics, and obviously
the old woman couldn't survive without her daughter-in-law. Who
would be foolish enough to throw two hundred rupees down the drain?
Aside from the two hundred rupees, one had to take into account the ex-
penditure of the marriage feast to satisfy the community. Who would
provide for all these expenses? Ramavatar's entire salary was spent to
pay the debt incurred at the time of his wedding. Due to inflation, today
a healthy wife like Gori would cost no less than four hundred rupees. After cleaning the entire mansion, she worked for four other houses in the
neighborhood! She might have other faults, but she certainly was very
efficient.

"Whatever the case," Mother warned her, "You had better take steps
to resolve the issues immediately, or Gori will not be permitted to live
within the compound walls of the mansion."

The old woman pleaded and begged. She went home and honored
Gori with the choicest abuses; she seized her by the hair and beat her up.
After all, wasn't Gori all paid for! She continued to grumble through the
day, and the next day she vengefully created even more work for her.

The cook, the man who brought water to the mansion, the washerman, and the peon, they all beat their wives up when they found out
what they had been up to. Even my stuck-up sisters-in-law had a tiff
with their respectable husbands. Telegrams were dispatched to their

parents' homes. To make a long story short, Gori became a porcupine's quill for the whole household, which had been tranquil until now.

Four days after this, Mehtarani's nephew came to see his aunt and stayed on. He began to help with the work of four additional mansions in the neighborhood. This was better than what he did before. His wife had not yet come of age and still lived at her parents' house. The ceremony which would bring about the consummation of his marriage had not been performed yet, and, therefore, Ratiram used to roam about aimlessly in his village.

Ratiram's arrival greatly improved the mood of the mansion, as if the strong winds had shattered and dispelled their dark and terrible gloom. Nobody heard Gori's musical laughter anymore. Her bracelets did not jingle now. It was as if the blimp had lost its air. Once again her veil got longer and longer. The untamed animal had been transformed into a bashful bride. The women sighed in relief. Even when the men in the servants' quarters teased her she shied away. If they made a pass at her she would signal at Ratiram from her veil and he would immediately come and hang around her, scratching his arms. The old woman now sat peacefully at the threshold pulling at her hooka, gazing around with half-closed eyes. An air of peace filled the hearts of the women in the compound as if the pus had been removed from the wound.

However, this time the menfolk of the mansion joined hands to create a new front against Gori. The cook who used to force all kinds of delicacies on Gori now began to scold her for not cleaning the gutters. The washerman complained that whenever he washed clothes and put them on the line to dry, she would come to raise the dust with her broom. The peon ordered her to sweep the men's quarters several times a day and still wasn't satisfied with the job she did. Before, the water fetcher used to be ready to carry as much water as she wanted for her to wash her hands. Now he completely ignored her pleas to sprinkle water in the yard to prevent the dust from settling on the drying clothes, so that the washerman could call her all kinds of obscene names for dirtying them.

Gori put her head down and worked silently, never responding to the vicious circle around her. But when she went home, who knows what she told her mother-in-law? The old woman would make enough noise to make people uncomfortable. In her view, Gori had changed into a pious and good woman.

Then one day the chief of staff came to our mansion to pay his respects to Father. Yes, the same one with a long beard who is the head of all servicemen. Supposedly he used to be quite informal with Father. He told Father the terrible story of the illicit relationship of Gori and that rascal Ratiram. The scandal had brought shame to the entire community of servicemen who worked and lived within our compound. Father handed over the case to the sessions, which means he dropped it in

Mother's lap. Once more the women's court was in session and the old woman was summoned and verbally undressed.

"You old hag, do you even know what games your wretched daughter-in-law is playing?" Mehtarani blinked around innocently as if she couldn't even guess who was being referred to. Thereupon she was informed in no uncertain terms that there were eyewitnesses who testified to the indecent relationship of Gori and Ratiram. They were caught redhanded in a shameful condition.

The women had expected her to show some sign of gratitude to her wellwishers, but on the contrary the old Mehtarani became very angry and upset with them. She began to threaten and scream that if only Ramavatar were here he would take care of those who uttered such false accusations about his innocent wife. Mehtarani claimed that Gori constantly wept because she missed Ramavatar so much. She worked so hard. She didn't give anybody reason to complain. She didn't even flirt anymore. People had turned against her unjustly.

The women of the compound tried their best to convince her but Mehtarani beat her breast and insisted that the vindictive people only wanted her life. She said she didn't have any idea why people were doing this to them. What in the world had they done to deserve this? She did not associate much with other servicemen and their families. She was everybody's confidant and she never divulged anybody's secret to others.

She said that she was not particularly fond of taking advantage of people's weaknesses. Didn't she know all that happened in people's back yards? Nobody could hide their secrets from a Mehtarani. These old hands had buried the sins of many a respectable person. If these hands had wished to, they could have toppled the thrones of a few queens. But no, she didn't hold any grudges against anyone. Only if her own life were in jeopardy, she might make a mistake or two, but otherwise she would let no cat out of the bag.

Well, nobody had the guts to challenge her statement. Who doesn't have a skeleton in his closet? And so they relented. The women competed with each other in defending her. Whatever Gori might do, their own forts were secure, so why bellyache?

For awhile there was no gossip about Gori's love affair and things appeared to have calmed down, though a few nosey people smelled a rat— a rat which even Gori's plump figure couldn't hide any longer. People renewed their efforts to counsel the old woman, but this new topic failed to get the woman's attention. She pretended to have lost her hearing completely. Mostly she would stay in bed and order Gori and Ratiram around. Once in a blue moon, she came out of the house to sit in the sun, and on those occasions Gori and Ratiram would bend over backwards to please her as if she were a great queen.

Respectable ladies repeatedly tried to tell her to get rid of Ratiram and have Gori treated before Ramavatar came back. Undoubtedly, Mehtarani was an expert in these matters and the whole thing would only take a couple of days, but the old woman would not respond to these suggestions. On the contrary, at these occasions she would go off on a tangent and complain that her arthritis was getting worse and worse and that the people at the mansions were eating a lot of fatty foods and as a result someone or other always had diarrhea.

Her reluctance to recognize the issue at stake really annoyed her friends. They said, "Agreed that your daughter-in-law is young. She is innocent and naive. Even women born in noble families make mistakes. But when this happens, a mother-in-law should not look the other way and ignore the issue completely."

All this good counsel was ineffective because for some reason the old woman had totally lost her sense of propriety. Had she wished, she could have dumped the nagging problem very easily in the bottom of a garbage can, but no, she chose to look the other way and let it grow.

Mehtarani waited for Ramavatar's return eagerly. She would threaten people saying she would tell Ramavatar about their teasing her and then he would deal with them. And now Ramavatar was coming home from the war alive! Everybody awaited his arrival with bated breath and looked forward to the entertainment in would inevitably bring.

To the community's chagrin, when Gori gave birth to a son, instead of giving her poison, the old woman grinned from ear to ear. It did not surprise her in the least bit to get a grandson two full years after the departure of her son. She went from door to door demanding old clothes and congratulations. Her friends tried to tell her that according to the calculations it was impossible for the baby to be Ramavatar's son, but the old woman refused to listen to them. According to her calculations, Ramavatar was taken to the war-front in the rainy season. It was then that she had slipped in the European style toilet of the yellow mansion. Now it was winter and she had suffered a sunstroke the summer before. She had barely survived by the skin of her teeth. Since that fall, her knees began to ache more and more. The doctor was a scoundrel to be sure. He mixed chalk powder in her medicine. She would completely go off track and babble nonsense. Nobody could make her address the issue she had decided to overlook.

When the boy was born, she had a letter dictated for Ramavatar. "After love and kisses, let Ramavatar know that all is well here and we pray to God for your well being. A grandson is born in your house so consider this letter to be a telegram and return as soon as possible."

People thought that this was sure to make Ramavatar's blood boil in anger. Their hopes were dampened when Ramavatar wrote back that he was bringing back booties and clothes for the baby. The war had come to an end and he was just about to come home. The old woman rocked her grandson on her knee and considered herself as lucky as a queen. What a way to grow old! The business was running smooth as silk. The interest on the loan was being paid regularly and to top it off, she had a grandson on her knee!

People had thought to themselves, "Well, when Ramavatar finally arrives and finds out the truth, then we will watch the fun." And now Ramavatar was coming home after the victory. After all, he was a soldier and had every right to foam at the mouth with rage. Their hearts beat with excitement. The air at the servants' quarters was abuzz. People expected at least a few murders and they looked forward to seeing Ramavatar cut the nose of his wife or mother.

When the boy was about a year old, Ramavatar arrived. The entire staff was up in the air. The cook put a whole lot of water in the pan so he could watch the show without having to worry about burning his dish. The washerman removed the pot of starch from the stove and put it aside, and the water-carrier tossed away his pot as well. As soon as the old woman saw Ramavatar, she clung to his waist and began to wail aloud. The next minute she put the boy in his lap and laughed as if she had never cried.

Ramavatar looked at the baby proudly as though he himself were its father. He quickly opened his suitcase and began to pull out the presents. People thought he was looking for a knife or a weapon, but when he got the red shirt and yellow shoes out for the boy, it was as if their own manhoods were challenged. Shame on him! The rascal, he only pretends to be a soldier. In reality he is just a eunuch!

And Gori? She was so bashful, just like a newly wed bride. She brought a large brass bowl full of water, removed Ramavatar's foul smelling military boots, and washed his feet.

People told Ramavatar the whole story, they taunted him and called him all kinds of names, but he just grinned as if he did not understand what they were telling him. In the meantime, Ratiram had left to bring his wife from her parents' place.

People were more angry than surprised at Ramavatar's shameful conduct. Even Father, who usually kept himself detached from his staff's affairs, got involved. Employing his own legal skill, Father now prepared to convince Ramavatar.

"Haven't you been away for three years?"

"I do not know exactly, sir, more or less ... it must be."

"And your child is one year old."

"He seems to be, but your honor, he has become very mischievous," Ramavatar replied, a little embarrassed.

"Come on. Can't you calculate?"

"Calculate? What should I calculate, Sir?" Ramavatar replied meekly.

"You clown, how could this be possible?"

"Now how am I supposed to know this? Children are God's bounty."

"Hum ... God's gift! You bonehead! This bastard cannot be yours."

When Father tried very hard to convince Ramavatar that the child was a bastard, he seemed a little convinced. Then he spoke in a very humble tone like a fool, "What am I supposed to do now, sir? I did beat up my wife severely." He balked, a little irritated.

"You are such an idiot ... why do you not throw the wench out?"

"Sir, how can I possibly do this?" Ramavatar began to plead.

"Why not?"

"Who will give me about three hundred rupees for a second engagement and another two hundred rupees to prepare a feast for our community?"

"Why do you have to feed the entire community again? Why should you have to pay for Gori's loose conduct?"

"This I do not know, Sir. Such are our customs."

"But I tell you Ramavatar, this child is not yours. He belongs to that bastard Ratiram," Father said dejectedly.

"What of it! Ratiram is my cousin! He is no stranger. He is my own flesh and blood."

"You are really stupid." Father lost his temper.

"Sir, when the boy will get older, he will help me out with his two hands," Ramavatar gently reasoned with Father. "He will succor, and in my old age I will seek comfort in him." Ramavatar bent his head low in shame. Suddenly, for some reason, Father also hung his head along with Ramavatar. Millions of pairs of hands seemed to cover the horizon of his thoughts. These hands were neither legitimate nor illegitimate. They were hands, alive, pulsating, busily cleaning the filth off the face of the earth. These two hands carried the majesty of Ramavatar's old age. They were adorning the earth with vermillion; these little, dust-stained, black hands.

—Translated from the Urdu by Naseem A. Hines

Ghodsi Ghazinur
(1943–)

GHODSI GHAZINUR WAS BORN in Lahijan (a northern city in Iran) in 1943. She is a widely read author of children's stories who lives in Iran. "Aboud's Drawings" was published in 1981.

Included in this anthology are stories of children who lose their homes and their families due to war, children who remember their terrifying experiences, and children who cannot or will not remember. "Aboud's Drawings" shows a child's courage and integrity. He refuses to join his peers in war games inspired by the Iran-Iraq War of 1980–1988 and insists that they all paint instead. One wonders if this story was written specifically for children since Ghazinur is a children's writer.

Aboud's Drawings

The twelfth person stood next to the others along the wall on the lefthand side of the alley. The rest of the boys were standing along the wall across from them. Mohsen and I were chosen by a drawing to pick our team-mates. We were going to play the "war" game.

The trouble started when the two teams were selected: one team was to play the Iraqi, and the other the Iranian soldiers; but neither team wanted to play the enemy.

We decided to pick the teams from scratch.

This did not solve the problem, either, since none of the boys wanted to be an Iraqi soldier. We tried casting lots, but everyone was willfully against it. Then we decided that smart and agile boys play the Iranian soldiers and lumpish, sluggish boys, the Iraqi soldiers.

"Then Javad, who is both a good student and the monitor of his class, should be an Iranian soldier and Mahmoud. ... " Mohsen began.

Akbar interrupted him, protesting that: "Who said being the class monitor makes you a good guy? Aside from Javad, monitors are all spies. They constantly watch us, and just to get some brownie points, they give our names to the superintendent so we get beat up."

"Let's ask the boys," Mohsen said. "Whoever is chosen by everyone will be an Iranian soldier and whoever we determine unworthy will be an enemy soldier."

But things were not as easy as we had expected. We were all friends; there was no reason to look for weak points in each other. We wouldn't be able to call this a game anymore.

We finally decided to arrange a race: the first twelve boys to reach the electric pole would be the Iranian soldiers and the rest the Iraqi ones.

Now we needed a referee. Akbar suggested one of the boys accept the job and in return for this favor he would be allowed to be an Iranian soldier. We consented.

"Look boys," Ali said. "Since Javad's brother is now fighting at the war front, let's make him the referee."

"My brother is due at the front any day now," I said anxiously.

The boys protested simultaneously, "But he hasn't gone yet. Anyway, everyone's brother is eventually going."

Finally, Javad was elected and we took our places along the line. Everyone was anxious. We were so nervous that we could hear our own heartbeats. Some of the boys were stalling; we were getting ready for a big race. Javad blew the whistle as we all stood straight. He counted, "One … two … three … "

We shot off like arrows. I don't know how long we ran but when Javad blew into the whistle again, my hand touched the post. Some boys were still far behind. The twelve of us who had made it to the post first were relieved. Our faces beamed as we moved towards the left wall and stood there like we had just won a war; the rest of the boys dragged themselves towards the other wall and stood there with lowered chins. They looked as if they were about to be hanged. Some of them leaned their backs against the wall and some shrank back like frightened geese. They glowered, as if they had been given a harsh penalty.

The teams were finally organized. Two teams, one elated and one indignant, stood facing each other.

After a short meeting we decided to play in the alley to the north of our own, since it had ditches on both sides. Some said they were fixing the electricity, and some said it was the telephone cables they were working on. Whichever it was, we didn't care. What was important was that we could use the ditches for trenches. When we arrived there, it was three in the afternoon. A few workers wearing bandanas and loose Kurdish pants were working under the oppressive sun. A group of women, clad in black clothes, entered the alley and disappeared through an open door. We heard someone reciting verses from the Koran. Javad said:

"Hey, look kids, there's a canopy!" And he ran towards the curtained canopy to read the framed obituary of a recently deceased youth. When he returned, he said, "One of the boys in the neighborhood has been martyred at the front. He was nineteen years old. The canopy is for him."

We looked at one another. It would be too embarrassing to play in the alley. Our mere presence had already annoyed them. We returned to our alley, concluding that although we wouldn't have any trenches there, we were sure no one would bother us. All the neighborhood kids, except for the girls and the younger children, were playing this game. Besides, our parents wouldn't object to our noise, knowing that it meant fewer kids in the house.

Our neighborhood is one of the oldest and poorest in Tehran. Its alleys are long and narrow. Each house is inhabited by a dozen people. The houses remind me of a story I once heard about an old woman who lived in a house with a yard as big as a match-box and a tree as tall as a match stick. This is why even one person's absence from the house was a godsend, and in this case, there were two or three boys from each house involved in our game.

When we were back in our alley, my younger brother opened our door and suddenly jumped out, screaming, "I want to play, too."

"No way," I retorted. "Our game is only for older kids."

But he stood firm and said, "I'm older, too. I know all your games. I want to be in this one, too."

As hard as I tried I couldn't discourage him. I could have forced him to retreat with a cuff on the back of his neck, but I knew he would get my mother involved, so I gave in.

The boys exchanged pleading glances. There wasn't much they could do, so they consented.

"Go stand in the line of the Iraqi soldiers," I said grudgingly.

"What?" My brother asked unexpectedly.

"You heard what I said! We're playing the 'war' game, and you have to play an Iraqi soldier," I said.

"No, I won't be an Iraqi soldier!"

"Either do what I say, or get lost!"

And I gave him such a mean look that he obeyed me instantly. As he walked towards the line of the enemy soldiers, he looked like a mouse with its tail curled up on its back. But the game wasn't as simple as we had anticipated. It was a "war" game and war requires preparation. First of all, we needed guns and other equipment. Most importantly, we needed to build trenches. To prepare it all would take time. We sat down to do the necessary planning. We had to find gunny-sacks, plastic bags, tin cans, and buckets. We stuffed the gunny-sacks with anything we could get our hands on, from mud to the garbage left outside.

When the sandbags were finally made, it was already dark. We decided to take the sandbags home at night, so the garbage man wouldn't take them. We had to be careful about this; if anyone saw the sacks, they wouldn't last a twinkle of the eye. My mother had made us promise that we wouldn't take any junk or garbage inside the house. How could we convince her that these sacks that were stuffed with trash weren't garbage?

My brother and I tiptoed in, each carrying a sack, both shaking with excitement. We hid the sacks in a corner of the yard and then walked into the house, relieved. But we still needed guns. Each boy was to have his gun ready by the next day. My problem was that I had to make my gun without my brother seeing; after all, he was an enemy. I didn't want him to copy mine. But he was still very young and couldn't understand my logic. He begged me to make one for him, too.

"You want me to make you a gun so you can kill my friends?" I asked. "Make one yourself! It serves you right!"

"You're the one who made me an Iraqi soldier! I didn't have a choice," he said with tears coming to his eyes.

He was right. I had forced him to join the line of the enemy. Since I knew that he wouldn't make a good soldier anyway, I didn't argue with him and he didn't insist because he was afraid I would throw him out of the game altogether. Nevertheless, he looked so dejected that when my mother's eyes fell on him, she said, "What's wrong? You look like it's the end of the world."

My brother didn't respond. He just sniffled and looked at me indignantly, as if he had fought against the idea of being an Iraqi soldier all day long. In the morning my mother told him, "You eat so much junk that you can't sleep at night. You were having this nightmare about a war and having been taken for an Iraqi soldier. I'm not letting you have dinner from now on so you can rest at night."

I couldn't help feeling sorry. I knew he hadn't touched his food the night before.

After my brother fell asleep that night, I got to work. I found a piece of cardboard, drew a picture of a J-3 gun, cut the picture out in the dark with a pair of scissors I took out of my mother's sewing box, then I took the half-ready gun to my room and painted it black with a magic marker. It turned out perfect, My brother cried his eyes out when he saw my gun the next morning. My mother who had lost her patience with him bought him a squirt gun. but my brother kept on crying that that was not a gun and that he wanted a gun and my mother, not knowing what was going on, ignored him. Eventually she got disgusted and started beating him. I felt so sorry for him that I had to rescue him from her, in spite of the fact that he was an enemy, and make him understand that a handgun was as good as any gun in a war.

When he was calmer, he stuck his gun in his pajama pants. His wet, stained face made him look so pitiful that I decided to make a fake holster for his gun with a piece of cloth. I was trying very hard to see him as a brother and forget that he was an enemy. Having noticed the color of his gun for the first time, he said, "But brother, this gun is yellow!"

And tears filled his eyes again. I said, "So what if it's yellow?"

He bawled, "Whoever saw a real gun that's yellow? This is no good, it's made of plastic."

Reluctantly I painted his gun black with my magic marker.

At eight o'clock in the morning, all of us reported to our posts, each carrying a gun on the shoulder and a bag in hand. We got stationed and marked our sandbags so that they wouldn't get mixed up. Akbar remembered at the last minute that we didn't have flags. We decided to find fabric and make the flags ourselves. Mohsen and Javad were assigned to draw the flags of both countries so that the flags could be made accurately.

At night I asked my mother, "Will you give me some cloth?"

My mother said mechanically, "Did you cut your hand?"

I said, "No, I want it for our game."

She said astonishingly, "Good Lord! You've run out of all other games and now you want to play with dolls? The trouble is you have nothing to do. Get up and bring some oil for the Samovar."

To keep her from getting more resistant, I jumped quickly. I ran and filled the oil bottle and hurried back. When I handed the bottle to her, I said, "Now give me the cloth!"

"Shame on you! Don't you know only girls play with cloth?" she answered.

"Just give it to me, I need it!" I said.

Murmuring, she left and brought back a few pieces of cloth and dumped them in my palm. My brother, having felt left out, demanded, "I want some, too."

My mother said, "For God's sake! ... Look how they get on my nerves!"

But my brother kept insisting. My mother said, "Share it with each other!"

I thought to myself, "Sharing with an enemy? No way!" I said to my mother, "I won't share it. If you want him to have some, you give it to him."

My mother was shocked. "What do you mean?" she asked.

"Just do it yourself, will you?" I said.

Irritated, she took a couple of pieces and threw them at my brother.

When we went outside, we saw Akbar's sister, Akhtar, standing with the boys, stubbornly demanding that she be allowed to play, too.

A female soldier, in our game? No way! But Akhtar wasn't going to give in. Her mother, a worker in the local mill, had asked Akbar to help his sister with her math in the morning. Akhtar was threatening that if we didn't include her in the game, she would tell her Mom that Akbar was loose in the streets all morning instead of working with her.

We had to choose between including Akhtar in our game and giving up Akbar if his sister meant what she said. Mohsen, believing himself smarter than Akhtar, tried to dissuade her by saying, "Akhtar, it's not proper for a girl to play in the alley."

Akhtar boldly shot back, "The only thing improper about it is that it will make your clumsiness more apparent."

Mohsen blushed. Akbar glared at his sister but Akhtar dismissed his threats lightly, concluding that, "You don't want to play with me because I'm not a boy, otherwise you all know that I am more clever than you are."

She wasn't exaggerating; she was a spark of fire. She ran faster than a bullet. None of us could beat her. We were left with no choice. She imposed herself on us, and to top it off, she refused to be an enemy soldier. She joined the team I was on. When we collected the pieces of cloth everyone brought, we found we had a large pile of it. Akhtar agreed to sew our flag. She bragged that her sewing skills were superior to everyone else's in her class. We thought she was bluffing, but when the flags were ready, everyone stared at our flag admiringly. It was truly gorgeous. We were all set.

With the explosion of the fire-cracker Ali had set up, the war began. We stood at attention. When Akhtar's fireworks flashed into the sky, the shooting began.

Akhtar had saved these fireworks from the last holiday and she volunteered to use them provided that we let her set them off herself. We agreed grudgingly. We all issued gun-fire noises from our mouths. Some boys imitated the sound of grenades.

There were no casualties till noon, since no one wanted to leave the scene. The game went on non-stop. At noon we all went home for lunch. We declared a cease-fire as soon as we heard the usual calling of the faithful to prayer at noon. Later that afternoon, the boys showed up one by one in the line in front of the bakery. Only Akhtar, who stayed home to prepare lunch, and my younger brother, who stayed home to help my mother, were missing.

We all forgot that we were in two opposing armies. We joked around and laughed the whole time. But I got into an argument with my brother at lunch when he told my mother, "I want the same amount of food you give Morteza."

I mumbled, "You miserable, enemy spy! What are you counting my bites for?"

My older brother, who had just arrived, broke in angrily, "Aren't you ashamed to talk to your brother like that?"

The news came on the radio, "The Iraqi enemies bombed several houses in Ahvaz today."

"May God strike them dead. They've killed so many of our young boys and made our people homeless," my mother said.

And she turned to me and added, "THESE are the enemies, stupid ass, not your brother!"

It was almost three o'clock when we resumed our game. Most of the boys came early and the rest showed up one by one. We occupied our posts and sat there alert. I don't know what made Javad raise his head and stand straight all of a sudden. Taghi took advantage of this opportunity and shot at him. But Javad sat down again behind his trench, totally ignoring him, as if nothing had happened. Taghi's screams filled the air:

"You must drop, Javad! I hit you right in the head."

Javad jumped like a gamecock, saying, "Not a chance! It didn't touch me."

"You bet it did and you must drop right now!"

Their argument was getting out of hand. They were at each other's throats, when suddenly the door to Javad's house opened and his mother, who had stuck her head outside, called, "Javad!"

Javad answered her from his hiding place, "Yes!"

"Come here, right away! I need you."

Javad got up and walked towards his house. Taghi shot at him again. Javad started running and ran all the way to his house, while Taghi kept on screaming:

"What's he going to say now? I hit him."

Javad returned a few minutes later, walking leisurely. When he reached the middle of the alley, Taghi opened fire at him again. Javad didn't pay him the slightest attention, calmly sitting behind his trench. Taghi exploded, livid with rage. He jumped out of his trench, threw his gun on the ground indignantly, and screamed:

"You call this a war? You're all cheating. I'm not playing this stupid game."

"No way! It didn't hit me," Javad responded.

"You're saying that I missed when you were in the middle of the alley, too?" Taghi shouted angrily.

Javad, realizing the situation was getting sticky, said gently, "When someone has to leave his post to go to his house, the game has to stop, even if as you claim he is hit by the enemy."

We had to interfere; it was decided that from that point on if someone was hit he should drop, but instead of leaving the game, he could enter as a new soldier. No more sweat! We also decided that if someone had to leave to attend to something urgent, he should get the group's permission so that a cease-fire could be announced. We were in business again.

Although everything was going smoothly on our war front, the real war was heating up. The neighborhood youth joined the soldiers at the front in shocking numbers. Some of the mothers also went to the front to provide what help was needed. They made clothes, wove, cooked jam, and in short did anything they were good at.

That day my older brother informed us that he was joining the army on Monday. My mother looked at my father. My father's hand, holding a cigarette, started trembling. They acted as if it were the first time they had learned it. I sat by my brother and said, "Brother, are you going so you can fight the enemy?"

He caressed my hair and said, "Yes."

"With a real gun?" my younger brother asked enthusiastically.

My brother smiled bitterly. My younger brother went on gleefully, "We're fighting, too. In the alley ... But our guns are fake."

I glared at him but it was too late. I expected my older brother to scorn us, to say that instead of engaging in nonsense like that we should be studying. But he gently said, "Sweet Mostafa! No one really wants to be in a war. You are too young to know what war is, otherwise you wouldn't be playing a 'war' game."

"What would I be doing then?" Mostafa asked astonishingly.

"You could be playing a 'school' game, for example."

I was let down. I thought to myself, "To Hell with school! We just finished nine months of it. Isn't that enough?"

"Then why are you going to the front?" I asked.

My mother interrupted, "Come! Can't you leave him alone?"

And she went and sat down next to my brother, as if she didn't want to share his attention with anyone else. "Do you really have to leave on Monday, son?" she asked.

"Yes, mother."

She started crying. My brother said, "You know, Mom, that most of the boys in the neighborhood are at the front now! You aren't alone, thank God!"

Mother said sheepishly, "I wasn't complaining, son ... "

My brother kissed her hair. She closed her eyes, trying to hold back the tears that poured down her cheeks. My father only smoked, non-stop. My brother moved next to him and started whispering something. I couldn't hear what he was saying. I could only see my father shaking his head helplessly.

My brother finally left. Since that day, my mother would leave the house in the morning with the rest of the neighborhood women and return in the afternoon. At home, she would constantly knit sweaters to send to the front. We dared not make noise when the news came on; she wanted to hear every word.

A few days later a new boy appeared in our neighborhood. He was our age, with a dark complexion and curly hair. We soon found out that his name was Aboud. Akbar was the first to meet him. He brought us the news that we would have a new play-mate the next day.

When we went to the alley the next day, we found Akbar and Aboud waiting with the rest of the guys. Akbar introduced him to us. When Aboud saw the sacks in our hands and the guns on our backs, he asked, "What are these for?"

"For the 'war' game."

He lowered his head and remained silent.

"Why don't you join us?" Ali asked.

"No, I don't want to play."

"Why?" Ali asked in an exaggerated tone.

"Because war isn't a game."

The boys looked at one another. What did that mean? Hadn't Akbar said Aboud was going to play with us? This kid didn't seem excited at all. Maybe he didn't know how to play. We were all annoyed. We searched Akbar's face for an explanation, but he was surprised, too. Aboud looked down and started walking away.

"Why did he come in the first place?" Taghi asked.

"How do we know? Ask Akbar, who invites everyone he finds on the street to play with us," Jafar said.

"Drop it guys!" Ali said. "It's no big deal! Just forget he's in the neighborhood. Back to the game!"

It wasn't a bad idea, particularly because Akbar himself looked confused and our teams were intact. We resumed our game, but to tell you the truth, I couldn't stop thinking about Aboud.

The next morning we went to the alley as usual. We hadn't finished setting up our sandbags yet when Aboud appeared. He was holding a big roll of cardboard under one arm. Everyone exchanged curious glances. I decided to act as if I hadn't seen him, but before we had a chance to discuss it among ourselves he came and stood in the middle of our circle and said, "Good morning, brothers!"

His tone was so friendly that everyone's attention went to him.

"Since I left you yesterday, I have been working on this. I worked on it all day so I could finish it in time to bring it today."

And he opened the roll. On the extra-large piece of cardboard, there were several pictures of war, each scene neatly drawn. On the top of the sheet he had written in bold black print, "The Damned War." A scene showing bomb explosions appeared on the righthand side. Aboud had drawn pictures of wounded birds on the edge of the scene, writing underneath the picture, "This is what war is all about." On the lefthand side there was a picture showing a few small children staring sadly at a demolished house. The words underneath the picture read, "This used to be Zaer Abbas's house." Another picture showing a classroom was pasted at the lower section of the poster. Aboud had depicted a teacher writing something on the blackboard. The words read, "There will come a day when wars won't exist, a day when all the garrisons will be transformed into schools and children will sing the song of peace."

We gazed at the pictures for a few moments.

"Who was Zaer Abbas, Aboud?" Jafar asked.

"Mahmoud's father," Aboud answered, squinting. "Mahmoud was a friend from school. An explosion destroyed their house. When my friends and I arrived at the scene, they had closed the alley off, preventing us from getting near the bombed house. The only thing we could find out was that none of the inhabitants had survived. They lifted the restriction in the afternoon after they removed the corpses. I walked towards the house. Mahmoud's sneakers were tossed outside and lay on a mound of dust next to his sister's plastic doll with its missing hands and eye sockets filled with dirt. I wanted to scream. I wanted to knock my head against the wall. All my memories of Mahmoud came alive in my mind: the days we used to set fire to car tires during the uprising; the afternoons we used to spend playing soccer; the days we used to go to the river bank and sprinkle bread scraps for the ducks and the fish. Now Mahmoud is dead. The river is contaminated with bodies of ducks and fish killed by bombs, and it stinks. There's not a single bird left. The explosions have scared away not only the people but also the birds."

"Where did they escape to?" Mostafa asked.

"God knows. They've become refugees, too," Aboud said. Then he fell silent.

"Aboud! Is this your school?" Ali asked.

"Yes, but it's now occupied by Iraqi soldiers."

"Then, they must have erased the board," Mostafa said.

Aboud smiled. Then he caressed Mostafa's hair and said, "I wish that was all they had done. They're going to destroy everything. When my younger sister heard on the radio that her school was taken over, she cried in her sleep all night."

In Aboud's eyes, we caught a glimpse of all the suffering of the world. We had completely forgotten our game. The sandbags lay piled up in a corner. The guns were scattered on the ground. No one said a word.

Mostafa took his beloved gun out of its holster, pitched it to the ground and said, "I don't want to play the 'war' game anymore."

Once again I stared at Aboud's drawings. All of the sketches showed a small boy with curly hair, resembling Aboud himself.

"Your drawings are beautiful, Aboud," I said. "Have you done all of them yourself?"

"Yes. Now we can color them together, and when it's done we can paste the whole thing up in the alley so everyone can see what War really means."

—Translated from the Farsee by Soraya Sullivan

Yasmine Gooneratne

YASMINE GOONERATNE WAS BORN in Sri Lanka and earned her Ph.D. in English literature at Cambridge University. She is an educator, literary critic, editor, poet, and short story writer. She has lived in Australia since 1972 and has written many of her works there. Gooneratne holds a chair in English at Macquarie University and is the director of the university's Post-Colonial Literatures and Language Research Centre, which was founded in 1981. In 1990 Yasmine Gooneratne was awarded the Order of Australia for distinguished service in literature and education.

In trying to envision and formulate a women's mythology of war and peace, we realize that the mythology of war is learned early in life, as seen in this poem, "The Peace Game." The tenacious myth that we fight wars to win peace, the dominating group's power to make rules, and the absurdity of associating the word "war" with the word "game" all appear in this poem, in which children, nearly always the most numerous of the innocent victims of military conflicts, play at war.

The Peace Game

"Peace" was a game we liked to play
as kids of six, or maybe seven,
it needs some players to divide
into two teams, of Odds and Evens.
The Odds were the children down the street
and miscellaneous scraps and strays,
the Evens were my brothers and
our friends, swell, upright, regular guys.

"Peace" was the prize the game was fought
(or played, perhaps I mean) to win.
Their object was to keep us out
and ours to get, and then stay, in
for since our fathers didn't want
rough-housing near the orchid sheds,

we fought our battles over their
parents' vegetable beds.

We Evens were a well-fed lot
and tough, so that the little patched
and scrawny Odds would never dare
to say the teams were not well matched.
That was the beauty of the game,
we chose the ground and made the rules,
they couldn't really do a thing
about it, stunted little fools,

Except to put up quite a fight
sometimes, against our guns and such.
We called the entertainment "Peace"
or "War"—I can't remember which …

Fadwa Tuqan

IN THIS SECOND POEM by the Palestinian poet Fadwa Tuqan, life under Israeli occupation is again invoked. However, unlike the "The Gull," "Song of Becoming" is a concrete evocation of an event. Eighteen years before the Intifadah, or Palestinian Uprising, broke out officially, this 1969 poem described its strategies: grass-roots happenings that pitted stone-throwing children against military tanks.

Song of Becoming

They're only boys
who used to frolic and play
launching rainbowed kites
on the western wind,
their blue-red-green kites
whistling, leaping,
trading easy laughter and jokes
duelling with branches, pretending to be
great heroes in history.

Suddenly now they've grown,
grown more than the years of a normal life,
merged with secret and passionate words,
carried love's messages like the Bible or Quran,
to be read in whispers.
They've grown to become trees
plunging deep roots into earth,
stretching high towards the sun.
Now their voices are ones that reject,
that knock down and build anew.
Anger smouldering on the fringes of a blocked horizon,
invading classrooms, streets, city quarters,
centering on squares,

facing sullen tanks with streams of stones.

Now they shake the gallows of dawn
assailing the night and its flood.
They've grown more than the years of a life
to become the worshipped and the worshippers.

When their torn limbs merged with the stuff of our earth,
they became legends,
they grew into vaulting bridges,
they grew and grew, becoming
larger than all poetry.

—Translated from the Arabic by Naomi Shihab Nye [with the help of
Salma Khadra Jayyusi]

Bibliographic Notes to Part Two

al-Amir, Daisy. *The Distant Country That You Love*. Beirut, 1964.

_____. *Promises for Sale*. Beirut, 1981.

_____. *Then the Wave Returns*. Beirut, 1969.

_____. *In the Vortex of Love and Hate*. Beirut, 1979.

Devi, Mahasweta. *Fires Underground*. Calcutta, 1978.

Garg, Mridula. *From the Glacier*. New Delhi: Rajkamal Prakoshan, 1980.

Gooneratne, Yasmine. *Relative Merits: A Change of Skies*, N.P., 1989.

Hosain, Attia. *Phoenix Fled and Other Stories*. London, 1953.

_____. *Sunlight on a Broken Column*. London, 1961.

Imam, Jahanara. *Of Blood and Fire: The Untold Story of Bangladesh's War of Independence*. Dhaka: Academic Publishers, 1990.

Khalifa, Sahar. *Memoirs of an Unrealistic Woman*. Amman, 1986.

_____. *We Are No Longer Your Slave Girls*. Amman, 1974.

_____. *Wild Thorns*. Amman, 1976.

Naamani, Huda. *I Remember I Was a Point, I Was a Circle*. Beirut, 1980.

_____. *My Fingers . . . No*. Beirut, 1971.

_____. *To You*. Beirut, 1970.

Qasim, Suraiya. *Lyrical Voices: An International Poetry Anthology*. N.P., 1979.

Samara, Nuha. *In the Swamp City*. Beirut, 1973.

_____. *The Tables Lived Longer Than Amin*. Beirut, 1981.

Shafran, Nessia. *Farewell Communism*. Tel Aviv, 1981.

Singh, Jane, ed. *South Asians in North America: A Selected and Annotated Bibliography*. Berkeley: Center for South and South East Asian Studies, University of California, 1988.

Tuqan, Fadwa. *Alone on Top of the World*. Amman, 1973.

_____. *Give Us Love*. Amman, 1960.

_____. *The Guerrilla and the Land*. Amman, 1968.

_____. *I Have Found Her*. Amman, 1958.

_____. *Night and the Knights*. Amman, 1969.

_____. *The Nightmare of Night and Day*. Amman, 1974.

About the Book and Editors

THE EXPERIENCES OF WOMEN in twentieth-century wars in South Asia and the Middle East challenge the concept of the separation of front and homefront and of family and society common to most modern western wars. Women there have not only entered into what was once considered male-only territory in men's roles wearing men's clothing, but more important, they have entered explicitly as women playing a variety of roles in the conflicts surrounding them. Their self-conscious, self-confident presence has changed the nature of that territory.

This anthology reflects the realization that through their writing, women have created a new mythology of the war-peace paradox—one that is grounded in the reality of their own lives. The works collected here illustrate the many ways in which women have become active participants in social conflict and military battles, speaking of war not only as an extraordinary but also as an ordinary experience of coping with violence and conflict on a daily basis. Women's involvement with the rituals of violence does not begin or end with traditional war; their daily struggles for survival stretch seamlessly into the more public arena of political war.

In this anthology, Drs. Cooke and Rustomji-Kerns offer a collection of journal entries, interviews, fiction, and poetry by twentieth-century Middle Eastern and South Asian women writing about war and political conflicts. Some of the works were written in English, but the majority were translated specifically for this anthology and are published here for the first time in English. *Blood Into Ink* is an important and much-needed addition to the rapidly growing literature on war and peace. The anthology will greatly enlarge our understanding of the role of women in one of the most central of human concerns.

MIRIAM COOKE is professor of Arabic literature at Duke University. She is the author of *War's Other Voices: Women Writers on the Lebanese Civil War* (1988) and coeditor with Margot Badran of *Opening the Gates: A Century of Arab Feminist Writing* (1990) and with Angela Woollacott of *Gendering War Talk* (1993). ROSHNI RUSTOMJI-KERNS is Emerita Professor, Hutchins School of Liberal Studies, at Sonoma State University. She has edited *East-West Literary Relations* (special issue of *Journal of South Asian Literature*, 1981) and *South Asian Women Writers: The Immigrant Experience* (special issue of *Journal of South Asian Literature*, 1986). She is the editor of the forthcoming anthology *Living in America: Fiction and Poetry by South Asian American Writers* (Westview, 1995).

CPSIA information can be obtained at www.ICGtesting.com
Printed in the USA
BVOW05s2106260814

364354BV00002B/176/P